STRANGER THAN
THE BULLET

STRANGER THAN THE BULLET

The Wild and Wonderful World of the Vote

JONATHAN SNELLING

ROBSON BOOKS

First published in Great Britain in 2002 by
Robson Books, 64 Brewery Road, London N7 9NT

A member of Chrysalis Books plc

British Library Cataloguing in Publication Data
A catalogue record for this title is available from the British Library

ISBN 1 86105 468 8

Typeset by SX Composing DTP, Rayleigh, Essex
Printed in Great Britain by Creative Print & Design (Ebbw Vale), S. Wales

Contents

Preface

An Apology for the Book

Not just an introduction, more of an apology. Some people may wonder why anyone should take such an unhealthy interest in elections and the eccentricities of voting. As you have picked up this book, you may not be one of them, but, just in case, let me give you a few clues as to what sparks this fascination.

First, I'm interested in people. There's not much that people do communally these days. Occasionally, a TV programme or a major event unites us for a moment, but it does not last. We live our lives surrounded by a fairly small supporting cast – possibly thousands of walk-on extras – but they barely count. Some play starring roles for a while, but then leave the show. But voting is something that most adults do together at least sometimes, and the outcomes of those communal decisions affect us all and tell us something about ourselves. The basic figures that tell us who won or lost may be all we notice, but the smaller details that I have picked on can be much more interesting. Even those who rarely or never vote can point us to some interesting insights and some funny stories – by opting out, they are part of the story, whether they like it or not.

Second, I have to admit that I am a man and I share that strange obsession that many men and mysteriously few women suffer from – love of statistics. Just as most train spotters are male, so are most of those who love to pore over the finer details of football or cricket stats to find that killer information byte that will dazzle their friends or give them an edge in their *Fantasy*

Football competition. Many retain a curious fascination with the pop charts long after they stopped actually liking many of the songs that got into them. Train spotting has never appealed to me, but I plead guilty to the other examples. Before any women put this book down, or others who do not share this compulsion – don't worry! The book is not packed with intricate statistical information and analysis. There is some, but that is mostly there to point out the really interesting stories that lie beneath. Number crunching is actually rarely interesting and never funny in itself, but it can lead the way to much more rewarding material.

A third reason for finding interest in this topic is the scope it gives for playing one of those favourite history games: 'What if . . . ?' Many of us like to play the game of conjecturing with the old favourites, such as 'What if Caesar had not crossed the Rubicon?' or 'What if the wind had blown the other way the day the Armada sailed?' Alternatively, it is often fascinating to hear historians hold forth on these questions with all their years of study and pointless gin-soaked debates in university common rooms. With elections, we have a glut of these kinds of cases – only it is the behaviour of ordinary people that provides the variable factor, and often bizarre and inexplicable behaviour at that.

This book concerns itself mainly with British elections, as that is where I have always lived and I know it better than anywhere else. There is a fair amount of material on the USA, including a whole chapter on the momentous presidential election of 2000, that served as a reminder to me as I started writing this book that I am not dealing with a topic of pure trivia here, but a topic that shows how trivia drives history, and drives the lives of all of us more than we admit. It is not just major socioeconomic upheavals and the actions of Great Men that change the world. It is also a bunch of elderly folk who can't punch a hole through a piece of card and a group of barely competent politicians and overpaid lawyers who can't decide what to do about it.

There is a reasonable amount of material on Europe and other parts of the world and some historical perspective, although the twentieth century dominates. Maybe, if we ever get around to a sequel we can explore other corners of the globe and periods of history in a bit more depth. There is more than enough out there to keep us going.

I have not attempted a chronological study of the topic, but have organised the chapters on a thematic basis – although the first chapter takes you on a brief voyage through the strange history of voting from the birth of democracy up to the arrival of universal suffrage. I have tried to think of all the different aspects of electoral weirdness and given a chapter to each. Within these I have included the various stories, anecdotes, facts, figures and observations that I have chosen.

There has been much that I have not included. I am sorry if I have left out your favourite election story, but if you know it you don't need it in the book anyway. I hope I have included some you have never heard before. I have done my best to ensure everything in the book is true. Where a story is based on a widespread rumour, or doubtful evidence, I have made it clear that it may not be true. There may be one or two minor details that are not correct. Where I have quoted electoral statistics or other factual data, I have tried to use two, three or more sources. Doing this, you discover they often do not agree, so I have tried to ascertain the most reliable report. Sorry if I have been wrong occasionally. I have named any sources I have directly quoted from. Much of the information is from original source material, newspaper reports or my own recollection. Some Internet sites have been very helpful. For more detailed data on the UK, I bow down to the mighty David Butler and Robert Waller, who are the twin giants of electoral statistics and modern electoral history. If those two agree on a fact I take it as gospel. Where they disagree, or don't say: I go hunting elsewhere.

In case you find the style a little cynical at times, please be assured that I did not set out to be so. Sometimes it is hard not to be, as you will see. But it would not be possible to write a book like this unless one loved elections, loved democracy and, frankly, loved people too. I hope it refreshes your interest in the democratic process and makes you feel a little better. If it does the opposite, then I have failed, but I hope you will have one or two laughs on the way at least.

When Abraham Lincoln observed in 1856 that 'The ballot is stranger than the bullet', history changed the word to 'stronger' thanks to some half-deaf reporter. At least that's my view on the matter. The thing is that elections are often crazy, chaotic affairs. Voters do the oddest things. Candidates and parties fall over themselves to make more ridiculous mistakes than the others, people think up weird manifesto promises and campaigning techniques. Sometimes you despair of the whole process. Democracy is a stranger principle upon which to base power and sovereignty than brute force and violence, but in the end they are really the only two choices we have, and I know which I prefer. Lincoln may have met his end by the bullet, but it was the ballot that made him and thousands more across the globe that have done something to improve our world. Several despots have used the ballot as well, but at least even they recognised the need for some kind of popular mandate, however distorted, and did not simply claim their divine right to rule. Many of them were eventually removed by the ballot, and, where it took violence to remove them, democracy usually rushed in to fill the void. The ballot is definitely stronger, but it is also much, much stranger. Read on.

Voting Early

The First Steps Towards the Future

'Vote early. Vote often.'
– Traditional Irish slogan

When did mankind first vote? We do not know of course. We know that power systems in primitive societies were largely based on brute force and that hereditary systems followed to develop leadership among the offspring of the victors in the 'survival of the fittest'. It suited most people to go along with this and accept their hereditary authority rather than fight constant battles for the right to lead. As long as there is peace and there is enough to eat, why rock the boat? However, boats have a habit of being rocked quite a lot. Many leaders did not provide peace and prosperity. Some turned out to be psychopaths or lunatics. Sometimes, alternative leaders would appear with great ambition, who would offer favours and promises to those who would support their struggle. Then the violent selection procedures would start again. Some early societies would have practised forms of what we would now call direct democracy over areas of their communal life, but we really know very little of the political ideas of the 'noble savage', however much Enlightenment philosophers liked to think they knew about them.

As mankind developed religious structures, a new hierarchy arose. In some civilisations this became the new hegemony, and a higher power claimed its precedence over mere brute strength. In other societies, it developed alongside the secular power

1

structure. Usually there was mutual support, as each endorsed the other.

But voting? A general level of public support has always been of some significance. A despot cannot rule unless at least a significant minority supports him, preferably the minority with the biggest weapons. If nearly everyone turns against him, he can claim hereditary rights, divine right or any other right he wants, but it won't stop his head rolling down the palace steps when the mob overthrows him. There might not be a formal general election, but the people still get to decide.

CLASSICAL ROOTS

Those good old Greeks! Clever lot, weren't they? Everyone concedes that they invented democracy. The truth is that we do not know. Much earlier civilisations may have employed some form of democracy, at least at some levels of government. There were early forerunners of parliaments in the Middle East centuries before Athens got its act together, but there is no evidence that there was anything very democratic about them. The Greeks certainly invented the word and the form of democratic philosophy that has been passed down to us. We may as well accept their version as our starting point. Our journey through the murky waters of the electoral process gets off to just the sort of dubious start we might expect.

We are all familiar with the idea that Athens was the first home of democracy. Today it is the world's most impressive home of urban carbon monoxide poisoning. As in other city-states of ancient Greece, this was a form of democracy that would look very limited to modern eyes. As long as you were a male citizen, you had a say. Women, slaves and any others who did not qualify as citizens had no rights at all, save those the citizens generously chose to give them. In one sense there was greater democracy than today. Many of the city-states held regular meetings that were open to all citizens, where important decisions were taken. This form of direct democracy can be observed today only in small communities, although some would claim that it is the purest form of democracy. The referendum is a descendant of this, several times removed after dodgy marriages in the disreputable side of the family. Some spotty types have bounced up and down eagerly and pointed out that the growth of the Internet and interactive TV may bring this form of Greek city meeting into modern democracy. Ignore these people. They are safer left floating around in *Blake's Seven* chatrooms or trying to hack into your bank account. You really do not need people like that running the country.

Greek elections would have looked particularly unusual to us, as their idea of equality among citizens meant that elections were commonly conducted by the drawing of lots. This practice, which we have come to call sortition, rid them of the vulgar unpleasantries they would have had from lots of men claiming they were better than the others and deserving of votes, making promises they were in no position to deliver, or just bribing and cheating their way into office. If all citizens are equally honourable and just, it makes perfect sense to decide elections by lottery. If we could combine our general election with the National Lottery we could all guess who would get the key cabinet positions and watch on Saturday night as the election results tumbled out of the machine. Who is to say the new government would be any worse than that elected by other means? This way one or two lucky voters would become millionaires. It seems like a very appealing idea.

If you want to read in detail about Greek philosophy and its relationship to democracy, you are reading the wrong book, but, in brief, it is worth noting that Aristotle had a grudging kind of acceptance of the idea. He thought all forms of government were bad, but democracy had more going for it than tyranny or oligarchy. In that respect he sounds like many people you might canvass at an election today. Plato does not seem to have much to say on the subject in his *Republic*. What views he did express about it were almost entirely negative. There does not seem to be anything democratic about his vision of Utopia. Admittedly, most of us would not think about elections if we were conjuring up our own idea of heaven. Mind you, Plato's Republic seems to be such a dull place that a few elections might liven it up a bit, as the occasional war seems to be his only idea of fun.

We all know the Romans had their senate and we like to romanticise figures like Brutus and the Emperor Claudius, who dreamed of restoring the republic, as if they were pioneering democrats. They may have been enemies of tyranny, but don't kid yourself that there was anything democratic about the old Roman republic. A small number of noble patrician families dominated the senate. Julius and Augustus simply showed that tyranny conducted by one ruler could be more efficient and effective than the tyranny of an overlarge and ponderous committee, which is all that the old oligarchical system had become. Admittedly, once you have gone down that road you wind up with Caligula and Nero, but just think of all those great movies we would have missed if they had never happened. You can't thrill to a spectacular epic in CinemaScope and Sensaround that is all about a bunch of old men in togas chatting to each other.

STUCK IN THE MIDDLE

There were numerous experiments with limited forms of democracy in the Middle Ages, particularly in some Italian cities, but they were usually quashed pretty quickly by kings or princes, priests or popes. The Eastern world and the civilisations around the rest of the planet knew nothing of the idea. Arab scholars would have read about it, but it did not impress them much.

Through the overwhelmingly undemocratic Dark Ages and

Middle Ages, the curious home for the memory of democracy became the Church. It was only here that any scholars remained to study and consider Greek and other classical thought. Strangely, it was also this largely authoritarian institution that preserved some elements of democracy. At the bottom some monastic communities practised democratic decision making in some areas of their life. At the top the pope himself was elected by the cardinals. Also a series of early church councils took democratic decisions on such issues as whether God was three persons or one, and which books belonged in the Bible. A few recounts on some of those votes really could have changed history to a greater degree than your average local council by-election.

Let's turn back to the struggle to bring democracy to the state. Who can claim the oldest continuously serving parliament, then? That is a strongly contested argument and the answer is not clear. The Althing was established in Iceland in AD 930, but it was disbanded for a while in the nineteenth century. So it disqualifies itself if we are strict about being continuous. The Tynwald on the Isle of Man has been continuous, and may be older anyway, but nobody knows exactly when it started. They both make 1241 look a very late start for parliament in England. Somehow, the English still claim to have the Mother of Parliaments. Don't mention it in Iceland or the Isle of Man. Were any of these democratic? In modern terms, of course, they were not, but there was some kind of electoral process, even if in most cases it was local nobles nominating their chosen appointees to represent the county. I suppose an electoral register of one name is still an electoral register.

It took a long time for democracy to establish itself as the consensual view among philosophers. Among the many great names who regarded it as foolish at best and satanic at worst was Thomas Hobbes, a brave man who showed how democracy was truly evil in his classic work *Leviathan*, but then had to flee from France because he had slagged off the Catholic Church as well.

He returned to England, said sorry to Cromwell for all the times he had annoyed him, and decided to shut up.

Even Jean Jacques Rousseau, who some would say was the father of modern democratic thought, tended to look back to the Greek city-state model. He did not seem to see much future in the 'elective aristocracy' of the modern nation-state. Still people puzzle over what exactly he meant by the 'general will' and his ideas were picked up by Hegel and others, who paved the way in the end for Hitler and Stalin. It's a confusing old road that democracy has travelled.

Through John Locke, Jeremy Bentham, John Stuart Mill and Thomas Paine, the British established the intellectual basis for liberal democracy. However, it was really the French and the Americans who started doing something about it.

BY THE DAWN'S EARLY LIGHT

The Americans included a commitment to popular elections in their constitution, but in truth their franchise was almost as exclusive as Britain's initially. The first presidential election was a triumph for disorder. Not only did the Americans have a limited franchise that excluded many men, as well as all women and all slaves, but several states were short-changed in other ways. It was on 4 February 1789 that the electors met in their respective states to choose the first President. In Connecticut, Delaware, Georgia, New Jersey and South Carolina there was no election at all. The state legislatures appointed the electors. Only Maryland, Pennsylvania and Virginia chose their electors fully through a ballot. Massachusetts managed to work out a complex way of combining a ballot with legislature choice. New Hampshire tried a ballot, but it got too confusing, so the state Senate opted to choose their own in the end. New York was to be the home of the new presidential administration, but they did not get around to choosing their electors in time. Two electors from Maryland and two from Virginia were held up by bad weather and North Carolina and Rhode Island missed the election because they had not ratified their state constitutions in time. Therefore, 22 votes out of 91 went missing.

The first presidential election of 1789 was almost as big a shambles as the one they managed to produce 211 years later, but at least the result was not in doubt. In those early days, the electors had two votes. Whoever came second got to be Vice-President. All 69 electors had cast a vote for George Washington – the only president to get unanimous endorsement. John Adams received 34 votes and gained the vice-presidency. These results were announced in the Senate on 6 April 1789, posing the question why it took two months to count 138 votes. It makes Miami Dade look like a model of speed.

LA BELLE FRANCE

The first moves towards universal suffrage were to be seen in those states that embraced revolutionary fervour. France quickly got the bug, and no sooner had they thrown off royal autocracy than we find they were electing mayors, local officials, judges and even priests. The elections to the new Convention in 1792 allowed the vote to all seven million men (in theory). Not women of course: France was not that revolutionary! The existing government did its best to set up a practical framework to make the elections manageable, but it is believed that the turnout was about 6 per cent. Even a nondescript local council by-election on a wet December day in Liverpool can manage better than that. Was Revolutionary France politically apathetic? Were the people truly monarchist and dismissive of this Girondist- and Jacobin-produced nonsense? We have no reason to believe either argument is true. Those Liverpudlian by-election dodgers might complain about the weather or their aches and pains, or might just think there is no point in their voting, but they could never match the excuses the French voters had in September 1792. War was still raging across much of the north and east of the country and two electoral assemblies had to move to avoid meeting in the middle of battlegrounds. In Paris, the assembly was convened at the Jacobin Club, home of the ultra-Revolutionary group. It was probably not a wise move to attend an open hustings and show your opposition to Robespierre, Marat, Danton and Desmoulins in front of everybody. Perhaps you might pass the guillotine on your way to the vote. In fact it was probably wiser to stay away altogether than even go to support them. Who knew which faction would gain precedence over whom and who would turn against the others? Safer to stay out of it. Most of the major cities were similarly charged with intimidation, fear and unrest – often virtual anarchy. In rural areas the more mundane matter of the harvest took precedence in most voters' priorities. Added to that, the lack of understanding that must have been widespread among such a formerly disenfranchised mass was surely a factor. Communication would have been incredibly difficult at such a time and illiteracy would not have helped. The vote went on chaotically over a few days while Parisians went on massacring each other.

One observation that could be made and that has been repeated often since is that low turnouts are good for extremists. The Jacobins and other radicals did extremely well and those moderate Frenchmen who stayed away in droves probably had a big part to play in ensuring there was no middle-way compromise to keep the new republic on line. The terror of the next few years and the eventual rise of Napoleon was partly down to good old stay-at-home voters. I would probably have done the same.

WAS JERUSALEM BUILDED HERE?

Democracy was slow to get established properly in Britain.

However, we know there were forms of local democracy going on in parts of England from very early times.

In *The Oxford History of England*, the volume on the thirteenth century (1216–1307) by Sir Maurice Powicke shows that elections of some sort or other were around in medieval England:

> The election or nomination of a few men to serve the interests of their community goes back very far. It can be seen in the reeve and four men of the vill, the twelve knights of the shire, the electoral system of a borough, and in the intercourse which linked the central to local administrations; it made possible the organisation of monastic orders and of the orders of friars.

He particularly points to the election of the portmen of Ipswich in 1200. There were even early examples of electoral law in those days:

> A statute of 1275 declared that elections should be free from disturbance by the great; while the writs to the sheriffs stipulated that those sent to this same parliament must be chosen from the more discreet and law-worthy knights of the shire. Some responsible method of election seems to be implied. In London, which was a shire with hustings as a shire court, elections from 1296 onwards, if not earlier, were made indirectly, that is, by the aldermen and deputations from the wards, acting probably on behalf of the hustings. Shire elections, of which nothing seems to be known for this period, may have been conducted in a similar but less formal way. A knight of the type required was certainly not a nonentity.

So only the more discreet and law-worthy knights of the shire were considered eligible for election. You have to wonder just when they revoked that 1275 statute. There is sadly little reliable historical evidence left of the real story of medieval elections. We can assume most appointments to Parliament and lesser bodies were made by powerful local nobles with no recourse to popular opinion at all. After all, when we reach the era of Oliver Cromwell there is plenty of reliable documentary evidence, and that was still the way things worked then. The all-time hero of the supremacy of Parliament never fought a proper election in his life. Anything approaching real democracy in Britain had to wait. Perhaps we can say 1832 was the start. Before that, the monarch and then the aristocracy ruled. Of course, Lord Macaulay did not see that as such a bad thing: 'Thus our Democracy was, from an early period, the most aristocratic, and our aristocracy the most democratic in the world' was his apologist position in his *History of England*. We might prefer to go with G K Chesterton in a *New York Times* article of 1931: 'Democracy means Government by the un-educated, while aristocracy means government by the badly educated.'

Simon de Montfort had insisted that MPs be elected when he summoned the Parliament of 1265. The pattern of membership of county and borough members was hardly changed between then and 1832. A few new boroughs got royal charters over the years, and occasionally one was removed.

Henry VIII even allowed Wales to have seats in Parliament, albeit severely underrepresented – apart from Monmouthshire, which was still mistakenly regarded as English until 1974. Scotland was also suitably underrepresented at first when it joined the Union in 1707. This was rectified, and overcompensated later. Then Ireland was given a hundred Members of Parliament, again an underrepresentation for a populous nation prior to famine and mass emigration. Oddly, the region of the country that was ridiculously overrepresented in pre-reform Britain was Cornwall.

TRUE DAWN?

So some form of democracy has been around for most of the time that we have known as history, even if it was little more than a theoretical idea for much of that time. In Britain we might take the 1832 Reform Act as the starting point of genuine parliamentary democracy. Women would still wait nearly another century for the vote and most men still did not have it yet, either, but at least the principle was established and the road to genuine democracy was begun. Maybe we have not arrived at the destination even now, and maybe we never will, but any rational person will now acknowledge democracy as the basic principle of government, and 1832 was a real turning point as the old, wholly unrepresentative system was reformed. Certainly something a little magical was lost by the removal of all those pocket boroughs and rotten boroughs – those places where few, if any, lived and which provided easy routes into power for the favoured appointees of influential noblemen. Never again will anyone represent the sheep of Old Sarum or the charming resort of Dunwich-under-Sea.

We will never again have an occasion like the Gatting by-election of 1816. Like most of these kinds of places, Gatting had always returned appointees unchallenged. It had only three electors and Sir Mark Wood nominated his absent son for the seat as a Tory candidate. Jennings, the butler, was the other elector. He objected to the choice and decided to stand as a Whig. Mark Jr never came back home to vote. Jennings did not vote for some reason. Perhaps he realised there were other butlers looking for a good job. The one vote cast for Mark Wood Jr was presumably that of his father. Isn't that much more appealing than most of the by-elections you get these days?

And the most famous pre-reform election in a rotten borough? The answer is obviously the election for Dunny-on-the-Wold in 'Dish and Dishonesty' from Richard Curtis and Ben Elton's brilliant *Blackadder III*. This was the story in which there was a plot to drop Prince George from the civil list, led by Pitt the Younger. Blackadder bought the half-acre of sodden marshland in Suffolk that was Dunny-on-the-Wold on behalf of the Prince, in order to place his faithful servant Baldrick in Parliament. The plan ran into a hitch as Pitt the Younger put his even younger brother up to stand against Baldrick in the by-election and Vincent Hanna, the sorely missed real-life by-election watcher from the BBC, went to report.

After Pitt the Even Younger and Mr Ivor Biggun of the 'Standing at the Back Dressed Stupidly and Looking Stupid Party' had learned that they had gained no votes, it emerged that Baldrick had gained 16,472 from the single elector, Blackadder. The original electorate had very sadly, accidentally, brutally cut his head off while combing his hair.

Like all the best comedy, it was funny because, while being absurd and surprising, it is only a small step away from the truth. Was Dunny-on-the-Wold's election really any more ridiculous than Gatting in 1816?

In the first of the book's top tens and the first of our magnificent and much-desired prizes, I give you the ten most sorely missed constituencies, swept away by the tide of history and the march of democratic reform; those romantic reminders of a pastoral, almost mythical nation. They conjure up a picture of a country before 1832 that was once beautiful, idyllic, splendid and utterly corrupt.

1. Dunwich: two members for the Suffolk seaport, long since vanished beneath the waves by 1832
2. Grampound: Little Cornish village that lost its franchise after bribery in 1820 election – shame!
3. Old Sarum: how could we forget two members for nowhere much in Wiltshire, now an airfield?
4. Beeralston: Tiny village in east Devon had two members (same as Bristol)

5. Cricklade: small town in north Wiltshire with two members since 1295
6. Tregony: minute village in Cornwall with two members (same as Newcastle)
7. Gatton: yes, this tiny Surrey village had two members (same as its county town of Guildford)
8. Ludgershall: little place near Andover with two members
9. Weobley: two members for village in Herefordshire with nice name
10. Melcombe Regis: two members were elected as a consolation prize for the runners-up in Weymouth

For the record, these places can still be found in an atlas, but don't blink as you pass through them. There is even still a tiny place left on the coast called Dunwich, but please do not attempt to visit the original city! A few places like Bewdley and Banbury were given only one member. Of course if you lived in Birmingham, Liverpool, Manchester, Glasgow or Belfast you had no MP, only a part-share on a couple of county MPs who probably tried to avoid your town at all costs.

Who Said Universal?

The Electorally Disappeared

'Well I called my Congressman, and he said – quote:
"I'd like to help you, son, but you're too young to vote".'
— *'Summertime Blues', Cochran/Capehart, 1958*

If democracy is supposed to be government appointed by the people, we need to decide who the people are. This is not as obvious as it may seem at first. There are plenty of people who have been disenfranchised in every era of history and in every country of the world, and, once you have dealt with the historical perspective, you realise there are many who still are. You do not have to look for electoral weirdness in the past. Try right here, right now. Let's look at all the principal groups who have struggled to be noticed and start with the biggest group of the lot.

WOMEN'S WORLD

Strangely it was the Pitcairn Islands that gave women the vote first, in 1838. This did not mean that women actually voted, though, which was a neat trick. Wyoming started in 1869, followed by the Isle of Man in 1881 (curious how a people so often looked on as sleepy and otherworldly as the Manx were frequently in the forefront of political advance) and New Zealand in 1893 (the first entire nation-state to join in). British women voted for the first time in 1918. The USA took until 1920 for federal elections. Indeed most of the developed, democratic world went along with this trend during, or in the few years following, World War One. As the women had essentially kept their countries running, while the men had been fighting and dying, there was little point in persisting with the belief that they were fragile little things, not fit to have their pretty little heads bothered with a nasty business like politics. Among the fears expressed by various politicians before female enfranchisement were: 'Fancy a member returning home and finding there a politician in petticoats ready to continue the debate!' and 'Our legislation will develop hysterical and spasmodic features.'

The first woman elected to Parliament, by the way, proved immediately that women were not entering politics as a genteel pastime activity. Countess Markievicz was a revolutionary republican, elected for a Dublin seat in 1918 for Sinn Fein, and she refused to take the oath to the King. That is why Nancy Astor was the first woman to take her seat, after a Plymouth by-election the following year.

Not all countries relented to female pressure at the time. Greece managed to keep women out of the picture until 1952. Liechtenstein even left it as late as 1984, but it took until then for many people to notice that Liechtenstein existed, anyway. The continuing battle for full female enfranchisement still goes on today in several Arab and other Islamic states. Women now account for over 50 per cent of the electorate in most countries, but the fight for equal representation goes on in nearly all of them.

BORN TOO LATE

I suppose everyone has to concede that there is a point at which people are too young to be given a vote. Those countries that have allowed children to vote have done so through either administrative incompetence or straightforward corruption. After all, if you know you have a neighbourhood's vote in the bag – you might as well let their children vote too.

For ten years Britain had different age limits for men and

women. From 1918 until 1928 men could vote at 21, but women had to wait until they were 30. There did not seem to be much that could justify that. Very few women were educated to a higher level at the time, but there were not that many more men, either; nobody has ever claimed that women mature later than men. The only serious argument put forward was that women needed the guidance of a good husband to aid them in their electoral responsibilities, and you could reckon that most of them would have found one by the time they were 30. Of course the political reality was that this was partly a sop to some of the MPs who had been uneasy about allowing women anyway. After ten years on trial, women had shown that they had not caused the country to descend into a pit of political turmoil, so they finally gained equal voting rights.

Britain reduced the voting age to eighteen in 1969, significantly later than several other countries, and a long while after Screaming Lord Sutch had made it one of his mad and nonsensical policies, which so frequently became law in the end. Many now argue that sixteen should be the age, but these arguments will never be settled. Most nations are happy to set age limits for tax, military service and criminal responsibility nice and low, while setting higher limits for anything that might involve fun or empowerment. Mind you, those places that try to set a common age for everything can look equally absurd. You do find some oddities around the world. In Bolivia and Colombia you must be 21 to vote, unless you are married, in which case you can vote at eighteen. It seems a little strange that a country should decide to actively encourage teenage marriage, and regard that as more responsible than, perhaps, finishing an education first. If that is surprising, try the Dominican Republic, where they will allow you to vote while under eighteen if you are married! In Iran and Guinea-Bissau you can vote at fifteen. Good old Andorra will not put up with this sort of thing at all. There you can wait for your ballot until you are 25, married or not.

THE COLOUR OF DEMOCRACY

Apartheid elections stand out as a massive aberration in any study of voting. An almighty great boil on the body of democracy. Do you put apartheid elections into a section of their own? We could equally have put them into the chapter on fraud and corruption, as that is all that they were ever about. We may as well deal with them here along with the other examples of voter exclusion.

Early independent South African politics immediately split along racial lines – English speakers against Afrikaners. Black people were not regarded as of any consequence at all. As a matter of fact, a few wealthier blacks did have the vote in Cape Colony originally, but that did not long survive the formation of the new South African federation. Many of the English speakers realised they could not get power on their own, so they joined with the bulk of the Afrikaners and formed what went on to become the National Party. Joining with the majority population did not occur to them as an option.

Was there any radical opposition to this consensus? Yes, there was a strong, working-class trade union movement who bravely took on their government, facing brutal oppression in 1922 with that famous Marxist slogan, 'Workers of the world unite, and fight for a white South Africa'. Hang on a minute – that wasn't what I remember reading in the *Communist Manifesto*. For most of the twentieth century, South African election manifestos concentrated on arguments over the finer points of maintaining racial purity (Marriages Act, Immorality Act, Group Areas Act, to name but three), or the balance between freeing labour markets to allow businesses to employ cheap black workers and ensuring that they did not threaten the jobs of the white poor, mainly Afrikaners.

Times move on and they could not go on with this chaotic, haphazard approach to democracy much longer. Modern sophisticated elections require properly maintained electoral registers and there are law courts to take up any issues of unfair treatment. You cannot keep someone off a register just because of your own blind prejudice, so do you change the system? Of course not: you set it up properly and legally with the Population Registration Act (1950). I feel another award coming on. Surely this is the winner of the 'Most Pernicious Piece of Electoral Legislation' prize. The population was carefully separated into four racial groups: Whites, Coloureds, Indians and Africans. The rights (or lack of rights) of each group were carefully laid out and the detailed descriptions of how each person could be categorised in the event of any dubious cases was systematic, obsessive and absolutely insane. Precise anatomical and genealogical tests were prescribed to ensure everyone went in the right pigeonhole. I am not sure whether Hitler would have been impressed or would have been completely baffled as to why they bothered. Just to put the icing on the cake they decided that the Whites formed a single nation – despite obvious divisions among them – while Africans made up ten different nations. That made the White nation the biggest, and consequently they had absolute control. It gets so mad it's almost impressive in a perverse sort of way, isn't it?

The National Party leaders tried all sorts of things to put the race question out of the way, trying to avoid majority rule on one side and international pariah status on the other. Tribal homelands came and went and were mostly rejected, save by a few leaders who found the power and riches very tempting. One thing they tried was to encourage local democracy in black townships. Most of the residents held their local councils in contempt. They had very restricted powers granted by national government. Their budgets were extremely limited, but that did not stop some of the councillors doing quite well from it. In the October 1988 local elections, the black voters surpassed themselves. Fewer than half of the 1,839 seats were contested; 183 seats were bereft of a single nomination. It is estimated that 3 per cent of the African population voted. That may be the most triumphant victory for abstentionists ever recorded. Coloureds and Indians were given their own parliamentary chambers with some governmental responsibility in 1984. Their turnouts as a proportion of all potential voters in the subsequent general election were 18 per cent and 11 per cent respectively. Many had never even registered.

When F W de Klerk and Nelson Mandela led South Africa to proper democracy in 1994, one aspect of electoral strangeness was gone for good, but there was plenty still going on. Across the country, some of the longest queues ever seen for any election were observed. Some people waited for eight hours or more and polling station hours had to be extended. Voting in KwaZulu-Natal was as fraudulent as everyone had expected. Not only were ballot boxes stuffed and children allowed to vote, but 'pirate' polling stations were set up – like pirate radio stations but without the irritating jingles. Significant widespread illiteracy was a problem in some areas, particularly in one remote rural community, where the locals could not read and had no television. The system was that party leaders' pictures appeared by their party names to aid illiterate voters. Unfortunately, as these ANC supporters had never seen Mandela in the flesh or on the telly, they had no idea what he looked like. The polling clerks helpfully told them that he had white hair. The South African Nazi Party picked up a number of surprising votes from an unexpected source that day. Despite cases like these, the elections were agreed to be predominantly free and fair. Democracy had come to South Africa and now they just had the same sort of stupid things going wrong in elections as the rest of the world.

Blacks in South Africa were the most systematically and ruthlessly excluded group, but the roll of dishonour is lengthy, including in the USA, which passed the 15th Amendment in 1870, declaring that the right of suffrage shall not be denied to citizens on account of race, colour or previous condition of servitude, but they still managed to exclude Native Americans until 1924 and some of the Southern states managed to exclude most blacks well into the 1960s (some people would say they have ways of doing it today). The USA played a brilliant trick in 1787 as they set up the electoral college. Some were concerned that the South would be marginalised by the more numerous Northern Yankies. Therefore, they were allowed to count slave populations in the college vote calculations, even though they had no vote. So slaves helped the South to maintain their power and put slave-owning Virginians into control for all but four of the first 36 years of the presidency, without actually having a vote themselves. The winning candidate is usually still the one who can carry the Southern white males.

Before other countries start getting smug, remember Aborigines in Australia, Palestinians in Israel, Kurds and Marsh Arabs in Iraq, unfavoured tribes in several sub-Saharan African states and all the others that we could fill a book with. Democracy is fine for some people as long as you can just keep it to your friends. Interesting to note how many of the dis-enfranchised ethnic groups were not immigrants, but the original indigenous people. If the aliens ever arrive, don't expect them just to give us the vote – we may have to fight for it.

BRING ME YOUR POOR

In the earliest votes in England the franchise for county seats was open to all men who owned the freehold of land to an annual rent of 40 shillings ('Forty-shilling Freeholders'). That made you a pretty significant member of the community – very wealthy in today's terms. There were various different arrangements in the boroughs. Then in 1603, King James I (VI of Scotland) decided some people could have two votes if they were members of Oxford or Cambridge Universities. Other universities were added later and that nonsense continued until World War Two. Alternatively, you could have had a second vote if you owned a business in a constituency other than where you lived. People were not supposed to vote in three places, but the bias in favour of the rich was considerable. It took until 1918 for Britain finally to abolish property or financial qualifications, and enfranchise all men along with the women. It took until 1948 to abolish all forms of plural voting.

One effective way some countries have disenfranchised the poor has been to set literacy levels as a condition for their being allowed the vote. Any countries that have tried to be more sensible have seen that party emblems can be used to get round that one, and maybe Britain has acknowledged its own falling literacy levels by introducing that now.

Another way in which the poor are still disenfranchised in many countries is through the problem of homelessness. An electoral register requires electors to have an address. Even overseas voters have to be able to pinpoint the place they have come from, otherwise we do not know where they are supposed to be voting. Campaigners for the homeless have long argued that they have been locked out of the political system. Recent legal change in British electoral law may remedy this. A homeless voter can now register any reasonable address where they can be contacted from time to time, such as a café that they frequent. It is too early to see whether this will have a significant effect in bringing the homeless into the electoral fold, but it is a very good idea and deserves to achieve something. It may also give us some of the most imaginative addresses ever recorded in registers, so watch out for a whole new area of electoral strangeness to be opened up.

WE KNOW YOU'RE THERE . . . WE JUST DON'T KNOW WHERE

Almost every country in the world conducts a regular census and has other ways of making population estimates. From these, we know that there are people missing from the electoral registers. There are at least a million people missing from the British register and some people estimate that it is far more. It is hard to be precise, partly because some people are registered more than once. The largest group that can legitimately be registered in two places are students, who are frequently named at their college address and at their parents'. People who have recently moved may be registered at both addresses for a year and people with more than one home may be registered at two, but residential qualification time limits mean that two would be the limit. So there is no point in spending your fortune on buying a home in each of the 659 constituencies and trying to spend about half a day a year in each of them. That would not get you anywhere. You are allowed to vote in only one of the seats you are registered in at a parliamentary election anyhow, and this is another factor that can artificially depress turnout. The most seats I have ever known anyone to be registered in illegally is twelve. But here is a warning to all those people who register at friends' houses around the country and try to vote as many times as they can – they have computers now: they will catch you in the end!

Anyway, back to the people who are missing. One point to keep in mind here is that, unlike the case with some countries, it is illegal to avoid being put on the electoral register in Britain. You do not have to vote, but you must be on the roll. The main reason for this is that the roll is used for making selections for jury service, and avoiding jury service without due cause is an offence. This is very rarely chased up by the authorities, which is a pity because it would be a good excuse to prosecute Geri Halliwell, after her manager's admission of this crime. So who else is missing? First, there are the lazy, the bone idle who cannot be bothered to fill in a simple form that would take them about thirty seconds, and they happen to live in the patch of an authority that is as lazy as they are and will not chase it up. Second, there are the highly mobile. As we said before, some people might be double-counted, but more will fall between registers, particularly some of the bedsit brigade who move frequently, including lots of bed-and-breakfast welfare recipients and single people working on short informal contracts. Thirdly there are the shady: crooks, villains, spooks, spivs, welfare cheats, tax dodgers, anyone who does not wish to advertise their whereabouts. If anyone wishes to remain secret because they are afraid for their safety, this can be arranged, but some of them may not be convinced that their anonymity will be protected. Then there are others who choose not to register because they do not wish to participate: anarchists, some religious fundamentalists or just regular members of the awkward squad. Most of these people still register even if they do not vote, but some go that extra mile for their cause.

The people who are not registered are more likely to be poor, young, nonwhite (particularly if they speak little English and have no help with their forms), poorly educated and urban. In other words, they are the same sort of group who tend to be the most generally dispossessed in society, the ones who are less likely to vote anyway, even if they are on the list. That is why society should be concerned about the missing names, and always looking for ways to get as many of them back as possible. It is now much easier for names to be added to the register at any time of the year, but even changes like that will not make much difference for most of these groups unless there are people helping them, chasing them and perhaps occasionally bullying them.

In the USA, registration can be even lower. The Democrats, in particular, have long realised that in some areas the registration drive is just as important as the election campaign. Certain inner-city ethnic-ghetto areas can have terrible registration records and it can take great effort from organisations such as the National Association for the Advancement of Colored People to get those names included. There are many people in Congress whose election depended on it.

OUT IN THE COLD

So who does that leave? Well of course, there are the foreign citizens resident in a country. They may be there long-term and have more interest in what sort of government is elected than the overseas voters who never come back, but if they are not citizens they cannot vote – unless . . . Yes, there are more complications. Sorry! First, Europe complicates things as usual. Any citizen of the European Union can now vote in other European States as long as they fulfil the necessary residency criteria. In the UK this provision covers local and Euro elections. Irish and Commonwealth citizens have had the vote in Britain for a long time, and there are some constituencies in western Scotland, Merseyside and London, where Irish citizens make a significant proportion of the electorate. There are some similar arrangements in effect in other parts of the world.

Then there is the whole complex issue of the mentally ill. Many countries have very strict rules, restricting the voting rights of such people. It is claimed that, if they are not capable of voting with full mental facility, it is not only pointless to give them the vote, but it could also lead to manipulation by those caring for them, and open up possible fraud. We could all start going on about how some of the most intelligent and sane people we have ever known have been mentally ill, while at least one in ten of the people rolling in at the polling station appears to be barking mad, but we will resist the urge here. As in most places, in Britain it is mainly those in residential care who are restricted. Mental-health charities still campaign for the extension of the franchise, and good luck to them.

More controversial are the prisoners. The idea has raised its head again in Britain that prisoners should be enfranchised. Two inmates have taken their case to court, but the politicians have not reacted yet. Curiously, in Europe it is only Britain and Luxembourg that forbid voting rights to all prisoners. At least some categories are enfranchised everywhere else. There are harsher regimes elsewhere. In many states of the USA, convicted felons are struck off the electoral roll permanently as part of their punishment. That brings us back to Florida again! Just leave that one to the chapter on the 2000 election. On one side, you could say it is part of their penalty and they deserve to have their rights taken away. On the other side they are still citizens, they still have rights and most of them will be out within a few years, so they should be prepared for their return to society. We will leave that debate to you to work out for yourself. It is a tough one, but there seems little doubt that the fact that long-term remand prisoners, who have not yet been convicted, are disenfranchised in Britain is definitely a disgrace, and there does not seem to be any way of defending that.

One group of people in Britain who are staggering into the promised land, their eyes blinking as they shield them from the bright light of enfranchisement, are hereditary peers. A few have remained in the interim House of Lords, until the government work out what on Earth they want to do with the place. The rest can now vote in parliamentary elections for the first time. They could vote in local and European elections before of course, but they had that little mark by their names in the register to say they were barred when it came to the big one. One oddity here is that the entire royal family are now entitled to vote. I bet they are thrilled.

Stranger Gallery
The Unusual Candidates

' "But I don't want to go among mad people," Alice remarked.
' "Oh, you can't help that," said the Cat: "We're all mad here.
I'm mad. You're mad." '
– *Lewis Carroll*, Alice's Adventures in Wonderland,
Chapter 6: 'Pig and Pepper'

Joseph de Maistre said that 'Every country has the government
it deserves' back in 1811. If you agree with that, and he seems to
have a point, take a look at your government. Are most of its
members dull people, uninspiring, lacklustre? Are they exciting,
wild, extraordinary? I guess I know which way most of you have
gone on that. We get the dull because we deserve the dull. But
it's not for the shortage of interesting candidates. Elections
attract some of the most amazing people in the nation to stand
for office. However, very few of them ever get elected, and the
few who do are pushed to the back benches as dangerous
mavericks. This book is a celebration of the strangeness of
elections, so these are our heroes and here are a few of them.

THE SUPERSTARS

Bill Boaks has to be one of the biggest heroes for any fan of
elections. He contested his first parliamentary election in 1951.
He immediately announced himself as a man of enormous talent
by standing in the wrong constituency. His intention was to
stand against the Prime Minister Clement Attlee in Walthamstow, but he discovered too late that he was in the wrong

division. Attlee was defending his seat in Walthamstow West, while Boaks had got himself nominated for the East seat. For the next couple of decades he involved himself mainly with direct-action politics on several issues, but principally on transport and road safety. In the process, he went to court several times as his own protests had contributed to danger on the roads more than anything he had been protesting against.

Boaks returned to the electoral fray in 1970, and then tried three seats in 1974, when he stood in his own constituency of Wimbledon, his former home of Streatham and in the Cities of London and Westminster. He had expected to win all three and make his own decision as to which to represent, but his combined vote barely topped three hundred. He continued his fight until 1982, contesting 28 seats at general elections or by-elections. He lost all 28 deposits by a mile – the 240 votes he won in Wimbledon in 1974 remained his high point. His twenty votes gained against Jeremy Thorpe in Devon North in 1979 is among the lowest ever achieved in a general election. The five votes he gained in Glasgow Hillhead was his nadir, and it shares the title of the lowest vote ever in a by-election. His description varied between polls, but they were generally variations on a theme of 'Democratic Monarchist Air/Road Safety White Resident'. Some were put off by the apparent racism in the title, but it was hard to feel antagonism towards this batty old campaigner.

In some of the places he stood, he stayed only long enough to secure his nomination, but when he did campaign, his favoured technique involved using his mobile office. This was basically a bicycle converted into a kind of pedal-driven car with pieces of wood covered in slogans, which he took to the busiest road in the area. He would then leap out in front of cars to enable old ladies to cross the street. He would write down the licence-plate numbers of any drivers he considered reckless and pass them to the police, who would ignore him. Amazingly, he survived these adventures and kept safe until his death in 1986 at the age of 81.

To many observers of electoral lunacy there is only one man

who stands out as the true hero above all others. David Sutch chose not to wait for ennoblement and added the title of Lord to the front of his name by deed poll. He became a noted figure on the 1960s rock scene as Screaming Lord Sutch without ever selling great numbers of records. The music was frankly not all that memorable, but the political campaigning was legendary. His first foray into politics came with the 1963 Stratford by-election, caused by the resignation of John Profumo after the Christine Keeler scandal. The 209 votes he received for the National Teenage Party was a promising start and he was on his way.

Over the next few years he contested various elections under different guises, including a contest against Harold Wilson in Huyton. He would have fought more, but occasionally had problems with getting his nomination papers organised properly and also forgetting to get his deposit safely in the hands of the returning officer before he went and spent it. The Monster Raving Loony Party was launched in 1983 and it was under that banner that he campaigned for the rest of his career.

The party was admired for the humour that it brought to many elections, but the big problem was that it proved to be too sensible in the end. Among the wild policies that Sutch introduced that were eventually enacted were: votes at 18; abolition of the eleven-plus exam; licences for commercial radio; passports for pets; honours for the Beatles; and all-day pub opening. Sutch's lunatic ideas have led to more changes in public policy than any high-powered think-tank. His party has also had some local councillors elected, had some proper party arguments and splits and have had a few respectable votes in parliamentary elections. They now have sister parties in the USA, Canada, Australia and Spain (Los Pumas). There was even a proposal at one of their Loony conferences to change their name to the 'Raving Sensible Party'. We still await the enactment of his proposal to use the European Butter Mountain as a ski slope and allow water skiing in the wine lake. That will come. And there was for years only one Monopolies Commission – a fallacy only

Sutch had noted. Whether its change of name to the Competition Commission in 1999 was anything to do with Sutch's observation we may never know.

Sutch's most significant contribution probably came in the Bootle by-election of 1990. He got 418 votes, which was one of his better performances. David Owen's SDP got only 155 votes. It was this result that settled the issue for Owen. There was clearly no future for the rump of the SDP who had refused to join the Liberal Democrats. The Lib Dems had reason to be grateful to Sutch for resolving a problem for them that might otherwise have rumbled on for another year or two. It was probably mostly local Lib Dems who voted for him.

In all, Sutch fought 41 electoral contests, concluding with Winchester in November 1997. He never saved a deposit, but polled a total of 15,657 votes with his best performance at 1,114 in Rotherham, and his worst at just 61 in Kensington. He died in tragic circumstances in 1999 at the age of 58, and we all miss him. His final achievement is that the party he formed goes on without him. In 2001, the Monster Raving Loonies fielded fifteen candidates, now led by Howling Laud Hope and his cat. Their entirely blank election manifesto was one of the most profound contributions to this dismal election. When they finally admitted they did have some policies, they showed they were still on form. Watch out for future enactment of central heating for bus shelters, replacement of the national anthem with 'Do the Funky Gibbon', sweets, chocolates and cakes free on prescription and compulsory carrying of small mirrors rather than an ID card, so people can identify themselves.

THE HIGHEST FORM OF FLATTERY

There is nothing illegal about changing your name by deed poll to whatever you choose. There may be some technical problems you might come across, and officials can caution against any idea they fear the applicant might regret when they regain their sobriety. Some countries have rules, banning names such as Adolf, Jesus, Satan or any type of obscenity. Not only can you choose a new name in Britain, you can choose an old name too – someone else's name. If you fancy using the name of a well-known personality, there is nothing to stop you having it. Of course you may run into problems if you use your new name for fraudulent purposes or to conduct a campaign of harassment against the original user. As yet there is nothing to stop you using it to run against the original user in an election. There have been attempts to find ways of dealing with this, but there does not seem to be a way of insisting that people have to stand for an election under a name they no longer use.

The idea of deliberately using a change of name to cause difficulty for a politician in an election was launched by a Mr Lambert in 1970, who decided that he would henceforth be known by the name of Edward J R L Heath. He just so happened to go on to stand for Bexley in that year's general election, which just so happened to be the seat of the Conservative Party Leader Edward Heath. Not being the official choice of the Conservative Party for this seat, our new Mr Heath stood as 'Conservative Consult the People'. He was making a serious point about the direction of the Conservative Party, but questions were raised about whether this was entirely ethical. In the event the new Mr Heath gained a respectable 938 votes (1.8 per cent). This was enough to beat another Independent Conservative by over a hundred votes, but together they did not much damage Ted as he charged to a majority of 8,058 over Labour and picked up the keys to Downing Street in the process.

One odd point here is to wonder why anyone who goes to all the trouble of changing their name in order to cause difficulties for a politician cannot go so far as actually to get the name right. The full name of our former PM is Edward Richard George Heath. It would have taken Mr Lambert only a few minutes to find that out.

A similar mistake was made when Douglas Parkin made a deliberate attempt to ruin the chances of Roy Jenkins in the vital Glasgow Hillhead by-election of 1982. If Jenkins had not won, his parliamentary career was likely to be over, and the future of the SDP would have been endangered about five years earlier than it eventually fizzled out. The party had many enemies, so the plan for a spoiler candidate was not surprising and it worried the SDP enormously, as it expected a very close fight. In the event it was helped when its opponent changed his name to Roy Harold Jenkins, failing to realise that the middle name should have been Harris. He then went on to describe himself as SDP on his nomination paper, instead of SDP/Liberal Alliance, which was the style of designation every Alliance candidate took at the time, so hardly a surprise. Perhaps it is good for democracy that people who try these tactics to confuse voters are always so slapdash with their research.

Of course, candidates can change their names for reasons other than to cause confusion. For example, there was Tarquin Fin-tim-lin-bin-whin-bim-lim-bus-stop-F'tang-F'tang-olé-Biscuitbarrel. Tarquin was not given that name at birth, as you may have guessed. He used to go by the more mundane name of John Lewis, but he borrowed his new one from the Monty Python character who won Luton for the Silly Party in the Python team's famous 'General Election' sketch. The new Tarquin stood in the Crosby by-election in 1981. Everyone knew that Shirley Williams was going to gain the seat for the SDP with ease. The only reason why thousands stayed up through the small hours to witness the result was to hear the returning officer read out Tarquin's name. The official had got very cross about this upstart, and had tried any way he could to get him off the ballot paper, or at least have his name changed, and he had threatened to refuse to read the name. It is customary for the returning officer to read all the names in full. In the event he read only 'Tarquin Biscuitbarrel' and even allowed himself a small smile as the audience cheered before announcing his total of votes as 223. Shirley was not greatly threatened, but the watching audience was short-changed by this officer who flunked his moment of glory and would not give us the full performance. It does not need to be reported that Tarquin was a student.

If you wished to confuse the electorate, an alternative has been not to bother with changing your name, but simply to confuse the electors through your choice of description on the ballot paper. The description box on the nomination paper has caused problems for some independent candidates who have not realised that was where they were supposed to give the voter a clue as to what they believed. Thinking they are just filling in another form as they would for the Inland Revenue or some other official body, they tell us about themselves. That is why you sometimes find people standing for office as 'insurance salesman' or 'retail manager'. I have not yet come across a ballot paper that had a candidate under the description 'quite tall with fair hair', but I would love to know of one like that. Unfortunately, returning officers are usually too helpful and they would probably point out that sort of error to candidates.

Many people over the years have masqueraded as Conservative, Labour or Liberal candidates without ever gaining the endorsement of the party they claimed to represent. Often, returning officers would succeed in getting them to take a description such as 'Independent Conservative' or 'Local Labour', but even these descriptions have caused confusion at times. The legal situation had been fairly unclear until the Political Parties, Elections and Referendums Act 2000 set out the new rules. Parties can now register their name and an emblem (one that the new Electoral Commission deems not to be confusing or obscene). They can then nominate an officer who will sign to show approval of any official candidate. Then the official candidate can use the party name and the emblem on the ballot paper. This should mean an end to deliberately confusing descriptions.

Most people have not noticed that in future, unless your party is registered, you must stand simply as an independent or with no description. This will probably mean an end to most of the joke parties that have stood over the years, as well as to people who wish to stand using slogans to publicise some cause. It will certainly stop you calling yourself a Conservative candidate when you are not, but if you call yourself a Conversative candidate, and people have, it is up to the Electoral Commission to decide if that is likely to cause confusion, in which case they will rule the name illegal. Anyone wanting to register a joke party will also have to decide whether it is worth naming a treasurer who will have to abide by the complex procedures that the law now requires of them. Getting rid of confusing party labels is all very well and good, but a lot more has been lost besides. Again, convenience takes precedence over democracy.

The most curious recent example of confusion through party labels was caused by Mr Richard Huggett, who chose to call himself a Literal Democrat. He first stood in the European elections of 1994, the last to be held with the enormous first-past-the-post Euro constituencies. He managed to get 10,203 votes in Devon and Plymouth East (4.3 per cent), which was astonishing for someone who was not standing for a recognised party, was unknown in the area outside his village and never produced an electoral address or engaged in any campaigning that anybody noticed. This would have just been an interesting curiosity were it not for the fact that Adrian Sanders for the Liberal Democrats lost the seat to the Tories by just 700 votes. As another candidate for the Liberal Party gained 14,621 votes as well, Sanders had a right to feel that he had been well and truly set up. Huggett could see no reason for complaint, claiming that he was not a Tory stooge, but someone campaigning for more use of new technology to involve people in *literal democracy*. There seems little doubt that some of his votes, possibly nearly all of them, were from mistaken Liberal Democrats, but the courts could find nothing wrong in what he did. Anyway, candidates who are nothing more than spoilers usually score well under 1 per cent, so something odd was happening.

The next odd thing about Huggett was his choice of seat for the 1997 general election. From his manor in Devon, he chose to stand in Winchester. This time he stood as 'Liberal Democrat – Top Choice for Parliament'. What was that about not trying to be a spoiler candidate, Mr Huggett? Where did the commitment to *literal democracy* go? He got only 640 votes this time, but somehow he seemed to be the only person in the nation who knew Winchester would be the closest result in the country. With a majority for the Lib Dems of just two, and all the fuss that is described in our chapter on spoiled votes, Mr Huggett's intervention could easily have been decisive again. It will be a real shame if joke parties and serious local single issues disappear from ballot papers in the future, but, if you want someone to blame, you know where to look.

ALWAYS READ THE LABEL

Many candidates have stood over the years with odd descriptions that need explaining to anyone who reads about them later and does not understand the context. For anyone who wondered what a 'Dog Lover' was standing in Devon for in 1979, this was the reason.

The greatest political scandal of the 1970s in Britain surrounded the Liberal leader Jeremy Thorpe. He was tried for conspiracy to murder Norman Scott, a gay model who claimed to have had an affair with Thorpe. Friends of Thorpe claimed Scott was blackmailing him. The story had rocked the nation when an apparent attempt on Scott's life had resulted in the fatal shooting of his dog. Another Liberal MP, Peter Bessell, had become entangled in the plot and was accused of planning an attempted murder on Thorpe's behalf. Thorpe resigned the party leadership, but remained an MP and won his court case.

However, he never recovered from the terrible publicity. He remained a regular target for satirists and he was not allowed to forget it as he attempted to hold his Devon seat in 1979. Auberon Waugh stood against Jeremy Thorpe as a 'Dog Lover' in Devon North. Waugh did not make much impact locally, but Thorpe lost anyway to the Tory candidate. The BBC joined in the joke by scheduling a Liberal Party broadcast to be immediately followed by *One Man and His Dog*.

A FEW MORE ODDITIES FOR YOU

Where do we begin to name the other curious characters who have found their place on the electoral cast list? We could mention Jonathan King, the irritating pop mogul who has waved his flag for his own brand of 'Thatcherite Cool Britannia'. Thankfully, that little adventure did not go on very long. More lasting were the candidates who liked to be more up front about their sleaze than most. Miss Whiplash (Linda St Claire) lit up many by-election campaigns with her 'Corrective Party', which raised many giggles but hardly any votes. Usually, more successful on the vote front was Cynthia Payne. She stood in a number of elections, sometimes for the Rainbow Alliance, a party that was a semiserious contender for many years. Cynthia became something of a media personality everyone knew. Her claim to fame followed from her 'luncheon-voucher' parties in a Streatham house that I used to pass on the bus on the way to school every day. She was so shameless in her defence of the intimate activities that went on within that that she became the figurehead for the liberalisation of sexual attitudes. It got her 193 votes at her high point in Kensington in 1988, easily beating Sutch, London Class War, an Anti-Left Fascist, a Free Trade Liberal, Fair Wealth, a Leveller, an Anti-Yuppie and the unfortunate Connell and Trevedi, who both crop up in our look at failed candidates.

Numerous nonentities have stood on silly labels over the years. They have rarely been funny, but have occasionally made a point, such as J Fox, who stood for the Silly Party in Dover in 1979. He admitted afterwards that the whole point of the campaign was to beat the ultra-right-wing National Front. This he achieved by 642 votes to 378. It was the strangled swan song of the National Front's glory days of the 1970s. A little earlier they thought they were becoming the third party. Now they were beaten in one of their target seats by the Silly Party. That probably achieved more than dozens of Anti-Nazi League rallies and concerts did.

The election of 2001 was lacking in curiosities by earlier standards. The Jam Wrestling Party was the most notable newcomer, and the candidacy of Jordan, the synthetically enhanced glamour model, in Stretford and Urmston was for no other purpose than to give the *Daily Star* something they could report. I guess being political editor of the *Star* must be the cushiest job in the world. Changes in electoral law may have had something to do with the lack of interesting novelties, as well as general lack of interest in the whole process. I guess we have to give you another top ten and another coveted prize. The best descriptions registered for candidates in parliamentary elections:

1. Church of the Militant Elvis
2. Freedom to Party Party
3. Correct Edification
4. Gremloids (leader Lord Buckethead)
5. Fancy Dress Party
6. No Candidate Deserves My Vote
7. Beautiful Party
8. Feudal Party
9. New Millennium Bean Party
10. Jam Wrestling Party

EURO ODDITIES

Odd candidates continue to emerge on the continent of Europe. Italy has set a high standard in attracting unusual people to politics. For example, it is quite normal there for football stars to move into a political career. The Italians have a love of celebrities greater than just about anywhere else. While Brits may be interested in stars, we like to knock them down as well and we are always suspicious. The most interest has been aroused (if that is the word) by the porn star La Cicciolina. She proved to be a very successful candidate by adopting such unique techniques as campaigning topless and allowing voters to shake more than just her hand. It is hard to imagine that in Britain. We have had similar candidates, but the police would not be too keen on walkabouts of that nature. We might laugh at them, but we would not elect them. Italians do. Alessandra Mussolini also got her break in the world of pornography, but she decided to move on from that when she entered politics. After all, she had the dignified example of her grandfather to live up to.

Following on from the success of La Cicciolina in Italy, France has made its move into that sort of territory. Cindy Lee announced her intention to stand for the Paris municipal elections in 2001. Cindy's more regular employment has been as a striptease artist and dancer. Her choice of the fifth arrondissement as her target was probably a deliberate one – it was the former political home of Jacques Chirac. The platform included a call for sexier uniforms for city workers, municipal wife-swapping clubs and a nudist section in the Jardins de Luxembourg. Her claim that normal candidates were not sexy enough must have hurt Chirac deeply, but can hardly surprise anyone else.

Under the new rules for party lists in France, her 'Paris Plaisir' list had to include an equal number of men, which presented a new set of problems, but not any greater than those facing the Green Party, whose second candidate on the list for the seventeenth arrondissement was a transsexual, entered officially as a woman, but still regarded by the law as a man. These are problems never dreamed of by Emily Pankhurst.

A well-known clown suggested that he might run for President of France in 1981. When some polls showed that he was already running at support levels above 10 per cent, he decided he had better drop out. It had seemed a good joke, but it was getting worryingly serious.

ON THE WILD SIDE

Election officials will not let you put an animal up for election in Britain. Several people have tried and it never works. There is an argument that they should be allowed to stand, even if they cannot take office. After all, known convicted felons have stood when everyone knows they could not take their seat if they were elected. Some people have stood for local councils who have been underage as well, but they have generally kept quiet about it. You cannot keep quiet about trying to put a cow up for election. It is obviously a cow.

The tradition of nonhuman political involvement was started by Emperor Caligula, who made his horse, Incitatus, a consul of the Roman Empire. Many countries have taken an enlightened attitude. Dogs have stood for election in several places and a duck has put in at least one appearance. A rhinoceros has been elected in São Paulo, Brazil. It was also in Brazil that a goat ran for mayor of a town as a protest against local corruption. Just to show how uncorrupt and wholesome they were, supporters of the ruling party killed the goat. It had been leading in the opinion polls at the time. There was once an attempt to put a pig into the American presidential race. This attracted some support, but the campaign fell apart.

Of course, we must remember to cherish our minor candidates. There may be no point in voting for them, but cherish them anyway. The major candidates might become even worse without them. As for the argument that a vote for a no-hoper is a wasted vote, remember the *Simpsons* episode when Clinton and Dole were replaced by two morphing aliens, Kang and Kodos, whose evil plans are revealed by Homer:

KODOS: It's true, we are aliens. But what are you going to do about it? It's a two-party system! You have to vote for one of us.

MAN IN CROWD: Well, I believe I'll vote for a third-party candidate.

KANG: Go ahead, throw your vote away! Ah-hah-hah-hah-haaaah!

(*Man in crowd punches hole in his Peron '96 Hat.*)

LET'S NOT BE CHILDISH

It would be puerile to conclude this chapter with a round-up of candidates with silly names. After all when Zimbabwe could elect a president with the name Canaan Banana, it is hard to find any more obscure examples that could compete. All right, then, we will try. The real stars when it comes to interesting names are the UK Conservative Party. Their opponents rarely match them. Sadly, the party has become more proletarian in recent years, and the wonderful names of the past are very rarely repeated any more. A quick look through the Tory candidates in the 1950 election gives us some mighty examples of the kind of names they used to find: Somerset de Chair, Sir Hugh Lucas-Tooth, Sir Harry Legge-Bourke (that sounds familiar), H J Scrymgeour-Wedderburn, Sir Oliver Crosthwaite-Eyre, and of course Leslie Hore-Belisha, formerly of the War Cabinet, who gave his name to the Belisha beacon. That sort of magic seems to have gone, but even among the more mundane names they field today they have still found a few fairly impressive contenders in recent local elections, with Richard Thick in Kent, Robert Conboy in Lincolnshire and Bob Sleigh standing in Warwickshire. Again they came up trumps in 2001, fielding Prudence Daily and Mark Reckless. Surely they should become a double act. I doubt whether the Tory Party will ever be able to top their former Scottish candidate, Humphrey Dumptie.

Empty Closets and Magical Words

Strange Manifesto Stories

'In one corner they found a closet that promised mystery, but
the promise was a fraud – there was nothing in it.'
– *Mark Twain*, The Adventures of Tom Sawyer, *Chapter 26*

Do voters really bother with manifestos? Obviously very few
read the full document. Apart from party members, opposition
politicians, journalists and academics, hardly anyone reads
them. They are important, though, and the general ideas do get
across through the papers and the election leaflets. Most voters
have at least a vague idea of what the parties stand for, even if
they can make some colossal mistakes sometimes. So do the
people get the policies they really want in the end? In his *Little
Book in C Major*, H L Mencken's view was: 'Democracy is the
theory that the common people know what they want, and
deserve to get it good and hard.' In fact most manifestos try to
avoid that. They usually try to aim for a reasonable middle
ground and not to scare the horses. Any party that really
offered the people what they wanted good and hard would
probably lose. People don't expect politicians to be as brutal as
them.

Was Robert Peel's Tamworth Manifesto (1834) the first true
manifesto? It was not specifically designed as an election
manifesto originally in the way we would understand it today,
although he fought on it over the next few years. It was also very
short on specific commitments. For all the fuss that is made of it
by historians, we should not forget that the Tories lost two

41

general elections on it. He struggled on with a very short-lived minority government, but he could hardly have claimed a victory. If Peel had gone through that today, he would have been ditched by his colleagues and focus-group research would have dumped the Tamworth manifesto in the nearest shredder, but this was not an age for spin-doctoring and it survived and laid the foundation for the Tories' victory in 1841 and established the first true Conservative Party political platform.

Margaret Thatcher noted in her memoirs that the central importance of the manifesto in British elections strikes foreign observers as slightly odd. Certainly party platforms in America are far more vague and are widely ignored by media, voters and the candidates who are supposed to be running on them. Newt Gingrich's 'Contract With America' arguably challenged this, but it does not seem as though he has started a trend. Thatcher always saw the manifesto as a leader's personal statement. That is how everyone else saw hers too.

John Major said of the 1992 manifesto, 'Every last word of it is me.' He did not actually write any of it, but he still felt it was him right down to all of its 350 pledges, possibly a record. Labour's manifesto of 1983 might have made more in its original form, before a few clouds of common sense strayed across the landscape and they took out loads of the pledges, including a lengthy section on dog homes.

REMEMBER ME?

New Labour would be delighted if you would be so good as to forget the 1983 Labour manifesto – 'the longest suicide note in history', as Gerald Kaufman MP put it in one of the most famous political quotes of modern British history. The party had torn itself apart over the previous three years, largely over internal reform. However, in those days the national executive and the party conference still had control over the Labour manifesto, and both those bodies were firmly in the control of the left wing at that stage.

It is a curiously nostalgic experience to look back through the document now and read about Labour's promises to withdraw from the EEC, renationalise all assets sold off by Tories, seek to phase out private schools, aim for the unification of Ireland by consent, borrow massively to finance more public spending and remove all nuclear weapons from Britain. Maybe you prefer 1980s Labour. Maybe you prefer 21st-century Labour. Maybe you find it hard to enthuse about either. Just don't try to pretend they are the same party!

Of course, it is the job of all party candidates to back their manifesto, isn't it? In fact, more senior figures like Jim Callaghan, Denis Healey and Gerald Kaufman made their contempt for it absolutely clear, but what about ambitious new candidates in County Durham? What did that personal election address for the new Labour candidate in Sedgefield say in 1983? 'We'll negotiate a withdrawal from the EEC, which has drained our natural resources and destroyed jobs.' Several candidates who wanted nothing to do with this policy did not mention it on their own leaflets. Not Mr Blair though. Nor Mr Kinnock come to that, who went on to work as a commissioner for this organisation that had 'drained our natural resources'.

There were a few concessions to electoral reality, as even more detailed commitments on industrial policy, equal opportunities and numerous other issues were excised at the last minute, but most of the left's agenda was allowed to stand. A national executive member, John Golding, was the only right-winger with any significant input into the document. Some of his friends were aghast at his work, but he already knew the party was heading for a thumping at the polls. He was reported to have decided to 'let them have enough rope to hang themselves with'. After all, if you know your party is going to lose, why waste your favourite policy ideas on them? They can have someone else's.

The one true success of the Labour manifesto of 1983 was that it was a big seller. Not only did it sell better in the shops than manifestos usually do, but it was also bought up in bulk by Conservative Central Office because they loved it so much. Do you want to know the real killer point on that? Labour gave them a bulk-order discount!

FAT CITY

Hunter S Thompson is a social and political commentator that some Brits have tried to emulate. The name Will Self comes to mind here. In truth, Britain can never produce anyone like him. His combination of radical independent political thought, twisted humour, vicious aggression and paranoia can be found only in America. The mix of gun culture, drug culture, beat generation culture and professional political activism that he represents just cannot happen anywhere else. If you want to read the most vicious piece of character assassination ever written about anybody, try his eulogy to Richard Nixon at the end of his book *Better Than Sex*. After any politician's death, everyone queues up to praise them. Not Hunter! Also in this book we are told about the manifesto that he wrote for his campaign for sheriff of Aspen, Colorado, earlier in his career. He stood as the 'Freak Power' candidate in 1970 and very nearly won. His platform contained many imaginative policies such as putting dishonest dope dealers in the stocks, but the highlight was to counter the invasion of Aspen by irritating outsiders by renaming the town Fat City. Those who lived there or chose to move there would have no problem, but the greedy rich who bought up the town for profit and all the other annoying trendy types who still descend on Aspen every year would soon be put off by 'Fat City Ski Fashions' and the 'Fat City Music Festival'. In a typical turn of phrase, he hoped these people would be 'driven across the land like the rotten maggots that they are'. If only more manifestos were written like that.

IT WON'T MATTER: NOBODY WILL READ IT!

In many cases it is just as well that hardly anyone reads the manifestos. The Green manifesto for their successful 1989 European election is a case in point. They gained by far the highest support they have ever earned in Britain, but it was only through a desperate last-minute rush that there was any real policy included on the environment. The Green Party had detailed policies on proportional representation and gay marriage, but nothing much on saving the Earth. It was for this reason that nine out of the ten leaders of environmentalist charities and pressure groups who were polled said that they would not be voting Green, and the remaining one, Jonathon Porrit, issued them an ultimatum to sort it out fast, or he would turn his back on them as well. Since then they have had time actually to make their policies green after all, but they have never had that many votes again.

The Tories succeeded in putting their policy emphasis in 2001 on the euro and asylum – policies that were not great priorities for most people. They really excelled themselves in 1997, when they announced that the polls would be turned around, because they had unveiled their vital policy that would bury Labour under an avalanche of voters rushing back to the Tory fold. Wait for it . . . They would save the royal yacht, *Britannia*! Many of them danced with delight as they had pulled the rug out from under Tony Blair and confounded the pundits. At least two daily newspapers went along with the analysis. It took a while for some of them to realise the royal yacht was not the key issue on many people's agenda. When it turned out that this was not the trump card after all, they tried introducing a complex new pensions policy a few days from polling. It was not a particularly bad policy, but was bound to lead to confusion and fear, and sure enough it did.

In looking at manifestos always remember to fear any that promise of 'Peace in our time'. They always lead to war. Any that promise economic regeneration usually lead to recession. The ones that tend to be more successful both in winning the election and in delivering their promises are the deadly dull. When it comes to choosing the dullest manifesto, Labour 1997 has to be in the reckoning. As for the most unsuccessful ones, let's just say those that could have been titled 'Come On, Turkeys: Vote For Christmas' have yet to win an election anywhere. Promises to raise taxes, remove liberties or reduce the advantages of the dominant sections of society can win some votes, can even win arguments. They don't win elections.

VOTING FOR A NEW SEED

The Natural Law Party have become a worldwide success story of a sort. They started making their mark in the 1992 UK general election. It is very sad to hear that they are considering calling it a day. Most people never really understood what they were doing. They were not a joke party, neither were they simply standing just to promote their religion. They had a serious and detailed programme for running the nation, and felt that the country would be happy to embrace this at the polls. When I say serious and detailed, I am not kidding. It came as a genuine shock and disappointment to the party that they polled so poorly.

For anyone who is not aware of the Natural Law Party, they are an offshoot of the Transcendental Meditation movement inspired by the Maharishi Mahesh Yogi. Many people know them as the yogic flyers, from their practice of leaping about with their legs crossed while in a higher state of transcendental consciousness. Their 1992 manifesto was a literary masterpiece. As other parties seek to make their manifesto more dumb every time (in a few years we will be at the level of 'We like doctors' and 'Being poor is bad'), the Natural Law Party gave us something we could all spend time trying to wrap our brains around. Try these quotes for a quiet moment of contemplation:

The Unified Field Theories of Quantum Physics ($N=8$ Supergravity and Heterotic Superstring etc.) from the standpoint of modern science have identified this ultimate reality of life, the Unified Field of Natural Law, the field of pure consciousness, or pure intelligence . . .

The subsequent eight lines complete the remainder of the first sukt – the next stage of sequential unfoldment of knowledge in the Ved. These eight lines consist of 24 padas (phrases), comprising $8 \times 24 = 192$ syllables . . . these 24 padas of eight syllables elaborate the unmanifest, eight-fold structure of the 24 gaps between the syllables of the first richa (verse).

We were treated to a series of immensely complicated charts and diagrams illustrating the impact of TM-Sidhi techniques and the principles of Vedic science. These principles would transfer into policies that would eliminate crime by getting people to act in accord with natural law and eliminate disease by training medical staff in the principles of Maharishi Ayur-Ved (presumably prior to making them all redundant). Needless to say, there are plenty more incomprehensible charts to illustrate all this.

When it comes to the prize for the most impressive manifesto promise, all other parties fail to compete. We could give it to the Natural Law manifesto for 'Great Britain will be the first great nation in the world to enjoy freedom from problems', or for the entire detailed section that shows how we will attain 'Heaven on Earth', but the prize has to go to 'The United Kingdom will enjoy the direct light of the sun and also the sunlight reflected from the moon.' Despite their rejection by the people, they have still delivered on that one and that shows remarkable generosity.

I must thank them for the line, 'The Natural Law Party holds that election is a national celebration.' That could be the publicity line for this book, and I go along with them entirely.

Just Say Cheese and Pray that it Works

Bizarre Campaigning Methods

'In War then, let your great object be victory, not lengthy campaigns'
    – *Sun Tzu*, On the Art of War

Do campaigns ever change anything? The answer to that is not as easy as you might hope. Sir James Ferguson, writing in the nineteenth century, certainly felt they changed nothing: 'I have heard many arguments which influenced my opinion, but never one which influenced my vote.' For most people that may be true, but for a few others things are different – and those few can be critical in a close contest. We will take a quick tour through some of the stranger cases of election campaigning. Some of them worked. Quite a lot of them, actually.

THE LOWEST OF THE LOW

For one of the most unpleasant and grotesque campaigns of modern times, let us not ignore the Smethwick election of 1964, in which Peter Griffiths won the seat for the Conservatives against the prospective new Foreign Secretary, Patrick Gordon Walker, with the unusual slogan, 'If you want a Nigger for a Neighbour Vote Labour?' Yes you did read that correctly. Younger readers may not believe it. Today, he might be arrested for campaigning tactics like that, and thank God, too. Back then it got him elected. Labour ousted the Conservative Government and won the election, but experienced a swing of over 7 per cent against them in Smethwick – well out of line with anything else in the country. In a famous 'welcoming' speech Harold Wilson remarked, 'Smethwick Conservatives can have the satisfaction of having topped the poll, of having sent a Member who, until another election returns him to oblivion, will serve his time here as a parliamentary leper.' Remarkably, Mr Griffiths, after moving to a safer home in Portsmouth, returned to Parliament after a break and remained until 1997, which is a long life for a leper.

YOU'RE BETTER OFF WITH A SLOGAN

It was not really until the twentieth century that campaigns became national. Before that, the local constituency battle was the key contest, and national ties between candidates were loose. Maybe the first proper case of a national campaign slogan was the Conservatives' 'Safety First', which sounds about as uninspiring a slogan as you could imagine, but they ran with it in 1922 and liked it so much they used it again in 1929. The voters had had enough of safety by then though and they voted for a bit of danger instead. Another top ten coming up. These are some of the particularly poor slogans British parties have come up with in general elections:

Worst party election slogans ever

1. *Crisis Unresolved*	*Liberal*	*1955*
2. *Keep Britain White!*	*National Front*	*1974*
3. *What a Life!*	*Liberal*	*1970*
4. *Only a New Seed Will Yield a New Crop*	*Natural Law*	*1992*
5. *Think Positive Act Positive*	*Labour*	*1983*
6. *Who Governs Britain?*	*Conservative*	*Feb 1974*
7. *People Count*	*Liberal*	*1959*
8. *Britain Will Win*	*Labour*	*1987*
9. *The Time Has Come*	*Liberal/SDP Alliance*	*1983*
10. *The Next Moves Forward*	*Conservative*	*1987*

Some inspiring little gems there. Sadly though, British parties cannot keep up with the world's best. The international award goes to Canada's NDP with their 1972 number, 'Corporate Welfare Bums!'

WE ARE GATHERED HERE TODAY

The campaign rally still exists. It is no longer the most critical meeting point between the people and the candidates. TV took over that role many years ago, and often rallies are just stage-managed events for TV anyway. They can still be memorable, though, and here is a classic piece of journalism from Alistair Cooke.

Twenty-odd years ago my editor asked me to go over to England to cover a British general election and make such comparisons with an American presidential campaign as occurred to me. On the way in from London airport I scanned the hoardings for election posters, for the billboards that would show cosmetic blow-ups of the two opposing leaders over some such slogan as 'Labor is Your

Neighbor' or 'Eden is Leading'.' I saw none, no hint anywhere that there was to be, or had been, a general election.

Next day I took off for the country, and in all my travels – from Reading to the West Country and up through the Midlands and on to Scotland and back to the wind-up in Manchester – I saw no buttons or bows, no surging mobs in football stadiums, no airplanes sky-writing 'Madly for Adlai' – or the British equivalent – at $1000 an hour. There were no motorcades – six cars, three press buses, eight police outriders – sirening into a city square with the candidate and his spread-eagled arms acknowledging the roars of twenty thousand people – like Hitler entering Vienna.

Much more typical was a day spent with Mr Attlee and his wife. They drove alone in a mini-car through the country lanes and in and out of villages and dismal suburbs and came to a schoolhouse or a marketplace. He would stand up before a hundred, sometimes no more than a dozen, citizens and make a sort of scoutmaster's pep talk and then drive off again to a rustle of handclaps. Certainly there were rallies, so-called, such as you might muster in the United States for a particularly heated parent-teachers meeting. But they were held in halls, not in Colosseums. There was no army of Youth for Eden wearing blue boaters, no flights of Attlee balloons, no flocks of waving banners to give the impression that you were present at an indoor Battle of Agincourt. There would be the novelty – to an American – of people standing up in turn, like schoolboys, to ask the speaker to claify this point or that. And another, startling, novelty: hecklers bawling out, 'Yaw, but 'ow about the pensioners, tell us that' and 'Not bloody likely, mate.' These intruders, if they started to warm up to a harangue, were politely shushed. Finally the man said, 'Thank you, one and all.' And that was it.

In the United States thirty thousand people pack into

Madison Square Garden or some famous stadium in Boston or Pasadena. They are all of one party, one mind. These are rallies of the faithful, and any interloper who got up and heckled would be hustled out by a couple of alert cops. I came to the conclusion that a British election campaign compared with an American campaign was as a prayer meeting to a Roman circus.[1]

It is regrettable that the old-fashioned British campaign meeting has more or less died. John Major tried to resurrect it in the 1992 general election with his soapbox tour. Proper public meetings without ticketed entry, elaborate stage choreography and ruthless stewarding are hard to find. When you do find them you find hecklers. The noble art of heckling and the equally great art of dealing with heckling has died out with it:

HECKLER: Vote for You! I'd as soon vote for the devil!
JOHN WILKES BOOTH: And if your friend is not standing?

HECKLER: Go Ahead Al. Tell 'em all you know. It won't take you long.
AL SMITH: If I tell 'em all we both know it won't take me any longer.

John Major remembered his experiences of this kind of campaigning in 1979:

A few hecklers followed me around. One, a Labour supporter, was a persistent nuisance, and one evening I responded pretty sharply to his comments. He rose from his seat, snorted disapproval and stalked out in high dudgeon. Unfortunately for him he was so intent on

---

[1] Alistair Cooke 'In the Meantime' May 6th 1979, published in *The Americans: Fifty Talks on Our Life and Times* Alfred A. Knopf 1980.

registering his disgust that he walked into the broom cupboard rather than out into the night air. The audience watched fascinated, then burst into laughter and applause as he emerged. Red-faced and embarrassed, he slunk out and did not reappear. I missed him – he had provided many a light hearted moment during the campaign.[1]

SECONDS OUT! ROUND ONE!

The campaign debate lives on as a traditional spectacle. In most constituencies there is at least one of these between the candidates. Often it is the local Council of Churches who organise the meeting that the combatants all agree to attend. Otherwise it might be a local radio station, local paper, educational institution or some community group, but there is rarely more than one that all of them will attend. The sitting candidate usually finds other vital things to do, and they 'regretfully decline' to attend more than one. The age-old theory is that the incumbent has most to lose. This is a practice breached only when the incumbent is particularly good at it, or their main opponent is sensationally poor, or the incumbent is so stupid they do not realise they are a public embarrassment and their campaign manager can do nothing to stop them.

There are plenty of good stories about these *Question Time* types of debate between the candidates. There was a classic encounter in a Northern town that was held in a school at which the sixth-formers were firing questions at the candidates. One young man came up with a probing question that occurred to him as he heard the debate unfold. The teacher who was chairing the event looked up and said, 'That wasn't the question you were going to ask.' The sitting Labour member refused to answer it and the others were nonplussed. They were happy to answer.

[1] John Major, *John Major: The Autobiography*, HarperCollins, 1999, p. 63.

Bewilderment started to spread over the faces of the candidates and other assembled hacks as the debate became more and more curious. Then the Conservative candidate could sit there baffled no longer: 'Does he [the Labour candidate] know what the questions are?' When it turned out that the Labour candidate did indeed have a list of all the questions in the correct order and the others did not, the temperature moved up a few degrees. He had refused to take part except under those conditions, as he was known to be poor at thinking on his feet (or indeed, in this case, on his arse). The teacher who had organised this event had decided to go along with his demands. The previously polite and impressed sixth-formers started to boo and heckle, but this did not diminish the majority in a safe Northern seat. This plank of wood still sits in the Commons today.

We could go on about the New Labour woman who always took her toy fluffy bunny to debates as well as to the count. There was the Tory councillor, who had to stand in for the MP who never attended these sorts of occasion, who liked to lecture questioners on intricate and obscure aspects of European history and point out to the audience how stupid they were. There was the Green candidate who was doing quite well until he admitted previous offences of criminal damage relating to animal-rights campaigns that no one had asked him about.

One of the problems of organising these events is deciding whom to invite. As the average number of candidates in a constituency has increased, it becomes difficult to invite them all. For a start, if you invite the BNP candidate, the others generally refuse to turn up, and that leaves the vicar hosting a rally for Nazis, skinheads and misfits and any opposing thugs who have come to beat them up. Coffee and biscuits are served afterwards in the church lounge. Then there are the minor candidates whom nobody knows anything about anyway. Is it really worth it? The joke candidates will run out of anything funny to say after about three seconds, then they are even more boring than the others.

The Referendum Party provided an interesting problem in 1997. James Goldsmith and his cronies were at pains to point out that theirs was a single-issue party that had no policies on anything other than the need for a referendum on Europe. Candidates were under strict instructions not to comment on anything else. As the party was showing some notable support in national opinion polls, had some high-profile candidates and attracted significant media coverage, event organisers all wanted to invite them. The party's general advice to candidates was not to attend. If no one asked a question about a referendum on Europe, they would look a bit silly sitting there saying nothing all night. You might think they could have trusted their candidates to go and speak sensibly about their personal views, as they were putting themselves forward for election after all. They could have made it clear their views were personal and not party policy. Someone in Goldsmith's high command was more sensible than that. They realised most of their candidates were novices, who would get torn apart by experienced politicians and would get pushed into making terrible mistakes. The candidates who were not novices were even more worrying. They were mostly ultra-right-wing nutcases, oddball mavericks who had already been thrown out of all three major parties or they were David Bellamy. It was important they remained as nothing more than names on a ballot paper and did not reveal themselves to be real people.

PIGGIES GO TO MARKET

It is unfortunate that so many people are still so naïve that they think their vote matters in the election. The truth is that only really 2 or 3 million votes matter out of the 30 million or so that are cast. Elections in the UK are won or lost in around sixty to seventy seats that are generally won by the victorious party – win nearly all of them and you have made it! If other seats change hands as well, because of a national landslide, local factors or particular campaign issues, that is of only incidental interest within the bigger question of who is going to run the country. So only around 10 per cent of the seats really matter. Many areas of the country have very few of these. They are concentrated around the outskirts of London, the West Midlands and in some of the small towns of the northwest. There are hardly any in Scotland or Wales and obviously none in Northern Ireland. It's even worse than that. In these target seats you might as well ignore those who will probably not vote and those who are staunch supporters of any particular party. You want only the swing voters. All you need to do is work out who they are.

Marketing is an amazingly sophisticated science. Some of it may be of dubious authenticity, but that doesn't stop it being sophisticated. Just as brand managers can specifically target exactly whom they are aiming their product at and aim their campaign directly at them with ruthless intensity, so can political campaign managers. They can work out exactly whom they need to concentrate on, and the rest of the country can be safely forgotten. Are you one of their targets? See how many of the following statements apply to you. Count up how many times you can say yes:

1. I am a woman
2. I am between 30 and 55 years old
3. My annual household income is between £25,000 and £70,000
4. I am white and English
5. I have more than one child
6. I am married or divorced
7. I run a medium-sized family car
8. I work in the service sector, possibly part-time
9. I live in the southeast of England, the West Midlands or the northwest of England
10. I live in a seat held by the governing party with a majority of fewer than ten thousand

11. I live in a small town or in the suburbs of a large city
12. I live on a new housing estate
13. I am buying my house on a mortgage
14. I read the *Daily Mail* or the *Sun* regularly
15. I use the NHS
16. My children are state-educated
17. I have a private pension and some modest savings
18. I have at least one living parent who is, or will soon be, retired
19. I have been, or I am scared of being, a victim of crime
20. I have usually voted in general elections and fully intend to do so in the next one.

If you could identify with at least sixteen of those statements, you are a target voter and consequently might wish to plan a long foreign holiday whenever a general election is called, or at least cancel all diary engagements, because politicians will be falling over themselves to get to you. You will be doorstepped, telephoned, surveyed, leafleted, target-mailed and generally harassed until it is all over. If you can say yes to all the questions there will probably be a television programme made about you. If you are sensible, you should take the opportunity to make as much of this as you can: get all the media to pay you for your opinions and call in as many favours as you can from the party workers – many of them will consider household chores.

If you could recognise yourself in only about six of those statements, or fewer, the political parties do not really care about you. They consider that you are either definitely going to vote for them, definitely *not* going to vote for them, or that you live in an area where it does not matter whom you vote for anyway. If any canvasser calls on you during an election, this will be because they are lost. You are not morally obliged to help them.

If you doubt that the politicians really understand this principle, take note of campaign manager David Wolfson's advice to Margaret Thatcher out in the campaign bus in 1983: 'Only wave in marginals, Prime Minister.'

THERE NOW FOLLOWS A WASTE OF EVERYONE'S TIME

Election broadcasts have a fantastically honourable history. They predate television for the masses, having started with short films for cinemas, which started to be used even before radio broadcasts. Of course Eisenstein made his name through short political films of this nature and became arguably the only key film director to get his break in this manner – but Lenin and Stalin did not go in for elections in a big way, so the political films that were the best in any artistic and historic sense do not really concern us here. Some American politicians got into this early, but probably the first truly professional and effective use of election films was by Hitler and Goebbels in 1932. I did tell you the history of election broadcasts was honourable, didn't I? Hitler was a great one for campaigning innovations: mass rallies; use of campaign music as psychological tool (generally Wagner rather than D:Ream); use of private planes for impressive whistle-stop national tours; use of entertainment as a means of electoral communication; coordinated spin-doctoring for the press; and organised gang warfare. Only the last one is generally avoided by most major modern democratic parties.

Radio election broadcasts in Britain go back almost to the start of the BBC. Now, they are minor adjuncts to the key TV broadcasts. Perhaps the most memorable and silly one was Winston Churchill's 1945 address when he said, 'No socialist system can be established without a political police. They would have to fall back on some form of Gestapo.' So don't say that broadcasts have got more ridiculous and negative recently. He may have led the nation through the war, but that broadcast exemplified the mood that he was out of touch, and the people gave Labour their first majority government. They took the risk on the Gestapo.

TV election broadcasts started in the UK with the general election of 1951. There had been a few 'peacetime' broadcasts before this that were the early forerunners of today's PPBs. The very first election broadcast featured Lord Samuel for the Liberal Party droning on with a dull speech he read from his notes without ever looking up. He went over time by several minutes and they eventually faded him out halfway through a sentence. The Conservatives came second and already the art of the PEB was established. Anthony Eden was interviewed by Leslie Mitchell and most people agreed that it was quite well done. The politicians learned early to ensure that their broadcasts were transmitted simultaneously across the channels, as the people would watch anything else given a choice. In the election broadcasts of 1955, with only two channels operating in the UK, Hugh Gaitskell lost 80 per cent of the available viewers to *Jack Solomon's Scrapbook*. Anthony Eden also achieved only a 20 per cent share, the viewers turning to *People are Funny*. So those who claim that broadcasts have lost popularity are wrong – they were always unpopular. The politicians have lost the right to have them shown simultaneously, but real enthusiasts can now spend most of their evening watching them on various channels if they really want to.

It is worth looking at some of the older broadcasts if you ever get the chance. The production values are poor, looking like homemade movies shot on a set the politicians had just built themselves. The scripts are dull, and the performances awkward and patronising in tone, but there is often an honesty and freshness in them that comes across much more than in the bland corporate videos we get today. The politicians seem actually to believe in something, and the best of them were surprisingly good communicators – check out Harold Macmillan for the Tories, the young Tony Benn for Labour and, a few years later, Cyril Smith for the Liberals.

Hugh Hudson started the move towards getting famous movie directors to make election broadcasts. 'Kinnock the Movie' was similar to his film *Chariots of Fire* and managed to be even more self-righteous. The choice of John Schlesinger to make the principal Tory broadcast of the 1992 election was promising: 'Joe Buck' the ambitious, but naïve, cowboy from

Huntingdon, comes to town to make his fortune. He meets the lowlife of society on the Tory benches, is ripped off and humiliated, until 'Ratso' takes him under his wing and helps him to a leading position, after teaching him how to be cynical and give up all his principles. Joe Buck feels empty at the dubious, squalid sort of success he has achieved. Ratso dies in his arms after losing his seat in Bath.

Sadly, however, we did not get *Midnight Cowboy II*, but a dull little film about John Major going back to Brixton.

Here we present you with the ten worst party political broadcasts ever shown, culminating with the prize winner. I have opted to let Lord Samuel off the hook. Maybe his performance was one of the very worst, but, as it was the trailblazer, we ought to excuse him.

10. Pro-Life Alliance, 1997 (censored version). This was one of those cases where a party deliberately fielded fifty candidates in order to get a broadcast. However, the broadcast they wanted to transmit was so thoroughly mangled by the censors that they might as well not have bothered. The footage of the foetus in the womb was deemed too sensitive for poor dear little adult voters who might be watching, and we were given a film that mostly featured blurred abstract patterns to the accompaniment of music. There was no logical reason for censoring it. If you believe that a foetus is fully human and deserving of full human rights, then you agree with the Pro-Life cause and you would have wanted the images shown; if you believe that a foetus is merely a blueprint for potential human life, and does not have full human rights, then there was nothing wrong with the images. As usual moral censors foul up everything they touch. In this case, they trampled all over free speech and they should all be thoroughly ashamed of themselves.

9. BNP, 1997. Somehow the far right have always eluded the censors, even though it is sometimes hard for supporters of

free speech to stomach them. In the National Front's heyday in the seventies, they were very quiet about their more controversial policies. I remember a broadcast in the 1979 election when they looked and sounded like the Liberal Party. They even had their own Cyril Smith lookalike in Martin Webster. By 1997, John Tyndall's BNP had done away with all the business of trying to appeal to everybody. This broadcast was made to appeal to racists and nobody else. We were told that millions had died for nothing in the nation's past as we were shown pictures of black people wandering around different parts of London. The floodgates had opened and Mr Tyndall was sure we did not want this vision of the nation's future. The BNP saved a couple of deposits in London, but the vision did not seem to be worrying people as much as he hoped.

8. Liberal Party, 1974. For some reason they devoted most of the time on this one to reading out telegrams from celebrities who were supporting the Liberal Party. There were messages from such as Alec Guinness and Honor Blackman. There was even one from Jimmy Saville, who once made a broadcast for the Liberals but has subsequently denied ever supporting any party. There did not seem to be a lot of point in this list of names. We were not told what it was about the exciting Liberal policies that attracted them. Perhaps it was just to remind the viewers that some people would actually be voting Liberal, and they need not feel lonely. Huw Thomas even enthused that Derek Nimmo had quoted Psalm 115 on his telegram. He didn't bother to tell us what that said, obviously presuming all voters can quote any scripture from memory. Perhaps it was verses 5–7: 'They have mouths, but they speak not: eyes have they, but they see not. They have ears, but they hear not. Noses have they, but they smell not. They have hands, but they handle not. Feet have they, but they walk not. Neither speak they through their throat.' A biblical prophecy about the average

Liberal paper candidate of the seventies? Or a prophecy about the state of Norman Scott's dog, after the Liberals had finished with it?

7. Natural Law Party, 1992. We had to include it, didn't we? Most connoisseurs agree this was better than their 1997 effort, by which time they were starting to look a bit too much like the other parties. We had never before seen how the nation's problems would be solved by a few people leaping up and down on gym mats with their legs crossed. It was a joy to witness and it was also full of baffling scientific evidence that might have proved their point, if anyone had understood what they were on about.

6. Conservative Party, 1992. 'John Major: The Journey'. Some still say the idea of devoting an entire broadcast to John Major and his climb from humble south London origins was a masterstroke. John Schlesinger lovingly filmed Major returning to Brixton to meet the people and see his old house still standing. He reminisced about how he used to stand on his soapbox in the street and people would 'engage in badinage' with him. Now I've witnessed plenty of arguments in the street in Brixton and people do not engage in badinage there. Major's own view was that the whole thing was an embarrassment. He said in his autobiography that he disliked using his upbringing in an attempt to win votes. If that is his view I don't see why anyone else should argue. Whether it won votes or not, it was embarrassing.

5. Conservative Party, 1964. Alec Douglas-Home was one of the nicest and probably one of the cleverest people ever to become Prime Minister. Unfortunately, he became PM about a hundred years too late. He was not a creature of the television age, and the Tories had an enormous problem with their leader's appearance in election broadcasts in 1964, as the sight of him on the TV at that time sent more people rushing behind the sofa than were sent there by an appearance of Daleks. He best summed it up when he later

admitted to a conversation with a make-up girl. D-H: Can you make me look better than I do on television? Make-up Girl: No. D-H: Why? Make-up Girl: Because you have a head like a skull. D-H: Doesn't everyone have a head like a skull? Make-up Girl: No.

4. Labour, 1987. Glenda Jackson and her potted plants. This one was really silly. Glenda must be the most glamorous star ever to go into politics in Britain. Her star quality has been wasted as she has just turned into another dull politician, but this was the one attempt Labour made to use her in front of a national audience. She stood in what may have been a greenhouse, surrounded by plants that she admitted she sometimes talked to, and proceeded to make a string of daft analogies between plant life and the economic state of Britain, illustrating the balance-of-trade problems by moving some shrubs around. You could not help but remember Peter Sellers in *Being There*, in which a gardener is mistaken for a wise political commentator through the trite observations he makes about his garden, and soon they are marking him down as a presidential hopeful.

3. Conservative Party, 1997. John Major had unilaterally decided to ditch the broadcast showing a Tony Blair lookalike making a Faustian pact with the Devil. Some of the loonier among the Tories claimed that they would have won the election had it been shown. That just proved that Major did not deserve to be surrounded by such a useless bunch. However, the last-minute replacement was the saddest election broadcast ever made. Major spoke to camera to plead not to be made to go into the European negotiating chambers naked with his hands tied (do not linger too long on that image). This was the first broadcast to go straight past the millions of electors and target nobody but the leader's own MPs. It was a personal message to three hundred or so people, who we assumed were voting Tory anyway. Even they ignored it. The Tories admitted defeat

with this broadcast, and it was a very, very sad little programme.

2. The Albion Party, 1974. The only reason this is not easily at number one is that the more pedantic among you will point out that it was not technically a party election broadcast. Although the Albion Party have fielded candidates, they have never had the fifty candidates required for an official one. This was a show on BBC2's public-access series, *Open Door*. I was very young, but I am one of the few who can remember watching it at the time. It has left a permanent mark on us all. The series producer, Mike Bolland, described it as both the most boring fifteen minutes ever shown on British TV, and also the most scary. That may sound impossible, but he could be right. We opened with a man dressed as a wizard, wearing a grotesque mask on his face and holding a notice, with the scribbled message: '45 million candidates. Sorry! BBC TV said not more than one person in the studio. We're going to let the tree represent everyone ♥.' The ugly wizard exited stage left and the camera focused on a small potted tree sitting on a chair, with a placard behind it that read, ALBION DANCES. There was nothing else for it to focus on and it zoomed in and out for the rest of the broadcast, while the two voices of a man and a woman, who were clearly auditioning for work on a self-hypnosis tape, mesmerised us with their strange messages: 'The only state is the state of your mind'; 'Albion is the other England of peace and love, which William Blake foresaw in a vision'; and 'If you want to be, you are.' It had to be the most memorable election broadcast of them all.

1. SDP, 1987. 'Rosie's Rabbits'. Rosie Barnes had recently triumphed in the Greenwich by-election and she was the new darling of the Alliance. Here she appeared on her lawn talking to her children and rabbits. The following is not a figure of speech, it really *was* shot in soft focus, like a 1970s ad for powder that washes whiter than white. She told us she

was a housewife who was concerned about her children's future and had decided to do something about it. Exactly what she was going to do about it neither she nor her rabbits would tell us. An election campaign that had started with great hopes for the Alliance was failing to lift off, and when the SDP wasted a precious TV spot on this tosh, Liberals all over the country were absolutely livid. The tensions started to come to the surface about this time in the campaign and the former allies spent the next two years arguing constantly and splitting into three parties. Most broadcasts have negligible impact, but this one must have had the most negative impact of any ever made.

As for the best broadcasts, there are several leading contenders, such as Saatchi's ground-breaking ads for the Tories in 1979, Hugh Hudson's 'Kinnock the Movie' in 1987 or John Cleese's classic performances for the SDP. However, one broadcast stands head and shoulders above any other ever made. The Green Party's 'Slime Child' broadcast of the 1989 European election was absolutely brilliant – clever, funny, moving and very effective. The Green Party started the campaign on around 1 per cent support and finished with 15 per cent. So, don't say campaigns never have an effect. Unfortunately for the Greens, there was still no PR for European elections at that stage, so their lack of elected members or any credible leadership, their shambolic national organisation and David Icke's re-emergence as the Son of God all killed the party off before it could build on that triumph. It was still a really good broadcast, though.

The year 2001 did not add anything ground-breakingly new to the catalogue of political broadcast art. There was nothing sufficiently bad to trouble my bottom ten, but the Tories' incessant, deliberately depressing snapshots of Britain going to ruin did not seem to do them any good. While most of their ideas came from American campaigning, they missed the balanced approach. Their broadcast on prisoner early release schemes was a straight take from the Bush advert against Michael Dukakis in 1988. Bush gave us lots of nice visions of a 'kinder, gentler America' as well, though. The Tory broadcasts just kept on with their distressing visions and would have probably encouraged more people to slash their wrists than they ever encouraged to vote Tory. It's a good job nobody takes these things too seriously.

Labour and Lib Dem efforts were the usual dull but worthy affairs. Of course, Labour scored a wonderful own goal with their final broadcast, which they chose because their research had shown that many young people had no idea about the process of voting. The *Hollyoaks* star Terri Dwyer turned the whole process into an exciting, sexy activity. Sadly, 90 per cent of the population have never watched *Hollyoaks* and had no idea who she was. The bigger problem was that the woman who was giving the young folk this lesson in civic education admitted she would not be voting herself because she was busy and she had never heard of postal votes.

The only real star turn that I saw was the broadcast of the Scottish Socialist Party. I do not know if Ken Loach was involved with this one, but the gritty mini-drama they put on about life in Scotland today was in a similar style. It was very well acted and filmed and featured a brilliant moment as the life of an unfortunate family was falling apart: Tommy Sheridan appeared on the TV screen in their room to say, 'If the class war is over, who won?' just before their power was finally cut off. Just as negative a broadcast as that of the Tories, but in a different league.

ON THE KNOCKER

Most voters do not really understand the point of canvassing. Some even get upset when an election passes and nobody has called to see them. They don't seem to realise that canvassers are not calling to have a nice chat or find out what the voters believe on the issues of the day. They may have ways of doing that on other occasions, but in an election there is not enough time – and they can't go changing their policies in the middle of the campaign if they find people don't like them. If the candidate or any national stars are in the area, they are there as a PR stunt, to get noticed and put their campaign in the news. If it is just common-or-garden activists who are calling, they are there to find out who is supporting them, who is wavering and who is against them. All they want to do is get the vote out.

The Tories' Gyles Brandreth admitted in his diaries that he was caught out by a woman who took him inside for the best part of an hour to talk about home births and all other manner of irrelevancies, before admitting she was voting Labour. Only the inexperienced fall for that. Every canvasser has favourite stories to tell. They tend to revolve around similar themes. Rather than go through them all, we can just give you the points table. If you have been a canvasser, score yourself for each time you have encountered any of these:

Door slammed in face	1 point
Asked a ridiculously obscure question by someone trying to be clever, or waste your time	1 point
Given a response that you could not understand after three attempts, then you gave up	1 point
Talked to someone who you know was only pretending they couldn't speak English	2 points
Given a hug or a kiss (possibly by someone who then realised you were someone else)	3 points
Told some intimate secret by a voter you wish they hadn't told you	4 points
Attacked by a dog or other animal	5 points
Attacked or chased by a voter	7 points
Canvassed someone who was in pyjamas or wearing only a bath towel	4 points
Canvassed someone who was naked	10 points

Any other unusual example can be awarded marks from 1 to 10. Bonus points can only be earned if the police had to be called. The Lib Dem candidate in Inverclyde who got shot with an air rifle can claim plenty.

Many claim that canvassing can be of limited effectiveness. It is probably a fair point that the reliability of response has gone down with the growth of phone canvassing. This method has much to recommend it and is the only option in some cases, but an experienced canvasser can spot a liar from fifty yards when they are working the doorstep. On the phone, there are no body gestures to observe and no eye contact (or indeed obvious non-eye contact).

There is also the specialised canvass. New Labour was always more sophisticated than people realised. At the Wirral South by-election just before the 1997 general election, they gained an impressive victory in Tory heartland territory that set them up nicely for the coming campaign. While their presentable candidate, Ben Chapman, undertook key campaigning tasks such as calling the numbers at the local bingo hall, they got Dennis Skinner, the leading mascot of the left wing, to hide from the public, but make personal calls to Labour loyalists who were threatening to withdraw support from the party in their relentless march towards the right. He got most of them to stay on board.

KNOCK, KNOCK, IT'S US AGAIN

The most important point of canvassing is to provide the records for the election-day knock-up. Some people learn the hard way that it is a bad mistake to tell all the parties you are going to vote for them, in the hope that you will get rid of the canvasser quicker that way. Of course some canvassers are smart enough to spot a liar, but some are not and, even if they are, the local campaign managers may decide to knock up anyone they think may be a possible vote. You are particularly at risk of being knocked up in a key by-election when the town is crawling with party workers on polling night. If you have not voted early you will be in for a hard time. In fact you may have voted, but some or all of the parties have not got your number for some reason and you are still in for trouble.

The art of knocking up is to get around to all your definite, or maybe even possible, supporters on polling day to encourage them to turn out and perhaps offer them a lift or any legal inducement you can think of. It is an opportunity to warn them that your wife-beating, child-eating opponent is currently winning by one vote (on no reliable evidence whatsoever).

At some by-elections when the parties have so many workers that they do not know what to do with them, they can start knocking up before 10 a.m. and harass the people at intervals until they either submit or murder the final visitor after five attempts at explaining that they intended to vote at 9 p.m. after everyone has got home, had tea and watched *Who Wants to be a Millionaire?*.

The sad character we mentioned, who thought he was clever pledging his vote to everybody, is in big trouble now. He voted early when there was only one teller on the door, did not give her his electoral number and has now had twelve visits from four different parties who all refuse to believe him. He was last seen strangling the lady from the catalogue delivery service.

I have had the experience of arriving to knock up a voter at the same time as someone from another party. I have heard of two examples where three parties arrived together. In one case, they made a moving gesture of political unity by ringing the bell and all standing there together to greet the man in his pyjamas. It is always men who make these mistakes. Most women realise that lying leads to more trouble in the end.

Knocking up can be a strange experience for a new political activist. Take a look at John O'Farrell's first attempt at the 1983 general election from his excellent book *Things Can Only Get Better*:

On election day I turned up at the committee rooms in the north side of Exeter eager to do my bit, knowing nothing of how elections are organised. They sent me out to knock on doors and although I knew I was on a council estate and that this should be natural Labour territory, I was actually pleasantly surprised by just how many Labour supporters I found on my way round. At the first door they were Labour. At the second door they used to be Labour but were voting Conservative this time. The next couple were voting SDP, but might vote for us 'if we got our act together'. Then another Labour voter, another Labour, and then one Conservative. On these figures we were ahead. I happily reported this news back to the committee rooms and they explained to me that the list of voters that I had been calling on was the Labour *promise*: the people who had been canvassed earlier in the campaign and had said they would definitely vote Labour. That's why I had only been knocking on every fourth door. If support was haemorrhaging like that across the country we were doomed.

Later that night he opened his new barrel of home-brewed beer that he liked to name after topical events. This was 'Labour Landslide Bitter' and it was undrinkable.

Another of those legendary knocking-up stories is the mythical dead voter. It does happen. It happened to me in a London by-election. You cheerfully ask the lady if her husband is going to vote, and she looks straight at you and tells you he died a week ago. I was about to enquire if he had cast a postal ballot before his demise when I managed to bite my lip just in time. It can be frightening how electioneering can dehumanise you. I remembered that what normal human beings do is to say they are very sorry and leave before they do any more damage. *The Times* reported a great case in 1991 of a canvasser who congratulated an elector on the excellent flower display in their hallway, and was told that they were from her husband's funeral.

The first experiments with computerised knock-up technology were eye opening. For many years all the parties used little tear-off slips with carbon sheets to cross the voters off as their numbers came through and take the top sheet off to go knocking. Many people still use this system and they are probably very sensible. When computerised versions started coming into use in the late 1980s they were carefully designed to be as useless as possible. First, they were very slow and labour-intensive to operate, update and produce new printouts, and this ensured that there were *two* party workers stuck inside committee rooms most of the time instead of the *one* that was necessary previously. Then the field length was so short that they gave only the voters' surnames and initials; so instead of knowing you were visiting Fred, Doris and Kevin and getting a picture of whom you were looking for, you were looking for F, D and K and you did not even know which sex to ask for. There was no option to feed useful information back into the computer such as, 'They will vote after 7 p.m. and if one more person calls on them before that they are threatening to switch sides!' The system was actually slower and less flexible than the old one and it led to groups of workers hanging around the printer waiting for the next list, which was already out of date. In short it was one of the best examples of inappropriate technology I have ever come across, and, although programs have been much improved since then, paper and pencils are still hard to beat in 21st-century elections.

KERB CRAWLING WITH LOUD-SPEAKERS

Some candidates feel they have not had a proper campaign until they have been around the streets in a suitably decorated car or van with a loudspeaker to tour the neighbourhood and annoy everybody. Bigger campaigns can even put on full-scale motorcades, cavalcades and the like, perhaps with a campaign bus,

colour-coordinated young enthusiasts with balloons and fancy
hats and all the rest of the paraphernalia. Ken Livingstone did
this in his London mayoral election with his purple bus. His
remarkable campaign manager liked to talk about giving the
voters their 'purple moment'.

There has always been the apocryphal story of the Range
Rover that goes around the housing estates at three o'clock in the
morning blasting out the message to vote for the other side.
Plenty of people have sworn that they know of a case when this
has really happened. I have never heard convincing evidence,
but I would love to know of it.

The Tory maverick right-winger Sir Peter Tapsell had a
lovely style with his loudspeaker street theatre in the 2001
election. He would announce to the public, 'Sir Peter Tapsell is
in your street. If you want to meet your MP, present yourself at
your doorstep.'

REFLECTED MEDIOCRITY

Some people wonder why politicians love to get the endorsement of celebrities during election campaigns. The answer is
obvious. Most politicians are very dull people who spend most
of their lives sitting in interminably boring meetings, trying to
read virtually unreadable draft documents about technical
arrangements for rate reviews, or discussing household drainage
problems with the kind of people who do not realise they would
be better off going to see a plumber. To be associated with pop
stars, movie actors, millionaire authors or even bit-part players
in a soap opera makes the politician appear to the public to have
a faint glow of reflected glory. More significantly, it makes the
politician think they are glamorous. This kind of delusion is all
that keeps some of them doing the job, and, if elected politicians
did not do it, unelected politicians would – and they are even
worse. So be grateful for celebrities who get involved in politics.

If they were not there, the only other kind of perks available for the average politician would be corrupt ones.

Beyond keeping the politicians happy the advantages are harder to pin down. They can provide money, but there are wealthy businessmen who can do that for little more than a peerage and then they will shut up and keep out of the way. A few committed and resourceful celebrities can be helpful through supporting party events, writing material or appearing in broadcasts. After all, when a company wishes to advertise its product it will pay a lot of money for a well-known celebrity to appear in the publicity. There have been a few cases of politicians appearing in advertising campaigns, but most of them suffer from low recognition or negative recognition. So a celebrity can attract attention and might make a campaign seem more attractive.

The likes of Gyles Brandreth, Seb Coe, Glenda Jackson, Michael Cashman and Clement Freud have even gained elected office, but in a way they all had to surrender a large part of their celebrity to become mere politicians. Of course the world's most successful celebrity politician was Ronald Reagan. For all the Americanisation of the rest of the world's elections, America is still different and it makes perfect sense for candidates to be celebrities. Whether there was any serious truth in the rumour that Warren Beatty was making plans to run for the presidency I do not know, but for all the comedy and self-deprecation in his movie *Bulworth* you could see someone in that movie character who was a natural, modern election candidate. Part of the difference is that American politics is more glamorous anyway. The President, as well as senators and large state governors, can lead lives that are not far removed from showbiz and well-known personalities can parachute into top jobs without having to work their way up. Even if party leaders run presidential-style election campaigns in the UK and other parliamentary states, they had to spend years as humble backbench MPs first, and maybe local councillors before that.

Somehow I could not imagine Reagan ever having done that.

Can the support of the famous make a real difference? Some people seriously claimed that the Bee Gees' intervention, when they said they might leave the country as tax exiles if Jim Callaghan had won in 1979, was significant. Callaghan lost and they still left the country. Of more significance were the rumours that Andrew Lloyd Webber and Paul Daniels would leave the country if Blair won. He did win and they never left, which was hugely disappointing for many.

The most organised attempt to get pop stars involved in election campaigning was the 'Red Wedge' campaign of the 1980s, backed by the likes of Billy Bragg, Paul Weller and the Communards. This was ostensibly a campaign to raise political awareness among the young and encourage more of them to vote. However, most of the contributors were Labour supporters and the title of the campaign gave a bit of a clue as to its goals. Margaret Thatcher won huge victories in 1983 and 1987, getting the biggest support for the Tories from young voters ever recorded.

One case that all the middle-aged pundits did miss was the Welsh referendum. Blair and most of the rest of the country were shocked at the narrow vote in favour of the Welsh Assembly. This central plank of the new constitutional agenda nearly fell at the first hurdle. Most of the wave of Welsh bands that had stormed the charts such as the Manic Street Preachers, Catatonia, Stereophonics and Super Furry Animals either specifically campaigned for a yes vote or implied support. The strong, growing sense of 'Welshness' among the young that they had done so much to encourage was surely a factor in the relatively good turnout among the young in a generally poorly supported poll and their clear support for the new assembly. In a narrow vote, it was very likely that it was decisive. Perhaps the involvement of U2, Ash and Barry McGuigan was important in the referendum on the Ulster peace agreement. It was certainly noticeable that no single celebrity would have dreamt of coming out for the other side. Maybe celebrities can be of more use in referendum campaigns. There are certainly some getting lined up on both sides ready for the Euro debate.

Conservatives have a problem with celebrities. In America, the only celebrities who will campaign for right-wing Republicans tend to be geriatrics from the movies, sport or TV, or walking caricatures of Neanderthal blood-and-thunder attitudes such as Arnold Schwarzenegger or Chuck Norris. The only musicians who will come out for them are country singers in enormous stetsons. All the cool stars support the Democrats. In Britain the problem is even bigger. The difficulty is that a celebrity is likely to be wealthy, and people will simply assume that they are rich people campaigning for self-serving low-tax policies. Greed may be considered good in America, but Britain is still a bit more puritan about it. It looks selfish and that is bad for a publicity-conscious celebrity. To support left-wing causes looks more socially aware and caring. Vitally for celebrity types, it is always more cool to be liberal or socialist. Generations of musicians have sung songs about oppression, racism, poverty and other social woes. Only one song from the Beatles has ever successfully tackled the issue of being fed up with paying tax. We have yet to be treated to the first attempt at telling asylum seekers to go home set to music. Right-wing celebrities tend to keep quiet about it.

For a time the now disgraced novelist Jeffrey Archer was in charge of getting celebrities to campaign for the Conservative Party. Don't those two concepts of celebrity political endorsements and Jeffrey Archer juxtapose to pinpoint the problem neatly? At one point he triumphantly produced a list of about forty celebrities who would be supporting the Tories in the forthcoming election. He even managed to get some of them together for a photo call to get press attention. I spoke to a friend some time later who had read the same article and had exactly the same thought as I had had: 'Out of this long list of names, the only one who makes me sit up and think that I am impressed that he supports the Tories was John Mills [who switched sides later anyway].' As for the rest, there was little one could say. Whether they could rely on the support of Lynsey De Paul or Christopher Biggins was of such monumental insignificance that it would be hard to measure. Knowing they shared a party with Michael Winner would surely have caused many Tories to tear up their membership cards. The fact that even he later defected to New Labour spoke volumes about British politics at the turn of the millennium. I had not been aware that half the people on Archer's list were still alive. Reflected glory? I think not.

While Labour attract more pop stars, young comedians and artistic types, Conservatives get the older D List has-beens and never-weres and a few retired sports stars. The Liberal Democrats tend to go more for nice, middle-aged intellectual types who appeal to . . . well to natural Liberal Democrat voters, really. So they do not exactly get them into new territory. You would expect Barry Norman and Nicholas Parsons to be Liberals, wouldn't you? Now if Marc Bolan had survived and had gone into Liberal politics, that might have been a different story. Of course the use of John Cleese in their campaigns did produce some of the best party political broadcasts of recent years. Labour have made some use of people like Stephen Fry in a similar manner, but have never really gone for it in a big way. A few seconds of Geri Halliwell making tea in a 2001 broadcast generated a lot of talk, but it was hardly a memorable performance.

The party who did go for it in a big way were the Scottish National Party. Many people regard Sean Connery as their leader, particularly since Alex Salmond retired and that bloke in the glasses took over. His broadcasts to his nation from across the sea in Spanish exile have become little treasures – rather like messages from Bonnie Prince Charlie to his faithful subjects back home across the water. The most unsuccessful use of a celebrity in a TV broadcast was the appearance of Leo McKern as the interviewer of Dr Alan Sked and his bizarre hair in the UK

Independence party election broadcast. 'Well, thank you, Dr Sked. I, for one, was most impressed. No doubt you were too,' he told us, as he fawned in the patronising manner of a 1950s children's TV presenter who had just interviewed some tedious scientist and was determined to tell the little people how grateful they should be that he had come to speak to them.

The Conservatives had to change their celebrity plans in the run-up to the 2001 election. They hoped to employ Jim Davidson more extensively than any celebrity they had ever used before. Comedian and game-show host, Davidson might make liberal elite types cringe, but they are not the target audience. To the aspiring working classes who embraced Thatcher and then turned their backs, he is probably as good a choice as anyone could hope to find. He is hugely popular with many from this kind of group, communicates well with them and is someone people like to identify with. As the Tory Party faced an election with only three front-benchers whom anyone had heard of (and not hugely popular at that), Davidson was to do his own national tour, glad-hand the public, front events, possibly even take an election broadcast. By polling day, William Hague, Ann Widdecombe, Michael Portillo and Davidson would have been the Tories ingrained into the nation's consciousness, for good or ill. Unfortunately, the numerous blue-rinse brigade of Tory old ladies were in two minds about Davidson. Some might like their own cheeky young man, but it seemed a bit too risqué for others. Those who had only seen him on *The Generation Game* were surprised at quite how rude he was when he made the financial appeal at the Conservative Party conference in 2000. It is just as well they have not seen his full stand-up act, or one of his 'adult pantomimes'. Once they had been hit by volley after volley of blue jokes, swearing and female body parts, the Tory Party would be missing a number of cardiac victims. Davidson was really done for by the growing influence of the new Christian right within the Conservative Party. He was certainly not their type and they were not going to put up with him. So the Tories sacrificed the one popular communicator they had available to take a leading role and his part in the campaign was significantly reduced. On the other hand to have opted for someone who has had even more wives than an average Tory Cabinet minister was always going to look a bit dubious for the 'family values' party.

TELLING THE PEOPLE WHAT TO THINK

Many democrats extol the virtues of the referendum. The biggest problem here is the great argument over what is the plural of the word. Is it referendums or referenda? I have heard people argue convincingly over Latin grammar far more knowledgeably than I ever could, and I am still torn between the arguments. So I shall write about referendi.

Hitler and Napoleon were great fans of referendi. We now refer to their invitations to the people to agree with them as plebiscites. The word says a lot. These were latter-day Roman emperors looking down and giving the mere plebs a chance to feel they were important. As a psychological tool it was powerful to get the people to take ownership of a policy for themselves and to support it with enthusiasm. Napoleon, Hitler and most Roman emperors desperately wanted to be loved and they felt that their own identity and that of their people were intertwined.

The important hint for any aspiring dictators among you is to remember that when you use a plebiscite, to remind the people that they are at one with you in some mysterious spiritual symbiosis, there are six important rules:

1. You must choose what is asked and what is not. Don't let others get at the agenda.
2. You must choose the precise wording of the question.
3. You must choose who gets to vote and who is excluded.
4. You must choose the method for counting the votes and determining the significance of the result.

5. You must choose whether to allow any opposition campaign and determine what they can do.
6. You must exercise extreme influence and preferably total control over all the key media.

If you can achieve all of those, you are a true dictator and you have got the idea of how to rig these things effectively. If you manage none, or only one of them, you are Swiss or Californian or from somewhere else that lets the people have control over the process. If you score four or five you are Harold Wilson or Tony Blair.

Hitler knew that control of the process was vital. The timing of the annexation of Austria was partly triggered by his desperation to halt the referendum that had been organised by the Austrian Chancellor Schuschnigg. Once the troops had gone in, he set about getting SA men to force Viennese Jews to rub out the slogans, notices, posters and any other clues to the existence of the referendum from their city. Crowds would gather to watch these 'rubbing parties' as elderly Jews rubbed them out with bare hands or toothbrushes. Having eliminated all trace of the earlier aborted poll, he set about organising his own by following the six golden rules. That way there was no question of losing.

UP ON THE BOARDS

One of the things that national parties spend a large proportion of their money on is their poster campaign. Getting these things designed, produced and then plastered all over the country is a very expensive business, even if some friendly companies offer billboard space. People often wonder why they bother. Usually the only advertising poster campaigns that make a big impact are the ones that are around for years and ingrain themselves into our brains without our realising, or the ones that really shock –

with disturbing images, near nudity or very surprising and off-the-wall humour. Party political posters rarely last more than a couple of weeks and they do not tend to go in for radical shock tactics. They may be cool for youth magazines or fashion clothes, but they are not worth the hassle for mainstream political parties.

Nevertheless, some posters are remembered for years. The best remembered of them all were the Conservatives' 'Labour Isn't Working' posters of 1979. We had had good slogans before, like 'You've Never Had it So Good', but this was a new kind of departure on visuals. Somehow the Demon Eyes campaign ('New Labour, New Danger') – won the *Campaign* magazine prize as poster ad of the year and it helped Maurice Saatchi and Peter Gummer to peerages. Most people thought it was pretty poor and it certainly had no discernible positive effect. I guess that says a lot about the advertising industry. At least the poster of the crying lion with its blood-red tear ('New Labour, Euro Danger') was called the worst campaign ever seen by Ken Dampier of Dampier Communications. Labour tended to go more for the straightforward classical approach to posters – clean and clear bland messages on primary-coloured posters with little fuss. In fact, they did have other ideas. We were spared a poster campaign based on the *Mr Men* series only because Tony Blair did not like it and they had problems getting copyright permission. In 2001 the most imaginative posters came from Labour's mock movie adverts 'Economic Disaster II' and 'The Re-Possessed'. These were followed up by the Hague/Thatcher morph. Whether they switched any votes was again questionable, but at least they were fun. The Tory ad men had long since despaired that they had ever taken on the job, and they produced nothing of any note.

In case you wondered why some of these posters that get launched at a promotional event shown on TV news never seem to appear on a hoarding near you, that is because in many cases they do not appear anywhere. This is the usual tactic of the

Liberal Democrats, who cannot afford this kind of campaigning. They paste up their poster on one site, get their stunt broadcast on the telly, and the poster is never seen again.

AFTER THE PARTY IS OVER

Campaigns are still not over after the last vote has dropped into the box. After that it is time to go to the count. There are no more opportunities to impress the electorate, but there are still other impressions to be made on people and plenty of opportunities to wreak havoc.

If you have not attended one of these, you must try to sometime. Small-scale counts tend to happen in school halls or council offices, but large counts for a whole local authority's council membership or for several different seats in a general election will take place somewhere suitably huge such as a concert hall or leisure centre. For example, the count for Birmingham's MPs takes place at the National Exhibition Centre. Just imagine how many of the weirdest people in the West Midlands you would meet if you attended in that vast arena.

Some are there to work and get paid, mostly council staff, police and other security personnel and bank staff who have been brought in because they know how to count, and that is helpful. Then there are the media – you can spot the young regional TV presenter planning for their two minutes of glory. Just tell them you are the leader of the council and you should get an interview with them before they are introduced to the real one. Then there are the hacks – candidates, their partners, agents and their tellers and guests. Some have come to eagerly scrutinise the boxes as they are emptied and work out precise percentage support from each polling station (strictly speaking, it is illegal for them to share this sort of information outside the hall, but the courts do not have a year spare to get around to prosecuting thousands of politicos). Some have come for the party atmosphere and to spot a famous face or two. Some have come for a good argument, and maybe a fight if they are lucky. Some have no idea why they have come, they just always do.

I have not yet attended a count at which there were fewer than three people who were hopelessly drunk. It is usually more than that. When you also remember that many of the assembled hacks have been awake for 36 hours and working all day like fury, and that most of the people there are about to be bitterly disappointed, while the others are going to be unbearably pompous and smug, you realise why there are so many policemen and security staff there. It is not usually fear of terrorists breaking in and burning the votes: it is fear of the mother of all after-closing-time pub fights.

Counts can be the most exciting and the funniest nights out you could have. The late Alan Clark had his own reasons for looking forward to them:

Bratton. Sunday 5 June
I'm madly in love with Frances Holland. I suspect she's not as thin and gawky as she seems. Her hair is always lovely and shiny. Perhaps I can distract her at the count on Thursday and kiss her in one of those big janitors' cupboards off the Lower Guildhall. [Frances Holland was the 22-year-old Labour candidate in the 1983 campaign for Alan Clark's Plymouth constituency.][1]

John Major remembered the Huntingdon count on the night of his 1992 triumph:

The atmosphere in the huge hall where the ballot papers had been counted was oddly subdued. Very few of my

[1] Alan Clark, *The Alan Clark Diaries*, Weidenfeld & Nicolson, pp. 7–8.

party supporters had been allowed in. Only the Monster
Raving Loony Party's Screaming Lord Sutch and his rival
fringe candidate, Lord Buckethead, added a spot of colour.
'I'm so glad you've won,' Sutch confided to me. I was able
to repay the compliment by telling him he had been the
most intelligent of my opponents. Since Lord Buckethead
was in his full fig I couldn't hear his comment, but he
seemed friendly enough.[1]

Martin Bell had his own fond memories of his election count:

There were three people whom I wished to avoid. Two of
them were Neil and Christine Hamilton. The feeling was
mutual. Christine always sidestepped me when she could,
except once on Knutsford Heath. They were looking
shattered. Nicholas Winterton, just re-elected as MP for
Macclesfield, walked past them without a word. I might
have felt some satisfaction; but their brokenness dismayed
me.

Miss Moneypenny the Transformer, representing the
Glamorous Party and a Birmingham nightclub, was not so
easily eluded. She pursued me down a blind alley beside
the counting tables, where she had me cornered. It is not
usual for a parliamentary candidate, at the climax of the
democratic process, to have to make small talk to a seven-
foot transvestite with flashing nipples; but I did my best to
rise to the occasion by standing on a chair.[2]

The key thing for the candidate to remember is always to
maintain their dignity. Others can cry or get into arguments and
fights, but not the candidate. This is most important for the
sitting MP who loses a seat. You have to remember to 'do a
Portillo' and go out with some style and even a bit of humour.

[1] John Major, *John Major: The Autobiography*, HarperCollins, 1999, p. 306.
[2] Martin Bell, *An Accidental MP*, Viking, 2000, p. 41.

The race for the most graceless concession ever made at an election count was enthusiastically joined in 1997 by Olga Maitland and David Mellor. Mellor compared most of his fellow candidates to animals and then harangued them, particularly Jimmy Goldsmith, while they all jeered and slow-handclapped him.

These latter-day election-night whingers have followed in the proud tradition of the former army heavyweight boxer, Brigadier Terence Clarke, who let his voters in Portsmouth West know exactly what form of lowlife he thought they were in his concession speech of 1966.

Getting Vicious – Getting Personal

'We may draw from it this useful lesson: that loss of virtue in a
female is irretrievable – that one false step involves her in
endless ruin – that her reputation is no less brittle that it is
beautiful.'

– Jane Austen, Pride and Prejudice

Reputations are there to be ruined. Loss of virtue can certainly
be irretrievable (male or female), depending on what exactly was
lost and where it went. But, if you want your opponent to be
dispatched to that endless ruin, they may need a helpful push,
particularly if they have not actually done all that much wrong,
and the electorate are going to need you to provide a mighty
powerful magnifying glass to show them what the fuss is all
about.

Grover Cleveland had to admit fathering a child out of
wedlock during the American presidential campaign of 1884.
Supporters of the Republican candidate James Blaine spread the
happy news about the son born to Maria Crofts Halpin, who had
been on very friendly terms with other politicians. The
opposition jingle went:

> *Ma! Ma!*
> *Where's My Pa?*
> *Gone to the White House*
> *Ha! Ha! Ha!*

There was also a leaflet that declared, 'One More Vote for
Cleveland' alongside a picture of a baby. Cleveland applied the
theory that a politician caught in a sex scandal should be honest

85

and remain dignified. Paddy Ashdown was one among many others who tried the same strategy later. This led to an increase in his popularity, as it usually does. Cleveland beat Blaine quite easily. Only by lying and squirming miserably does the politician lose votes in these cases, which makes you wonder why so many of them go for that option.

Louis B Mayer got involved in one of the silliest attempts to discredit a candidate when he made his theatres show a newsreel about Upton Sinclair, Democratic candidate for Governor of California in 1934 (a year so good for dodgy elections it has been challenged by only a few – 2000 for example). The film included a poor old dear showing us the modest little house that Sinclair's policies would ruthlessly take away from her and a bad actor making some sort of attempt at imitating a Bela Lugosi type Eastern European accent. He endorsed Sinclair, saying that 'his ideas had vorked vell in Russia'. The Republican candidate Frank Merriam spent a record $10 million dollars on a campaign that was full of masterstrokes like that. Sinclair thrashed him.

STILL AT IT

For those who think this kind of crude personal approach to elections died out years ago, just look at Britain in 1997: David Evans, the Conservative MP for Welwyn Hatfield, told a meeting of sixth-formers at Stanborough College that his Labour opponent, Melanie Johnson 'had three bastard children' and had 'never done a day's work in her life'. Evans prided himself that he always shot from the hip. Later on the voters shot from theirs and that was the end of him.

Evans was probably not the worst. In Exeter, the Tory candidate Adrian Rogers described his gay opponent, Labour's Ben Bradshaw, as 'sterile, God-forsaken and disease-ridden'. One of his leaflets warned parents that their children would be at risk if

Bradshaw was elected. Tories around the country breathed a deep sigh of relief when Rogers was easily beaten in this former Tory seat. They had enough problems without someone like that getting elected.

It is always good to see that America still leads the way in vicious campaigning. The desperate attempts to defeat Hillary Clinton in the New York senatorial race of 2000 included tactics such as implicating her in the bombing of the American ship in Yemen that had resulted in many deaths. A congressional candidate in Washington State was even accused of child molesting by telephone canvassers. The Land of the Free still sets the standards when it comes to campaign filth.

HALL OF FAME

Here we go, then, with another of our top tens, and another highly desirable prize. This time we have the most memorable election campaign insults. General insulting remarks about politicians do not count. They have to be made during a campaign, or be comments made about a campaign and its candidates. Let's take them in reverse order:

10. Norman Tebbit canvassing in the 2001 election and noticing a shop advertising a sale on flip-flops: 'Oh look, they're selling liberals.'

9. Hubert Humphrey campaign advert in 1968 consisting of nothing other than someone laughing helplessly at a TV screen that displays the message, 'Spiro Agnew for Vice President'.

8. Fiorello LaGuardia (1882–1947), former Mayor of New York: 'I could run on a laundry ticket and beat those bums any time.'

7. Dame Barbara Cartland, author, in 1992: 'If you vote for Kinnock, you are voting against Christ.' (I think we have to

take that one as an insult rather than an acclamation of Major as the Messiah.)

6. Democratic Party response to Barry Goldwater's campaign slogan, 1964, 'In your heart you know he's right': 'In your guts, you know he's nuts.'

5. A candidate for Congress conceding defeat: 'This is democracy. The people have spoken – the bastards.'

4. Anonymous leaflet in Ynys Mon 2001: 'If you vote for Bennett you will be electing a cheap drag act.' (Dishonourable mentions also for an anonymous leaflet in Bermondsey, 1983, with pictures of Peter Tatchell and the Queen: 'Which queen do you want?'; and for David Dimbleby referring to Ronnie Fearn as 'a pantomime dame, a Liberal dame' after his victory on election night 1997.)

3. On hearing that Walter Mondale said that he did not have the manhood to apologise – George Bush: 'Well, on the manhood thing, I'll put mine up against his any time.'

2. P J O'Rourke from his book *Parliament of Whores*: 'To call our system of primaries and party caucuses a beauty contest is to slander the Miss America pageant. No Miss Texas ever had a voice as grating or diction as tangled as George Bush. No Miss Massachusetts ever plucked her eyebrows as incompetently as Michael Dukakis. And neither Mike nor George could twirl a baton. If you want to get really depressed about the quality of our presidential hopefuls, think of it this way: What if you were wrongly accused of murder, and any of these men showed up as court-appointed attorney? Hello, lethal injection.'

1. For the winner, we take an example of the candidate who insults his electorate. Step forward Stephen Pound, Labour MP for Ealing North, who surprised a constituent by leaving the following message on her answerphone after she had called him to raise queries about Labour's manifesto policies: 'If there is one thing that really pisses me off, it's middle-class whingers going on about fucking tuition fees

and as far as I'm concerned, if that's your attitude, you can shove your vote up your arse'. Labour used several different slogans during the 2001 campaign, but, after much discussion and focus-group research, they decided to drop 'You can shove your vote up your arse'. Mr Pound was re-elected with an increased majority.

Remember, if the electorate still get it wrong even after your carefully planned smear campaign, you can always toss a literary quote or two at them: 'Let them assemble, And on a safer judgement all revoke your ignorant election' (Sicinius, from Shakespeare's *Coriolanus*, Act 2, Scene 3).

THE BITCHING IS BACK – A ROUND-UP OF SUSPECTS

Vicious character assassination was common currency in British politics until round about the middle of the nineteenth century. Then things tended to get more civilised, until the notorious period when MI5 went dotty in the Wilson years. There has been much said about the concerted campaign by senior figures within the secret service to destroy the Labour government. During the 1974 elections this included trying to spread rumours that Tony Benn had smoked cannabis, a senior Labour MP had stabbed rabbits while taking part in an orgy, Harold Wilson had fiddled his income tax returns and the Labour Party had been behind the rumours about Ted Heath's sexuality (a nice piece of Watergate-style reverse smearing). This was on top of all the stuff about Rhodesian deals, communist plots and other financial or sexual sleaze that had been circulating for a while. Little of this surfaced during the 1974 campaigns in the end. There were some hints and rumours, but most of the public heard nothing of them. This was partly because MI5 were so useless at the time, they could not produce smear campaigns that anyone could believe, and partly because in those pre-Thatcher days the trade unions were still powerful enough to threaten to stop the presses of the *Mail* and the *Express* if they tried to print a word of it.

Vladimir Zhirinovsky has written his own chapter into the book on vicious campaigning. The party he leads in the Russian Duma operates under the unlikely title of 'Liberal Democrats'. Paddy Ashdown, Charles Kennedy and crew might have considered suing over this, but Zhirinovsky believes in more basic ways of settling arguments, and they were well advised to ignore him. The Russian Liberal Democrats are an ultra-nationalist group. The term 'fascist' would not be unfair. Zhirinovsky is openly anti-Semitic, opposes all religious groups in Russia other than the Orthodox Church and wants to extend the Russian Empire to India's border and take back Alaska into the bargain. He claimed that it was his intention to bury Germany in nuclear waste, which would save them from doing it to themselves. He is so right-wing that even Pat Buchanan was embarrassed when he got an endorsement from him. Vlad was very upset when his offer of friendship was rebuked.

Zhirinovsky came to prominence with his scarily good third-place performance in the Russian presidential election of 1991. Thankfully, he has not progressed much since then. His macho image is a major part of his appeal to disillusioned Russians. He enjoys a good fight with opponents and once threw a glass of orange juice over a liberal opponent during a celebrated TV debate. His anti-West tirades have found a great deal of resonance, such as his campaign remark that 'Yeltsin and his administration should all retire to their dachas and stuff themselves with Snickers bars'. In his much less successful campaign for President in 1996 he said of his rival Yavlinsky that he had lost his ability to think through the time spent in his youth as a boxer. His analysis of the situation was summed up in the words, 'I am the single honest contender for President whom it is impossible to buy or to frighten. If voters prefer Boris

Yeltsin, then we really are a country of idiots and there is nothing to do, this is the final diagnosis.'

American presidential elections have concentrated on negative techniques almost since they started. Lyndon B Johnson's campaign against Barry Goldwater and Richard Nixon's against just about anybody stand as some of the clearest testaments to that. Maybe George Bush Sr's campaign against Michael Dukakis in 1988 was the most personally vicious. Not only was he generally rubbished as a lightweight candidate of no stature, his record as Massachusetts Governor was savaged in a series of campaign adverts. He was attacked on crime, the environment, pensions, economics and his views on defence. Fair political debate? It would have been, if it were not that nearly all the criticisms were untrue. There can rarely have been such a bogus advertising campaign in the USA since the last medicine man rode out of town, but the mud stuck and Dukakis's protestations could not wipe it off. His campaign was at its most effective when it went negative and attacked the soft target of Bush's running mate, Dan Quayle.

Worryingly, character assassinations often work. They rebound on the perpetrators only when they attack someone whom the public hold in some affection. That does not include many politicians. Perhaps one case when this did happen was with Labour's attempts to portray Churchill as a warmonger in 1951. This may have had some effect in encouraging the British voters to put him back into office six years after his stint as war leader.

It's only fair that the last word in vicious campaigning goes to Joseph Goebbels: 'Throw the scum out! Tear the masks off their mugs! Take them by the scruff of their necks; kick them in their fat bellies on 14 September and sweep them out of the temple with trumpets and drums!'

That was taken from the key Nazi breakthrough campaign of 1930, after the period when they were just a small bunch of thugs and social misfits and before they became a major political force.

As you can tell from the tone, this was the period when they were trying to appear moderate and reasonable, before they started being offensive to their opponents. Over the next couple of years anyone who stood in their way discovered it was not just rhetoric after all, and election campaigns really could be fought face down in the gutter covered in blood.

Corruption, Fraud and Winning Dirty

'Corrupt are they, and have done abominable iniquity: There is none that doeth good'

– Psalm 53, v. 1

The Rev. John Strachan (1778–1867) was not a great fan of the ejection of the British and introduction of democracy to Canada: 'Nobody would ask for the vote by ballot but from gross ignorance; it is the most corrupt way of using the franchise.' Throughout history many have rushed in to try to prove him right. The last chapter concentrated on attempts to destroy the characters of opponents. There are far more ways of fighting dirty than that.

DIRTY PAST

No less a star than William Pitt the Elder's start to his parliamentary career was touched by shameful corruption. His elder brother Thomas 'inherited' the famous seat of Old Sarum, the one your history teacher always used as the textbook example of a 'rotten borough'. This was once an ancient community, but was now a large field in Wiltshire, with five voters and a lot of sheep. It returned two Members of Parliament, while sizeable towns in the North of England returned nobody. Thomas Pitt won a triumphant victory in Old Sarum in 1734, but also won in Okehampton (a real town where real people lived). This was common in these days and the double winner could choose which seat to represent. Invariably, they chose the place where there was more money, privilege and influence. So there was not much choice this time, really. In brotherly love, Thomas offered his seat to little William. Then in brotherly spite he changed his mind and offered it to Thomas Harrison for the principled reason that he could promise more money. William refused to stand down, and Harrison decided to look elsewhere and leave him alone. The five good people got Pitt for an MP unopposed. Pitt carpetbagged his way around the kingdom standing for various pocket boroughs and rotten boroughs. He was offered a seat in Bath by the corporation, who owned the franchise. Yes, this is parliamentary democracy, not a fast-food chain! Okehampton, Buckingham and Aldborough all provided easy routes back to the benches, with no votes required – only the occasional bit of cash, a nod, a wink and a few favours. Only in Seaford in 1747 did William Pitt actually have to fight an election. He and his running mate, William Hay, gained 49 votes each. The others got 23 and 19 votes. The losers petitioned, claiming the poll had been unduly 'interfered with' by the Duke of Newcastle. He got away with it. That was the complete electoral biography of one of Great Britain's most respected prime ministers, known as 'a man of the people' – a renowned war leader, founder of colonies and opponent of corruption.

The journalist Matthew Parris took a look at John Wilkes in his study of Parliamentary scandals:

> John Wilkes made his first attempt to enter Parliament in 1754, standing in Berwick-on-Tweed. Part of his election strategy had been to bribe the captain of a ship bringing opposition voters from London. A generous inducement persuaded the captain to encounter navigational problems during the journey and the ship docked in Norway rather than Berwick. By the time it reached Berwick it was too late for the passengers to cast their votes. But Wilkes still lost the election.
>
> His wife left him in 1757, fed up with his lechery. Wilkes redoubled efforts to deal with his mounting debts; his plan

was to get elected to Parliament, where as an MP he would be free from arrest for debt. At a cost of £7,000, largely spent on bribes to the voters of Aylesbury, he was returned as an MP later that year.[1]

Through British general elections of the twentieth century, we have had numerous dirty tricks – Conservatives have claimed that the 'Chinese slavery' scare was partly responsible for their rejection in the Liberal landslide election of 1906. Certainly trade unionists and Liberal politicians made a lot of the example of Lord Milner. He was the South African High Commissioner whose decision it was to import large numbers of Chinese workers to fill labour shortages in his colony. This upset some who fancied the idea of emigrating there themselves and others, who were affronted by the apparent movement of people across the globe like cattle without any say in their future. Prime Minister Arthur Balfour was at pains to point out that the Chinese workers were not slaves, but actually treated and paid relatively well, but his arguments were somewhat undermined by Milner's sanctioning of flogging by the labourers' bosses. The Conservatives lost a lot of their working-class support in that election, which never really returned to them en bloc, as it went to the emerging Labour Party in future elections. That some candidates raised fears about the Tories as slavery enthusiasts was regarded by some as a dirty trick, but if Balfour could have managed things a little better the problem would never have arisen.

What was a more clear-cut example of an electioneering dirty trick was the case of the Zinoviev letter in 1924. The said letter was supposed to have been sent from Zinoviev, the President of Comintern, to the British Communist Party, advising them how to bring about revolution, and undermining Labour's policy of greater cooperation with the Soviet Union. The letter was

---

[1] Matthew Parris, *Great Parliamentary Scandals*, Robson, 1995, p. 18.

bought by Conservative Central Office from a delighted middleman and formed a major part in their election victory in that year. Using the red-scare tactic against the Labour Party, which had just had its first brief spell in minority government, worked a treat and Stanley Baldwin won a convincing victory. It took many years for confirmation of what most had suspected all along – the letter was a total forgery.

HOMES FOR VOTES

Let us be very clear here. Dame Shirley Porter is a deeply wonderful human being. She has never presided over any council that has attempted to win elections by corrupt means. Deliberate targeting of key wards with regard to housing policy was not a feature of her administration, nor was it detailed in council committee minutes. The fact that council housing was sold off to upmarket yuppie flat developers in the wards that Labour had to win to take control is of no significance. The fact that thousands of homeless people in temporary accommodation in Westminster were moved away to Labour boroughs and off the local electoral register was merely incidental to what was a well-considered, socially responsible policy. It is important that we remember these facts when we consider the matter of the Tories and their flagship London borough of Westminster in the 1980s and 1990s.

Their other flagship in Wandsworth took the much more direct approach of ensuring re-election by providing all their council services for free, which was a tremendous bonus for the lucky residents. The fact that there was nothing corrupt about Westminster did not stop successful prosecutions against some councillors and council officials, leading to several bankruptcies and one tragic suicide. Porter should not be blamed for this at all, because she rose regally above it all and she has sued people who say otherwise. To give some credit to her administration, it should be noted that they won re-election easily, gaining bigger swings in wards that were not under suspicion. Make of that whatever you like.

Of course, adapting local council policy for electoral purposes is not new at all, particularly with regard to housing. How many Labour authorities blatantly expanded council estates into key marginal wards in the 1960s in particular? Quite a lot of them in fact, and they did not even feel the need to be all that coy about it at the time. They were proud of it. For balance, we should attack the Liberals here. There is a problem. Many Liberal authorities have had brushes with controversy over the years, but this is one area where they are quite blameless. Labour expect most council house tenants to vote for them, Conservatives expect most luxury yuppie flat owners to vote for them. Liberal Democrats and their predecessors spread their vote more evenly. What kind of housing policy would give electoral advantage to Liberals? Is there a way of encouraging more Cornish Methodists to move into key wards?

So do we ignore those little tricks that the candidates might play. It is all part of the game after all. Back we go to the dawn of democracy again to get the view of Demosthenes: 'There is one safeguard known generally to the wise, which is an advantage and security to all, but especially to democracies against despots – suspicion.' That view from Philippics 2 gives us pretty clear guidance on this issue that we should still stick with today. More recently, G B Shaw had a more positive view in his 'Maxims for Revolution': 'Democracy substitutes election by the incompetent many for appointment by the corrupt few.' Shaw seemed to favour incompetence over corruption, but is there really a choice, or do we have to watch out for both? I tend to go more with Demosthenes on this one.

LAND OF THE FREE

Back to the good old USA again. You might ask yourself why the bastion of world democracy features more in an exploration of electoral corruption than anywhere else. Whether you believe this is because it is the most corrupt nation on Earth, or because it has the nearest thing to a genuinely free press, indicates exactly what your opinion of the country is.

Kansas City was dominated by the Democratic Party machine in 1934. The machine was dominated by Thomas Pendergast. However, a challenge emerged in the municipal elections that year from a combination of Republicans and independent Democrats working in an alliance. Pendergast was not going to let his control slip. He was an expert in advanced campaigning techniques. There was already the advantage of having 50,000 bogus names on the register in his pocket, but in case that was not enough he hired a large contingent of gangsters who killed four voters, beat up hundreds of tellers and opposition workers, shot at their headquarters and hospitalised a journalist among a dozen or so others. In a ringing endorsement of committed political campaigning, Kansas City returned the bulk of Pendergast's slate of candidates. This was a great relief for him as it enabled him to continue to direct the career of his protégé Harry Truman all the way to the Senate and then the White House.

On the subject of American presidents who got off to a wonderfully encouraging start, Lyndon Johnson looked like he was heading for defeat in Texas for his Senate Primary election against his fellow Democratic contender Coke Stevenson in 1948. Thankfully, he was saved when he got 202 extra votes at the last minute. These enthusiastic Johnson fans turned up a minute before the polls closed and voted exactly in the order in which they appeared in the electoral roll. The military precision of these voters was truly remarkable. This was enough to give him a majority over Stevenson of 87. It was 30 years later that one of the election officials admitted the vote had been rigged, as if we needed to know. Most of the interested parties were dead by now, as well as all those who fell in Landslide Lyndon's Vietnam War, so that was all right, then. In the campaign for office that followed, Johnson was alleged to have ordered his campaign manager to accuse his opponent, who was well ahead in the polls, of having had unnatural relations with his farm animals. On being told that he could not do that because it was not true, Johnson replied, 'Of course it's not, but let's make the bastard deny it!'

American presidents? Corrupt electoral practices? Just remember those magic words: 'The Committee for the Re-Election of the President'. Yes, the whole Watergate saga started with those overzealous Nixon officials seeking to get the dirt on the Democrats early before Nixon's re-election campaign of 1972. Donald Segretti stepped forward to lead by example and he rubbished the Primary campaign of the Democrat Ed Muskie by spreading rumours that he was in favour of extending unpopular bussing policies for schools and that he had written rude leaflets about French Canadians. Rather cleverly, Segretti saw that earlier campaigns had failed when politicians had tried to stick untrue accusations on to opponents, and then taken a beating when the electorate did not believe them. He managed to get Muskie blamed for untrue rumours that he spread about other candidates. It worked a dream and Muskie fell out of the running. In the end the Democrats were left with George McGovern as their presidential candidate in 1972 – a candidate so weak he could not even win his home state. Only candidates as poor as Al Gore can manage that. The committee, 'CREEP', overstretched themselves when they had the bright idea of bugging the Democrats' national campaign office. Jeb Magruder tried to hide the evidence of involvement in the bungled break-in. Nixon and several of his cabinet knew what was going on from an early stage, but carried on lying about it. The rest, as they say, is history.

As we conclude our look at American electoral corruption, it is worth mentioning the victory of Rutherford Hayes in 1876. He lost the popular vote in the presidential election to the Democrat candidate Samuel Tilden by nearly 300,000 votes. The Republicans were on the verge of conceding as it appeared that Tilden had soared past the electoral college margin required. Then the news arose of suspicions regarding the votes in Louisiana, South Carolina and Florida (yes, there again). Immediately the Republicans sent representatives to the three states, backed up with lawyers and plenty of cash. All three Southern states still had Republican administrations, imposed on the South after the Civil War. With their backing, the arguments about voter fraud, improper conduct and mal-administered elections raged on for months until a stalemate was achieved. Tilden was short of the electoral college margin required by a tantalising single vote without the three states in question. There was then the further complication that an elector from Oregon was found to be ineligible. The election was secured by one vote in the House of Representatives and Rutherford Hayes became known as President Rutherfraud thereafter. There were suspicions over the Southern Democrats, who eventually gave up and agreed to the ruling of the electoral commission, a body that had been pretty much fixed and had ruled that the contest should be so determined. The suspicion was that this was in exchange for a speedy end to Recon-struction. They wanted to wrest control of the South back from the Yankies and start a new era of segregation almost as bad as the era of slavery that had recently been ended.

FIXING FOR FUN

General Alfredo Stroessner of Paraguay holds an impressive place in the list of most brutal dictators of the twentieth century. Not in the same league as Pol Pot, but probably a couple of places ahead of Pinochet. Apart from executing opponents and socialising with Nazi war criminals, his favourite pastime was to hold presidential elections. He loved to go through the motions of having his leadership endorsed every few years by his grateful people.

Stroessner knew that one of the most effective ways to ensure there was no prospect of losing at this game was to maintain control of the electoral register. In Paraguay, the register was regarded as a state secret. It was not open to inspection in a public library as it might be elsewhere, and any journalist who wanted to make an issue about this would rapidly find themselves running short of body parts. When you have complete and secret control of the register, there is nothing to stop you keeping the names of supporters on the list long after they have died – just for memories' sake you understand. He even took a surprisingly enlightened view on allowing children to register, provided they were members of supportive families. After Stroessner was deposed in 1989, all of this was revealed. Western democracies had stuck up for him before as they usually do for anyone who maintains a veneer of democracy while opposing communism, however vicious they may be. I wonder if any of these governments were genuinely surprised when the truth was discovered.

Stroessner was no Saddam Hussein in that he enjoyed having an opposition to fight. After all, winning a game against nobody is very unsatisfactory. He paid the expenses and salaries of opposition politicians, who mysteriously got round about the same number of votes and seats in Parliament every time. There was never a great interest in the outcome of a Paraguayan election among gamblers. It would have been a bit like betting on yesterday's race.

DRAWING THE LINE

Constituency boundaries can be enormously significant. In a

country that employs some form of proportional representation, they are not so important – depending on the exact system used. In a first-past-the-post election they are vital. There is no point in seeing vast majorities getting run up in some seats, or in significant votes being wasted in seats that you still cannot win. If you are going to get beaten in all the closely contested seats this will mean you will lose the election, and the exact drawing of the borders can determine the outcome here. This leads us to consider the art of 'gerrymandering', or seeking to ensure that constituency borders are drawn up that suit your party interests and are inimical to the interests of your opponents.

From 1264 until 1832 in England and, later, the rest of the UK most counties and boroughs returned two Members to Parliament regardless of the size of their electorate. In most countries early democratic systems were viewed as a means to represent areas, not individuals. It was not until the Representation of the People Act of 1918 that the general principle of roughly equal division of electors among seats was established. It was only in 1950 that the last two member seats were abolished, as were the university seats. It was also this election that first saw the work of the Boundary Commissions come into force. Since then the four National Commissions have set the boundaries and they are now required to review them every eight to twelve years.

What has this to do with corruption and fraud? Before 1832 it had everything to do with it. From then until 1950 it was a mess, and corruption was still a feature, at least for part of that time. John Bright led the fight for further reform. He commented in a speech in 1858, 'I was looking down a list, the other night, beginning with Tower Hamlets, the largest borough population, and coming down to the smallest. I found that there were 71 boroughs, not one of which had a population of 10,000 persons. The whole population of the 71 boroughs is only 467,000, which is not very much more than the present population of Manchester and Salford; and yet these 71 boroughs return 117

Members to the House of Commons, while Manchester and Salford return only three members. These little boroughs are very little better than what we used to describe by the unpleasant term of rotten.'[1]

Bright succeeded in helping to see the second Reform Act through despite much opposition from such good folk as the writer Francis Hitchman, who complained about the reform campaigners that they were 'vast mobs of the great unwashed marching in procession to the discordant strains of brass bands'. He was particularly upset that crowds of protesters had trampled the flower beds in Hyde Park, but the price of reform can be that high sometimes. Even this further reform still did not finish the problems about unequal representation. Gross inequality persisted and nobody could bring themselves to resolve this mess finally until after World War Two. Since then, the Boundary Commissions have done a good job and stayed distant from the political parties commendably well. That does not mean there are not still some curious stories to look at. There are still plenty of anomalies. Why does the Isle of Wight still have well over four times as many voters as the Western Isles? Because the Isle is deemed too small to have two seats and none of the interested parties want part of it annexed to a mainland seat; while the Isles are deemed to be a very distinct and distant cultural region that should not be mixed with other islands or part of the mainland. It all sounds reasonable, but it is still unfair. The Western Isles case also illustrates another query. Scotland has smaller constituency electorates on average because they are guaranteed a set minimum of parliamentary representation as part of their constitutional settlement. Now they have their own devolved Parliament, I have yet to hear anyone explain satisfactorily why they should still have this advantage.

---

[1] From John Bright's speech at Manchester, 10 December 1858, quoted from *The Radical Tradition*, edited by S MacCoby, Nicholas Kaye, 1952.

Politicians have to keep their hands off the Boundaries Commission, which is now under the aegis of the new Electoral Commission, but they cannot resist trying. Every few years the map is drawn up again and the politicians panic. They have due cause to do so. It is usually the inner-city MPs who suffer, as declining populations mean their seats disappear. David Alton retired as Liberal Democrat MP for Liverpool Mossley Hill in 1997 partly because he had become disillusioned with his party, but the final straw must have been to see his seat ripped into pieces – cast into three different seats, which were all safely Labour. He was effectively retired by the commission. Many others have seen their best areas of support lost and unpromising territory added and have had to decide whether to stand and fight or go on what has become known as the 'chicken run', that is to look for somewhere safer, as many did in 1997 in particular. The parties make submissions to the relevant commission to try to influence the civil servants in a helpful direction. I have studied several of these works of art in different parts of the country and I here offer a fictional version of a submission that includes much of the kind of material you would observe in the real world. It is followed by a translation to show what it really means:

'Dear Sir/Madam,

With regard to the Boundary Review that you are presently undertaking in Wobblyshire, may we respectfully recommend the following course of action. We believe that Squalid-Dump ward should be removed from the seat of Safetown and placed in the seat of Wobbly Valley. This is because Squalid-Dump is positioned on the very edge of the town and the people form a natural community with some of the outlying communities and small towns of the valley rather than with the centre of town. Few of them work in town or use its facilities and many of them have historic or family connections with other parts of the county. Safetown itself has grown because of the new housing estates to the north, which have no other natural home to go to, and so numbers could best be reduced by removing Squalid-Dump.

Further to this, the electorate in Wobbly Valley can be restored to its target total by then removing the villages to the south of the motorway. These might be placed in the proposed new seat of South Wobblyshire that has been provisionally designated to take account of population growth in the county. These villages have little in common with the rest of the valley. The people here are more likely to commute to Wobbly-on-Sea for work or leisure facilities, and few of them use local county schools. The motorway also provides an obvious choice for a constituency boundary. We respectfully offer these suggestions for your consideration.

Yours etc.,
XYZ Party Executive Committee, West Wobblyshire Area.

This letter translated into straightforward English reads as follows:

Dear Pen-Pushing Toady,

Safetown is one of our party's safest seats in the country and it would take a national humiliation for us to lose it. We do not need the votes from Squalid-Dump to bump up the majority any further. Our local MP also thinks the place is an appalling hole and he is sick of the casework it generates as he would rather spend more time climbing the ministerial greasepole. Wobbly Valley is a highly marginal seat that we are scared of losing. We could use the extra votes from Squalid-Dump there. The people there do not work or spend leisure time in Safetown, because they do not work at all, and have no money to go anywhere. Some of the lads from outlying villages do come on to the estate, though to join in with the burglaries and heroin abuse – so there is a kind of natural community there. Please do not move the nice new housing estate out of the seat instead, as the MP now lives there and has many of his friends and favourite party members around him, and there are too many opposition votes to put into Wobbly Valley.

We would dearly love to lose the southern villages from Wobbly Valley as we have no members there and are not able to campaign properly. We closed down their local schools, so their children are no longer educated in the area. They keep stropping about the motorway extension we supported that cut them off from everywhere else. There are also a few people down there who are a complete pain in the arse, always writing bolshy letters to the local press. We would like them to become someone else's problem. If you want you can throw them into a new seat with Wobbly-on-Sea, as we have no chance of winning there anyway.

Yours with a patronising smirk, thinking we might get away with it,
XYZ Party Executive Committee, West Wobblyshire Area.

It is then the job of the commissioners to sift through all the submissions and the relevant data to decide what are genuine factors that should be considered in drawing sensible boundaries and what are corrupt, underhand attempts by politicians to fix the decision in their favour. They will take more notice of submissions from nonpolitical organisations such as local community groups, Councils of Churches or Chambers of Commerce. Smart politicians realise it is more useful to infiltrate groups like these and get them to do the dirty work for them.

One of the particular worries for the Conservatives at the boundary review prior to the 1997 general election was their fear of 'doughnuts'. Doughnuts were very scary to Tories, as they could spoil a neat division of seats that had helped them out for ages. There are many towns in the country that form the focus for a local area that includes outlying rural areas and maybe another small town or two. In many cases the town and its environs are too big for one constituency and they have traditionally been split in such a way as to mix main towns with rural areas. This suited the Tories perfectly in places like Colchester, Lincoln and several others. Then came the dough-nuts. The commission had to add extra seats in many of these counties and took into account that the advent of unitary authorities in many of these towns made it less relevant for them to be mixed with rural areas. We would now have seats that stood alone as purely urban cores surrounded by predominantly rural seats – doughnuts! There was no indication as to whether this meant the urban cores were to be regarded as jam or as holes. The Tories fought this tooth and nail in many of the cases, as they feared this would leave them with one safe rural seat and one urban seat that would be very hard to win, rather than two winnable seats. In the end, their rout of 1997 showed that the doughnuts saved their bacon in the end, if you can excuse the quite sickening food metaphor. They needed as many safe seats as they could muster and the old arrangements would probably have led to their losing even more. Gerrymandering is all very well, but you still need to win votes to get it to work.

Many believe mistakenly that the term 'gerrymander' comes from Ireland. It is actually taken from Governor Elbridge Gerry of Massachusetts, who drew up a new electoral map of the state that was very helpful to his cause in 1811. Some thought that the new map reminded them of a salamander – the animal, not the fire poker. There was one division in particular that twisted and turned in all sorts of curious directions in order to make sure the right people were living in it. It still looked nothing like a salamander, but then the constellations in the sky look nothing like animals or mythical gods, either. Anyway, the name stuck and, later on, the prefix 'gerry' and numerous appalling cases from the Emerald Isle combined to make Ireland become universally known as the spiritual home of gerrymandering – the northern part of Ireland in particular.

According to the new settlement for the six counties that remained in the UK after partition, all elections to local councils and to the Parliament at Stormont were to be conducted by proportional representation. Only the elections for the Westminster Parliament were supposed to continue using first-past-the-post elections, as there were was no wish to have mixed methods across the UK for elections to the Commons. British politicians knew that a simple plurality system in single constituencies would exaggerate the Protestant and Unionist majority in Ulster. There had been plenty of evidence of dubious boundary drawing in Ireland before partition, but even honest division could lead to isolation of the nationalists, as they would be poorly represented. Unionists shared this analysis entirely. Only they actually wanted to marginalise the nationalists, so they scrapped PR as quickly as they thought they could get away with it – from 1923 for local councils and from 1929 for Stormont.

This move soon wiped out most of the Independents and the nascent Northern Ireland Labour Party. The British Government were so cross about this, they decided to do nothing about it. The Ulster Prime Minister, James Craig, was free to get the constituency borders set up however he wanted them. The extent of gerrymandering in local government was absolutely huge and it ensured that Unionists held sway in most of the province's town halls until Ted Heath imposed direct rule in 1973. It was less blatant for Stormont, although the larger size of the constituencies made it less necessary. One place that was a shining example though was Fermanagh. The area had a slim Catholic and nationalist majority, but a good number of them could be tidied away into Fermanagh South, where they would outnumber Protestants by nearly three to one. This enabled the other divisions of Enniskillen and Lisnaskea to be so drawn that there were modest, but reasonably safe, Protestant majorities. As long as the Unionist vote did not get divided they would always win these seats. Three seats for an area with a nationalist majority. Two seats for the Unionists. Bingo!

If this seems like a trivial concern when set against all the terrible problems of Ulster, remember that the Troubles began with the civil-rights protests. Gerrymandering was one of the protesters' complaints, as were discrimination in education, housing and public-service employment – all of these under the control of the electorally fixed administrations. Local government and the Northern Irish Assembly now use proportional representation and the Irish and UK governments will not countenance anything else any more.

WE'VE GOT YOUR NUMBER!

I know many people refuse to give their electoral number to the party tellers on the door of the polling station, thinking that they can trace how they voted. There is no reason why you should give them your number if you do not want to, but there is no way that the party tellers can trace how you voted. There are other ways of doing that, however.

Many people who pick up their ballot paper do not even notice the code number on it. They are even less likely to notice the same number appears on the counterfoil left behind in the book on the clerk's desk – where the clerk writes their electoral registration number on the stub that is left behind. If people do notice this, they may think it just means that they have been given free entry to the raffle. This would be another interesting method of tackling low turnout, but it is not the reason they do it.

Do we have a truly secret ballot in the UK? The answer is that we usually do, provided we can avoid the opinion pollsters hanging around the door, but we are not guaranteed it. Our vote can be traced, if there is a need for someone to find out what we did. All the ballot papers, counterfoils, marked registers and other administrative detritus are collected and stuck in a big warehouse under the Seal of the Lord Chancellor's Department. They can be inspected only by order of the High Court or by Parliament. This would happen in a court case, where they provided necessary evidence. Most commonly this has been put into effect in cases of corruption. If a large number of dead people have voted in a marginal seat, we can check if they all happened to vote the same way and that can help the judge to decide whether a result should be invalidated. This procedure can also help in investigating cases of contested spoiled papers, personation, unauthorised proxy voting, or any of a number of different ballot-rigging ruses. There is a good example of one of these investigations in the chapter on unusual results ('What Was That Result Again?').

That's OK, then? No, it isn't. This is a very difficult area and civil libertarians have rightly been very concerned about it. Clearly there are legal cases where there is good reason to check particular papers, but it is an open secret that it has been abused. This is not really an area of conspiracy-theory paranoia. There have been numerous documented cases of evidence that have shown that agencies such as MI5 and Special Branch have gained access to ballot papers to investigate the voting records of anyone they wanted to keep tabs on. These would range from 'subversives' to terrorist suspects to civil service applicants. This went on throughout the 1950s and 1960s. It is believed that the practice has been much reduced, if not completely eradicated, in recent times. This is probably not so much out of a respect for privacy, fundamental democratic rights and general decency. It is more likely that someone realised that it is a completely stupid waste of time and taxpayers' money. Those agents who made it their work to collect lists of communist voters from around the country, might as well have collected lists of *Reader's Digest* subscribers for all the good it would have done them. They did not seem to notice that the British Communist Party ceased to be any serious revolutionary threat to the constitution early in the 1920s. After that it was a tiny party mostly supported by some trade unionists (often militant but not truly revolutionary), harmless intellectual romantics and ordinary people registering a protest vote or a joke. If there were any dangerous left-wingers in the country they were working from within the Labour Party until the mid-1980s. Perhaps they could have kept lists of 13 million or so Labour voters – just to be sure. As for crooks, they are either too busy to vote or they probably vote Conservative to keep the taxes on their ill-gotten gains nice and low. This sort of activity by our 'intelligence' community was a very scary encroachment on our liberties and did nothing to protect any of us.

Most of us do not really mind if people know how we voted, some might be mildly embarrassed by others knowing. In some elections in Northern Ireland over the last few decades, secret ballots allowed people to vote with their conscience and retain their homes, their kneecaps and their lives. We should remember that is what the principle is all about.

WHO DO YOU DO?

Personation is the art of voting on behalf of other people without their consent. It saves them a lot of trouble of course, but that is not the main purpose of the activity. 'Benign personation' takes the form of voting on behalf of the dead or otherwise absent. If they do not want their votes, someone else might as well use them. 'Malign personation' occurs when votes are stolen from people who turn up to the polling station to discover someone else has voted for them. In most places this is not a big problem and voters are rarely challenged to prove they are who they claim to be. If it happens occasionally, aggrieved electors, whose votes have been pinched, can be given tendered ballot papers to be checked later if necessary. However, this is taken so seriously in Northern Ireland that even the insistence that voters carry proof of identity is not considered to be enough. In some places the parties appoint 'personation agents' to check that voters are who they say they are and to challenge anyone they deem to be suspicious.

This would not be possible in London, where most people would have difficulty in recognising the difference between an impostor and their actual next-door neighbour. This issue has been one of the main sources of argument between the SDLP and Sinn Fein, the former accusing the latter of being the main perpetrator of this crime. We do know that there were 949 tendered votes issued in Northern Ireland for the 1983 general election, indicating that the number of personation cases was probably larger than that, as many disenfranchised voters gave up and did not bother, especially the dead ones. Rumours flew around in the 2001 election. No longer was it necessary to turn up to the polling station pretending to be someone who was dead. New regulations made it much easier to cast the illegal votes by post from the comfort of your own home. Mid-Ulster and Fermanagh come forward again as the perennial candidates for accusations of fraud. This leads us to the next problem.

THE DIY MAKE-YOUR-OWN-VOTER KIT

The recent changes in the law that have made it much easier for people to join the register at any stage of the year have drawn a lot of criticism about the lack of any checks on this. Some journalists have shown how easy it is to put nonexistent, or nonqualifying people on to the register and then claim their postal votes, which are also easier to obtain under the same legislation. These moves to help improve turnout are laudable enough, but they have exacerbated the problems with potential corruption. Most of the local authorities do not have the resources to investigate this, and most of the local parties no longer have the structures to check on each other's misdemeanours.

Everyone seemed to assume we would all play the game like gentlemen until two Hackney councillors were sent to prison for fraud in this regard in 2001. After claiming that a ruined old garage was someone's home, a boarded-up house contained seven voters and giving votes to American citizens as well as two votes to the brother of one of the conspirators, they had pushed their luck even further by claiming dozens of proxy votes from pensioners who knew nothing about it. Expect to see plenty more cases. There have been isolated incidents of similar things over the years, particularly falsifying proxy votes and overseas votes. The old favourite of 'granny-farming' has appeared a number of times. That is signing up loads of postal or proxy votes from old folk's homes, sometimes without the old folk knowing what you are doing, and then casting the votes yourself. There was a big suspicion of this in St Ives in 1992. Now the law provides new and better opportunities for similar ruses and the checks are inadequate. The police are looking into dozens as we go to print. From the most recent election a lot of the fingers have pointed at Bradford. There has also been some surprise as to why over a third of the voters in Stevenage chose to have a postal ballot. If most of these people used them, the polling stations that day must have been like ghost-town saloon bars, as turnout was near the miserable national average.

THERE'S NO ACCOUNTING FOR IT

Anyone who has been involved in accounting for election expenses, or has seen the completed forms, will know these are ridiculous. We quite rightly put a spending limit on individual candidates' expenditures to stop wealthy parties or individuals swamping the people with a lavish campaign their opponents cannot match. However, the truth is not so simple. The exact amount a candidate can spend depends on the size of the electorate and whether it is a borough or a county seat. It amounts to only a few thousand pounds less personal expenses, which are accounted for but not included in the total. The agent has to keep account of the smallest detail and ensure it goes in the return. Even if a service is provided free or at reduced rates, they are supposed to show a reasonable charge was made. This is not a problem in a no-hope, no-activist, no-real-campaign type of seat. Some expense forms have been submitted showing expenditure on nothing more than a few sheets of A4, Sellotape and a couple of stamps. However, when we look at target marginal seats, where a full-scale onslaught will be staged, the picture changes.

Consider four weeks of salary for six party workers who are employed full time; a commercial rent on the HQ and on any other properties used; full expenses for all cars, computers, and other equipment used; and full payment of all relevant telephone bills. Realistically, we have soared over £10,000 and way past the expenditure limit before we have printed a single leaflet or even given one kid a balloon. There are certain conventions to which all parties acquiesce. As long as agents do not do anything as silly as forgetting to include a leaflet that was produced, or something of that sort, they can frequently get away with murder. Not always, though. The Labour Party nearly lost two seats in recent years through expense irregularities: West Lancashire and Newark. In Newark, Fiona Jones MP was told that she would have to relinquish her seat after being convicted of making a fraudulent return, but she won on appeal. Labour also nearly lost Glasgow Govan after accusations of bribery of minor candidates, so they have had a few accounting difficulties of late. The Liberals lost their one seat on the Greater London Council in Richmond in 1981 after failing to declare a leaflet in their expenses. The last loss of a parliamentary seat, given Newark's narrow squeak, was Oxford in 1924, where the candidate exceeded the limit. The Scottish National Party tried to get the Conservatives thrown out in Perth in 1964, as they argued that they should have included the cost of a party political broadcast in their expenses. It came as a relief to all the other parties when that was thrown out.

There are now new rules for national campaigns in Britain, following the Political Parties, Elections and Referendums Act of 2000. For the first time there will be national expense limits. This will set a limit for the amount a party can spend in a year up to an election at less than £20 million. It does not include many things such as general running expenses and constituency campaign spending. Most people agree this sounds like a good move, but I am looking forward to the day when an electoral commissioner tells the winning party a few months later they spent too much and asks them to please leave government as quickly as possible.

The USA has its own complex rules, which include limiting individual donations. As you can imagine, there are hundreds of ways of getting around that. They also have federal funding of parties. Many other countries have a similar arrangement and there is a lot to commend it. It is something that most politicians in Britain would love to have, but none of them would ever dare put it in a manifesto!

A FEW OTHER IDEAS

The Philippines has been one of the premier places for dirty elections over a number of years. Ferdinand Marcos knew a thing or two about the electoral arts, or at least he thought he did. When Ronald Reagan threw down the ultimatum to Marcos that America's patience with his regime was at an end, he decided to show how much they had misjudged him by holding a presidential election in 1986. He would show that his people still supported him and that the Americans should, too. If the people were not going to oblige he was going to cheat. As he had feared, his opposition came from Corazon Aquino, widow of Benigno Aquino, the opposition leader murdered on Marcos's orders. It was obvious to anyone in the country at the time that a landslide victory was heading Aquino's way. Apart from the revolutionary groupings that were boycotting the election and Marcos's own favoured interest groups, it seemed that everyone was for Cory.

Despite all the attempts to frustrate her, Cory managed to organise incredibly impressive rallies – possibly the largest political rallies ever staged. Marcos loved a good show. It gave him and his wife Imelda a chance to sing. So he responded with rallies of his own. The crowds came. They were paid up to $2 each to do so and that was money worth having. Many of them came to the rally shouting Cory's name and showing the 'L' with their fingers, her campaign sign. They behaved themselves while they were there, but many of them left before Marcos spoke.

The world was perplexed as to what was going to happen. There was an enormous, high-powered team of international observers in place, but unless Marcos was going to pull off an outrageous con trick it seemed clear that he was going to be completely destroyed on election day. There were communities that owed him favours, but there were not nearly enough of them.

Election night turned out to be one of those interesting occasions for following election results. Occasionally ITN and BBC might disagree over the odd result or exit poll prediction, but in the Philippines, the radio carried the results from the National Movement for a Free Election, while the television carried the figures of COMELEC, the government's official agency. Anyone with an eye on the screen and an ear to the radio gained an education in media news manipulation that night. The radio was announcing victory after victory for Cory. Bigger majorities than she had hoped for in region after region. Results were trickling in on the TV and they were not looking too bad for Marcos. Then the TV figures stopped altogether and everyone knew something was up. Marcos had tried every corrupt trick in the book to rig the election and it was still not enough. Now there was a news blackout and everyone knew that meant ballot boxes were about to go missing. There followed an almighty great struggle to find ballot boxes and protect them, often led by monks and nuns. Some people lost their lives as a result. The computer operators at COMELEC walked out, having seen what a fix this was, but they would not give evidence to the observers for fear of their lives.

At the end of this farce Marcos claimed victory, but Cory Aquino moved fast to claim victory as well. Most of the world jumped behind her straightaway. The Americans waited until the two leading figures in the military switched their support to Aquino. As Marcos held his inauguration ceremony, the television broadcast broke down and a few hours later a mass movement of people power had swept Cory Aquino into office with a force that Marcos's remaining loyal marines knew was not worth opposing. Ferdinand and Imelda Marcos and their family were rescued by the Americans, but Imelda had to leave her enormous shoe collection behind. Maybe this was one of the greatest triumphs of democracy. One attempt at ballot rigging that included every trick in the book failed in the face of millions of real people who refused to be tricked any more.

There are many ways of fixing an election, and we are not going to go through them all here. Simply buying an election is a good way. Of course, in most free democracies the parties know that they will get found out if they attempt bribery on a grand scale, and they could not afford it anyway. The lesser crime of treating can be more effective (not strictly bribing, just offering nice inducements without directly asking for a vote in return). These days they realise that they will have far more money at their disposal when they are elected, so the bribes can take a more subtle form as targeted tax cuts or special spending initiatives. The last elected MPs to lose their seats on a charge of treating received the boot from Hull Central and East Cork in 1910. The last to go down for bribery was the MP for Worcester in 1906, with a narrow escape in Plymouth Drake in 1929.

In Thailand they have not been so shy about it. In 1988, the going rate for a vote was $4.50, with a bonus of $450 to any entire village that could deliver its vote en bloc. That can be quite a lot for an average Thai citizen in a poor rural area. How much would you sell your vote for? If either of our two biggest UK parties spent their entire vast election expenses on giving us all bribes we would still get less than £1 each, and I'm afraid that I, for one, would come a little more expensive than that.

Crude ballot-box stuffing on a grand scale long ago became regarded as far too clumsy and old-fashioned a method. Then the overthrow of Slobodan Milosevic in Yugoslavia in 2000 led to the discovery that the Parliament building was full of – guess what. The old methods were still in vogue in Milosevic's Serbia, and the evidence of thousands of ready-prepared, filled-in ballot papers was just lying there ready for the protesters to discover.

In most countries, the reigning party stay in executive control of government while the elections take place. They may not be able to pass new laws, but control of the military and police can be very successful ways of making sure opposition meetings are broken up and their voters intimidated. Anyone from central African militias to Florida traffic police knows the methods that can work most effectively. The legal system may be amenable to cooperation as well. Malaysia's Prime Minister Mahathir was spared the trouble of an election in 1999 for leadership of the United Malays National Organisation, which would have led to loss of the premiership. Conveniently, his former deputy, Anwar, whom he had sacked, was rendered unable to compete because he was put on trial for several charges ranging from abuse of power to sodomy. Whether Anwar was guilty of any, all or none of these charges, it all looked just a bit too contrived to believe.

Indira Gandhi was well aware of the powers of executive office. When her victory in the Indian election of 1971 was declared invalid by the courts four years later, she realised that she was still in power for the time being. So she declared a state of emergency, arrested hundreds of opposition leaders, postponed the upcoming elections and changed the law to make the illegal electoral practices that had been discovered legal. Now that is statesmanship of the highest order. As long as you win, the others can complain all they want. All the levers and buttons are in your hands.

Of course, violence is the oldest and most reliable form of electoral fixing. Fear of severe injury or death can be much more effective than any other method as a factor in influencing your vote, or your decision not to vote at all. We could easily take the massive election victory of Benito Mussolini's Fascists in the Italian election of 1924 as an example here. He was carried into power on a wave of enthusiasm by a public fed up with national decline and fearful of communism. As he was clearly going to win, one can only assume that his faithful Blackshirts carried out their ballot-box stuffing and maiming of opponents for fun. When the Socialist leader, Giacomo Matteotti, called for the election results to be annulled because of the widespread violence and fraud, he sensibly remarked 'And now get ready for my funeral.' Sure enough his funeral was soon forthcoming.

Terror still frequently accompanies elections in some parts of the world. If you are considering a holiday, the following are the places in order of danger that you must be most sure to miss if there is an election happening: Democratic Republic of Congo; Zimbabwe; anywhere in Indonesia or Malaysia – particularly Borneo; Colombia; El Salvador; Israel; the Palestinian Autonomous State; Philippines; Kosovo; Chechnya or most former Soviet Republics in that part of the world; Haiti and much of the Indian subcontinent – especially Kashmir, parts of Uttar Pradesh and anywhere in Sri Lanka. You might want to think carefully about Florida as well.

Violence occasionally flares in Britain still – and we are not just talking about John Prescott. Of course some degree of terrorism from Irish Republicans has accompanied almost all elections since the 1970s, and some further back. Interesting little punch-ups still spark up as the crowds jostle around politicians on walkabouts. However, you would have to go back to pre-Victorian elections for the serious violence. Hardly anyone had the vote, but elections were worth fighting for, and sometimes dying for. The early nineteenth century was a volatile time. There was tremendous violence in the elections in Westminster in 1818, Retford in 1826 and much of the country in 1835. The mood of the time can be seen in the writings of Dickens and the earlier pictures of Hogarth. It was probably just as well there were not more seats contested. For the most parts candidates have kept out of it if they can. The last MP to have an election result overturned for intimidation was kicked out of County Kerry in 1910.

THE INEVITABLE PRIZE

Of course the most bent election in the history of the world was the famous re-election of Charles D B King as President of Liberia in 1927. His opponent, Thomas Faulkner, must have been the most unpopular politician ever, as he was defeated by 234,000 votes. As there were only around 15,000 registered voters in the country at the time, they must have been really sure that they did not want him – voting at least fifteen times each. Many of them may have voted continuously all day.

Senegal made a good attempt at beating this in 1988, when the result of the presidential election was completely fixed. They made a big mistake when they announced the fixed result the moment the polls closed, not predictions but the actual result. That was a bit of a giveaway. The people rioted for a couple of days, but the government got away with it in the end.

OCTOBER SURPRISE

Here is a public health warning! We are now about to enter the world of American conspiracy theory. This is the world of *The X Files*; Chinese UN troops based in Idaho; Elvis on the moon; the Roswell incident; and JFK assassinated by Pat Boone on the orders of the Dalai Lama. Actually I made up the last one, but if you all go and spread it around the Internet we can soon get it to the same status as the others I mentioned. However, a good conspiracy rumour starts to pick up some credence when it deals with a curious factual incident that no official explanation has dealt with adequately; there is some genuine, compelling evidence to back it up – and it seems to be just about believable rather than completely fantastic. It is for those reasons that many believe the 'October surprise' theory.

It was 1980 and it looked like Jimmy Carter's reign as President was coming to an end after one term. Ronald Reagan was preparing to coast into the White House after years of American economic problems and foreign-policy setbacks. However, the Republicans were worried. They knew that Carter still had a lot going for him on an individual basis and that many voters were very concerned about Reagan's lack of relevant experience and intellectual ability, and about the extreme right-wing characters who had attached themselves to his entourage. The poll leads were not insurmountable and Carter could pull it back if he could manage a last-minute propaganda coup.

The final humiliation for the USA had been the kidnapping of the hostages at the American embassy in Tehran by Iranian militants in November 1979 shortly after the Islamic Revolution. Carter's abortive attempt at a military rescue was the lowest point of his presidency. Nevertheless, negotiations were now under way through the UN and other international mediators and there was a real chance that the hostages would be freed, giving Carter his last-minute coup – the October surprise.

Here comes the theory. Hold on to your hats! The

Republicans knew this could blow their chances and the release
had to be delayed. They could not afford to let Carter be the hero
before election day. It had to be Reagan after election day. The
story is that William Casey, arch-spook and later chief of the
CIA, led the negotiations with the Iranians to delay any release
of the hostages until Reagan was elected. There were secret
meetings in places such as Paris and Madrid involving various
emissaries such as Mehdi Karrubi for the Iranians and the vice-
presidential candidate George Bush for the Republicans. The
Iranians were promised that their frozen American-based assets
would be released and $150 million of military hardware already
bought by the Shah, and now withheld, would be exported.
Israeli Secret Service agents were brought in to provide the
necessary backup, as these people were not in Government yet
and did not have the resources. The Iranians also would have the
satisfaction of stuffing Carter after his attempted raid on their
capital and his leadership of the world's opposition to the
revolution, and they may have hoped there would be some
covert sympathy from the new US government for Iran in their
developing struggle with Iraq. Publicly they would still have to
express animosity towards each other, but there would be a lot
they could do together privately

If there was any truth in any of this, it might just be the most
shameful case of electoral corruption in modern history.
Fiddling expenses or telling voters your opponent is a secret
transvestite are not in this league. Is it just more silly paranoid
nonsense like most of what you would read in the American
supermarket tabloids? Perhaps it is not true, but consider the
following:

1. Reagan was elected on 4 November 1980, just as the Iranian
   Parliament had approved the conditions for release. The
   public terms were set by Ayatollah Khomeini two months
   earlier, but this move was delayed for some reason. The
   hostages got on board their Algerian plane to freedom almost

to the minute that Reagan delivered his inaugural address on 20 January 1981.

2. Despite protestations by the Secretary of State, Alexander Haig, that no arms would be sold to Iran and that earlier orders had been cancelled, the later revelations of the Iran-Contra scandal and the testimony of Oliver North, a military aide to the National Security Council, showed that secret arms deals with Iran had gone on for years. Did they start in 1980? That much is still secret. Iraq, rather than Iran, became the eventual target for Western aggression, just as Iran had hoped. Bush had a bit to do with that.

3. Numerous eyewitnesses have reported seeing Casey, Bush, leading Iranian figures and other suspects in Paris at the time of the supposed secret meetings in October 1980. There is no other explanation as to what they were all doing there. Former President Bani-Sadr of Iran is among those who have testified to this, after he went into exile.

4. The relevant dates from the late William Casey's journals and other documents are missing.

5. French intelligence officials have anonymously admitted to French and American journalists that they helped to facilitate meetings between Casey and the Iranians in October 1980.

6. Various Congressional investigations into this and other related issues have not come to any satisfactory conclusion. They have found that secret arms deals were set up with Iran and that the Republicans did gather intelligence both on Carter's dealings on the hostage crisis and on his campaign strategy. They have rubbished the evidence of some of the wilder conspiracy nutters who made obviously false claims, but have not dealt with some of the other evidence and they simply declared the case closed.

7. Even during the campaign Reagan had commented on his 'secret plan' to release the hostages. He spoke about his quiet diplomacy. What was he on about? They were in opposition and it was not their job to be involved in secret diplomacy. In

1991 he spoke to reporters about how, in 1980, he had 'tried some things the other way' while discussing the hostage issue. He said that 'some of these things were still classified'. Why should the activities of an unelected campaign team be classified? He later claimed to have no memory of what he was talking about. This was all put down to his sad decline into Alzheimer's disease and the resultant memory loss and confusion. He has made no further comments of significance on any topic in recent years for this reason, but was the onset of his illness partly responsible for his candid admission of something he was supposed to stay quiet about?

So what can we make of this? Something strange was going on and Casey's fingerprints seem to be on it, but the real truth is still unknown. Numerous alternative theories, including some of counterconspiracy aimed at discrediting Reagan and Bush, have muddied the waters further, as has false evidence from obvious liars and fortune seekers. As conspiracy theories go, it has more going for it than most. Make your own mind up.

What Was That Result Again?

'The People's Voice is Odd. It is, and it is not, the Voice of
God'
– Alexander Pope, Imitations of Horace, Epistle II, 1

Now we will take some time to look at some of the odder results
to litter the history of voting: the close calls, the low turnouts,
the candidates no one supported, the deeply suspicious results
and those that were just plain weird. Some of the stranger cases
are detailed in other chapters. There is an unsurprising
connection between some of these cases and those that illustrate
corruption and fraud or unusual candidates, for example.

I FEEL THE EARTH MOVE: THE DAYS OF THE EASTERN LANDSLIDE

One of the disappointing outcomes of the fall of the Iron Curtain
was the loss of the tremendous election results we used to get
from Eastern Europe. I am sure most Eastern Europeans do not
miss them at all – indeed they probably never took any notice of
them – but election watchers loved them. The 1960s was the
period when our European comrades had this down to a fine art.
Prior to that, elections were nonexistent, ludicrously badly
managed or actually gave some sort of a chance to opposition
parties. Later on the move towards *glasnost* was already
beginning and the chinks of light were starting to gleam through
the Berlin Wall. In the 1960s they got it just right. Take the East
German general election of 1963. I do not know if they had a
German Dimbleby brother to take the nation through an

exciting night of election coverage, but it would have been riveting viewing.

All 434 seats of the Volkskammer were up for grabs. A party list system was used for the whole country and, to make things nice and easy for the voters, there was only one list. The National Front (no relation to their British namesake – but come to think of it . . .) was dominated by the Communists with a few friendly additions thrown in. One constituency with a 434-name list to vote for and no opposition. Not an inspiring prospect for the average voter you would think. Not a bit of it. Out of an electorate of 11,604,626 the turnout was 11,517,241 (99.25 per cent). 11,511,500 of these enthusiastically backed the list (99.95 per cent). So let's get this straight: 11,511,500 voted for the Communists; fewer than 6,000 spoiled their ballots or ticked a 'No, Thank You Very Much' box; 87,385 failed to vote. A landslide victory if ever there was one. Peter Snow's swing-ometer would have gone around a complete circle and be about to disappear back up its own rear end. The lesson to learn here, however, is, 'If you are going to fix an election result, make it believable or the whole world will laugh at you.'

First, turnouts of 99.25 per cent just do not happen. Even if there is compulsory voting or the secret police are keeping a close eye on the list of names that have not been marked on the electoral register. For one thing, even the most up-to-date and well-produced electoral register will yield at least a 2 or 3 per cent vote for the Dead Party. Add to that those who cannot or will not vote for various reasons and a genuine turnout of 95 per cent would be a remarkable result, even for the most rigorously enforced compulsory ballot. I know Australia claimed 98 per cent on at least one occasion, but Aussies are a very fit bunch who do not die until after they vote, and I don't believe their figures either.

Secondly, to believe seriously that only one in two thousand voters opposed the single list is absurd. As you would guess after reading the chapter on spoiled votes, you would expect more than that to cock up their ballot. Presumably there was some actual opposition as well! Were their votes simply counted as support for the party list anyway, whatever it said on the ballot? Or were their votes counted even though they did not turn up, as they were busy that day trying to dig their way out of the country? We will never know, because these votes were never left lying around for any old international observers to turn up and inspect them. All we know was that all the East European elections of the Communist era stank to high heaven of a fix, but what a brazen and magnificently bold collection of fixes they were. The East Germans were among the very best at concocting these record-threatening landslide results. And the 'contests' were every bit as clean as their Olympic swimmers. I remember having conversations with Western communists who actually believed these were genuine fair results. They really did – I kid you not! They don't make lefties like that any more. How I laughed!

Saddam Hussein has been among those who have kept the flag flying for this kind of overwhelming support. He was re-elected President of Iraq in 1995 with 99.96 per cent of the vote. Not a single vote from Kurds or Marsh Arabs of course, but an impressive result albeit without the inconvenience of an opponent. Would you have stood against him?

Of course North Korea has given us 100 per cent turnouts with 100 per cent votes for the government, but that is just silly. There is nothing clever about that at all. Albania tried an interesting one when they claimed one voter spoiled their vote in an otherwise unanimous acclamation of the ruling Communist Party in 1982. That must have created uproar when they found that ballot paper. What did they make of it? What happened to the voter? Actually, in the one day of my life I spent in Albania a few years later, I think I might have met that single opponent of the regime about a hundred times. Oddly, I did not find any of the supporters.

Now that democracy had come to Eastern Europe, voters in

the municipal elections in Prague in 1994 had the joy of selecting
55 candidates from a choice of 1,187 on a ballot paper measuring
roughly twice the size of a broadsheet newspaper. Isn't real
democracy inspiring?

NUL POINTS

Norway has managed it with style four times in the Eurovision
Song Contest. There is always the sad character in the election
for student union executive/office staff association/golf club
committee and so forth whom nobody votes for. But, if they
were eligible to stand, they were usually eligible to vote, so they
should get one at least. In public elections, the feat of achieving
no votes at all has become the holy chimera of the study of
electoral strangeness. It is virtually impossible to achieve. In the
UK, a candidate for any office has to be nominated by at least ten
electors from the constituency in which they intend to stand.
They do not have to be registered there themselves. In theory,
that should mean ten votes in the bag, even if the candidate and
their immediate family cannot vote. Actually, they are not
guaranteed these at all.

Many have known the same experience as I have. The party
decides to fight a ward they have not contested for years. There
are only two members living there. One of them went fishing
with Lord Lucan and hasn't been seen since. The other is 98
and has lost all grip on reality. She is nominally the ward chair.
As there are no canvass records, you have to go house to house
to get people to nominate your candidate, who has no chance of
winning, has never set foot in the ward and has no plans to do
so. It is one of those situations when you really wonder why
you bother, but it turns out to be incredibly encouraging. At
least one in three households is quite happy to sign your
nomination paper. You think that with this level of support,
you are likely to pull off an amazingly unlikely victory. In

reality, a third or more of voters will sign your forms because:

- It seems to be the quickest way of getting rid of you.
- They have no idea what you are talking about and they will sign almost anything someone brings to their door: 'Lifetime supply of nuclear waste brought to your home?' 'Your own death warrant?' 'Yeah, all right, mate, where do I sign?'
- They take pity on you, or genuinely wish to support your democratic right to stand even if they don't support your party.
- They do support your party and don't mind admitting it. This is the least likely alternative in these circumstances.

The blessed Screaming Lord Sutch followed a similar line when getting nominations for all the by-elections he fought. He had a fundraising gig in a local pub, collected as much money as he could towards his deposit and collected as many signatures as he could for his nomination papers. He could go over the electoral register later to see if ten of these people were actually on it, and there were usually enough.

These cases illustrate that you cannot rely on your ten proposers. There have even been plenty of cases of supposedly more reliable party members signing papers and then turning their backs on the official candidate.

So how low can a candidate's vote go? Well, it can go pretty low, but I have not found an instance of zero in any UK election since the secret ballot was introduced in 1872 and subsequent reform greatly increased the size of the electorate. It may be possible in a parish council election with a very small electorate and a low turnout. After all, only one person voted in the Machars Community Council election of 1973, but that sort of level of micro-election scarcely counts. I would love to know if a genuine zero has ever been achieved. In the days between the 1832 Reform Act and the 1872 Ballot Act, there were eight candidates who received no support at all. These were four

Chartists, three Liberals and one Conservative. The Tory and one of the Liberals both managed it in Tewkesbury, which claims special honour as a result.

ALL-TIME HERO

The last known case of a parliamentary candidate getting no votes in the days before the secret ballot was a Mr F R Lees in Ripon, Yorkshire, in an 1860 by-election. Mr Lees was a Temperance Chartist. The Chartist movement had more or less wound up by this time, having achieved some of its goals and given up on some of the others. Those who remained in politics had mostly joined the Liberals by now. Unfortunately, Mr Lees's other stated principle ruled out the chance of a consoling drink to cheer himself up afterwards. Lees was a true believer in the cause who spotted his chance as the Liberal MP J A Warre died and precipitated a by-election. Lees stood against the new Liberal candidate, R A Vyner, on 22 December 1860. There was a 54.5 per cent turnout among the North Yorkshire electorate of 343, which was good for three days before Christmas. Unfortunately, all 187 of them voted for Mr Vyner. No Conservatives or any others stood, but it was of no help to our hapless hero. Ripon remained safely Liberal for many years.

Having already settled on his place in history (he was not to know his record would stand for over 140 years and probably for ever), Lees moved on to new triumphs. Ripon was clearly not a happy hunting ground, and the Chartist movement had had its day. Lees recognised that late-nineteenth-century Britain was a Tory-Liberal battleground. He converted to Liberalism and fought the seat of Northampton in 1868 under his new designation. There were two seats available, but four Liberal candidates against two Conservatives. C Gilpin and Lord Henley won as Liberals. Guess who trailed in last with less than half the vote of the third Liberal, who himself finished well behind the Conservatives. Not to be put off, Mr Lees moved back to Yorkshire and contested Leeds in 1874. He felt he had paid his dues by now, and Leeds was a growing major city of the Empire, now awarded three seats. 'Lees for Leeds' was bound to be a winning slogan. This time there were only three Liberals, so no split vote. Carter topped the poll for the Liberals with 15,390 votes. Wheelhouse came in second for the Tories with 14,864 votes and Tennant grabbed the third seat for the Tories with 13,194 votes. The Liberal candidate, Baines, was edged out with 11,850 votes. There was no third Conservative candidate. There was no candidate from any other party. Guess who trailed in last, way behind with 5,954 votes. Just to rub salt into the wound, Gladstone topped the poll in Leeds six years later, and he turned the seat down, preferring to sit for Edinburghshire. But Gladstone was Gladstone and Lees was a total and utter failure and one of the greatest heroes of parliamentary democracy. Never an MP, but always an inspiration. May he rest in peace.

THE NOBLE POOR

Those who have followed in the footsteps of the great Lees in recent years have never quite managed to repeat his pathetic record, but some have done incredibly well. Bill Boaks is investigated in detail in the chapter on unusual candidates ('Stranger Gallery'), but must be mentioned here as the holder of the title of lowest parliamentary vote in the twentieth century with his five votes from the Glasgow Hillhead by-election of 1982. While the rest of the country watched Roy Jenkins fight his way back into Parliament to lead the SDP, Bill fought his own fight and no one else really cared. His vote was equalled six years later by Dr Kailish Trevedi in the Kensington by-election of 1988, where he gained five votes as well. It is not unusual for parties to pick the wrong constituency to raise their banner. Here the Janata party picked entirely the wrong country! Rather like Plaid Cymru fighting Dagenham, or the Ulster Unionists contesting an uncharted region of the Amazonian rainforest, there was little clue as to what this lone candidate was doing here parachuted into an alien election away from the party's traditional home in India. Clearly, the people of Kensington had no idea. The only others to fall below the magic ten mark were J Connell (seven votes for the Peace Party in Chesterfield 1984), Dorian Vanbraam (also seven votes as a Renaissance Democrat in Putney 1997 – 0.02 per cent of the vote) and Esmond Bevan (Independent in Bermondsey, 1983, with eight votes) These were all high-profile elections with well-known, star-name candidates and colourful personalities. Connell, Bevan and Vanbraam were neither. Poor Connell was beaten by the Acne Party, a 'Prisoner: I am not a Number' candidate, 'Elvisly Yours Elvis Presley' Party, a furniture-shop owner running as an advertising stunt, an Independent Welshman, 'Yoga and Meditation', someone who wanted the *Sun* classified as a comic, Screaming Lord Sutch, seven other odds and sods and Tony Benn. It was possibly the weirdest collection of by-election candidates ever assembled and the Peace Party came last, which may be a sad indictment on Chesterfield.

The 2001 general election was remarkably short of poorly performing candidates. The reduction in numbers standing was an issue. There was no Referendum Party or Natural Law Party. However, that was largely offset by more UK Independence candidates, as well as more Greens and more far-left candidates. What we were lacking were the tiny parties and fringe causes who either caught the wave of apathy that swept the nation and did not bother, or were caught out by the new registration rules, and were told to change their descriptions or drop out. The lowest vote I could find was the reasonably creditable 43 votes for A Klein standing as an Independent in Hampstead. That would get nowhere near meriting a mention on the all-time lists. A little ahead was J Middleton standing in Kingston for 'Unrepresented People' and gaining 54 votes. Either there are very few of them or they are happy to remain unrepresented. The most pathetic party performance was the dreadful showing by the Workers' Revolutionary Party – a party so committed to its precise niche in the Trotskyite market that it could not join with all the other leftists that came together for the first time under the Socialist Alliance banner. Its handful of candidates mostly failed to struggle into three figures.

An interesting variation on the low-vote theme was achieved in America in 2000. David Palmer intended to run for the House as a Green Independent Party candidate. Although there was no other challenger for this title in his district, he still had to win the Primary election to be eligible to stand. Unfortunately, he did not get around to voting for himself in the Primary poll to select the 'Green Independent Party' candidate. Neither did anyone else. There being no votes cast, and therefore no plurality of the vote as required by law, he could not stand in the full election in November. Watch out for David Palmer. America may have discovered their very own F R Lees.

CATCH ME IF YOU CAN

While some candidates attract overwhelming indifference from the public there are also the candidates who cannot be touched. The winners who won by an embarrassing margin over an utterly crushed opposition. There are not as many examples of this as you might expect. In earlier elections, candidates who were unbeatable were usually left alone. The last MPs to be elected unopposed strolled effortlessly into Parliament in 1951. In recent years, it has become unusual for a seat to be contested by fewer than four candidates, making enormous winning margins rare. Society tends to be more heterogeneous and pluralistic than it once was, wherever you go in the country. Many councillors are still elected unopposed, mainly in rural areas. Some parish councils cannot even find enough candidates to fill the places.

In looking for impressively one-sided contests, you might be tempted to look to Labour in Rhondda or Conservatives in Sutton Coldfield, but the real home of the walkover is Ulster. This is curious as we can also find oddities like four-way knife-edge contests in the next-door seat, but everything is different in Ulster. In overwhelmingly Protestant North Down, J Campbell of Sinn Fein decided to take on George Currie of the Conservatives in the 1955 general election. In those days the Ulster Unionists were still united with the Conservative Party, although most of them were at least semidetached already. There may have been some difficulty for Sinn Fein in finding the ten nominators. Walking through the streets of Bangor trying to get signatures for Irish republicanism is not easy. However, Sinn Fein ensured there was a contest. Currie got 50,315 and Campbell got 1,637 – 96.8 per cent against 3.2 per cent. 'Give up, for goodness' sake!' Campbell was made of sterner stuff. Back came Sinn Fein in 1959. Again it was a two-candidate field. There were 5,000 more electors in the constituency and Sinn Fein had a base of support to build on now of course. Currie got 51,773 and Campbell got 1,039 – 98.0 per cent against 2.0 per cent. 'Giving up now?' Yes. Sinn Fein left North Down alone for forty years after that.

Ulster came up trumps with devastating results again on 23 January 1986. The unionist MPs were agreed in their revulsion towards the new Anglo-Irish Agreement. Ian Paisley had denounced Margaret Thatcher as 'Jezebel' from his pulpit and made millions of Britons who had previously despised her wonder whether they had been wrong all along and she was actually quite admirable. In a province known for centuries of futile gestures, here came another one. All fifteen unionists resigned their seats in order to force by-elections. This would bring about a kind of mini-election in Northern Ireland to show opposition to the agreement. The nationalists held only two seats at the time. There was a problem here. The nationalist parties and all the nonsectarian parties rejected the exercise as a propaganda tool for Unionism (which was exactly what the Unionists had intended it to be). There was no point in their joining in to fight elections they could not win, so they were threatening that they would not play this game. As the close of nominations drew near, it looked worryingly as if a number of these MPs would be returned unopposed. This would neutralise the propaganda effect, especially as the likely seats were, by definition, in the strongest unionist areas. There was no point in the unionist parties standing against each other as they normally would. That would not say much for this display of unity. So what to do? Someone had a bright idea. As it turned out, at least one candidate came out of the woodwork to oppose them in most of the places, but in four of them Plan B went into operation. One Ulster Unionist changed his name by deed poll to Peter Barry (the name of the Irish Foreign Secretary) to stand as 'For Anglo Irish Agreement'. He got 6.1 per cent in East Londonderry, 5.9 per cent in South Antrim, 5.8 per cent in Strangford and managed 2.6 per cent in North Antrim (Paisley 33,937, Barry 913). There was never too much danger of his getting very close to victory in any of these. The only question was: who actually voted for him? Surely most of the nationalists in these seats stayed away. Were 913 North Antrimites either off-message Catholics or accidental ballot spoilers? Or were they just having a laugh? Of course the whole thing backfired on the Unionists horribly. While the others triumphantly threw themselves into this campaign knowing their seats were safe, Enoch Powell and Jim Nicholson sat at the back saying, 'Excuse us, actually we have marginal seats to fight, thanks.' Powell held on to South Down by 1,842 votes, while Nicholson lost Newry and Armagh by 2,583 to Seamus Mallon of the SDLP. Mallon would go on to become Deputy First Minister in Northern Ireland's devolved government years later. He got his leg-up into Parliament through a unionist stunt that flopped. The other big question I never found an answer to was whether 'Peter Barry' took a liking to his new name and kept it, or decided to change to something else as soon as the election was over – John Paul II, perhaps, or Madonna.

It is impossible to give a definitive, historical answer as to the question of what was the most emphatic victory ever achieved in a fair democratic election conducted under universal suffrage. There are too many imponderables there, and too many records lost in the mists of time and dusty library shelves around the world. Ian Paisley will be up near the top. One candidate is the former Pakistan Prime Minister, Benazir Bhutto. After losing office on corruption charges, she stood again in her seat in Larkana-III. Her voters clearly did not believe there was anything corrupt about her. She got 94,462 votes (98.48 per cent). The runner-up got 718 votes (0.75 per cent). That is about as emphatic as it gets.

The Conservative MP Sir Cooper Rawson achieved the largest majority in the UK, getting 62,253 more votes than his rival in Brighton 1931. That was more than many entire electorates. Curiously, the 1964 general election saw Brighton Kemptown (covering much of Rawson's old seat) have a record seven recounts, before Dennis Hobden won the seat for Labour with a majority of seven votes.

THEY LONG TO BE CLOSE TO YOU

So to the other extreme. Those nail-biting contests where the electorate refuse to give a ringing endorsement to anybody. The closest vote possible is a tie of course. This has not been achieved in a parliamentary election in the UK since 1886 in Ashton-under-Lyne. It often occurs in local council elections where electorates and turnouts are generally much smaller. Most years there is one of these somewhere. There is some confusion and a lot of 'modern myth' over what happens when it occurs. First, there are a number of recounts of course. Even a small number of votes can easily produce the occasional misplaced ballot.

There is always going to be at least one very dubious ballot paper that will get the parties arguing. See the next chapter for the best modern example of that. When the tied vote is agreed, matters turn to the returning officer. In parliamentary elections, this is often the local mayor; otherwise it is usually either the council chief executive or the electoral registration officer, who manages all the elections in the local area anyway. They do not have their own casting vote, or follow some kind of precedence, as some people believe. Since 1948 they have been instructed to cast lots between the two top candidates. This is just exactly the method used by Christ's disciples in deciding whom to appoint as their new member in Acts, Chapter 1. Nowadays, the outgoing member is not Judas. Not usually, anyway.

The last MP to get elected with a majority of one in Britain was H E Duke as a Unionist in Exeter in 1910. A J Flint won in Ilkeston for Ramsay MacDonald's National Labour in 1931 by just two votes. Mark Oaten's two-vote majority in Winchester 1997 was overturned, as is discussed in the next chapter. Three-vote majorities were achieved by F D Acland for the Liberals in Tiverton 1923, Sir Harmar Nicholls for the Conservatives in Peterborough in 1966 (Nicholls had majorities of just 22 and 144 in other fights here and he is, therefore, the king of the knife-edge contest) and Gwynoro Jones for Labour in Carmarthen in February 1974 (he lost it to Gwynfor Evans, former leader of Plaid Cymru, in October 1974 by over 3,000 votes).

Zanzibar managed to elect a government by a majority of one seat in 1961. The Afro-Shirazi Party crawled past the winning post thanks to their victory in Chake-Chake on Pemba Island, where their candidate was returned with a majority of one vote. When someone tells you individual votes do not count, tell them to think about Zanzibar and watch the look on their face.

Close votes still keep on happening. On February 25 2001, Pedro Verona Rodrigues Pires of the African Party of Independence won the second round run-off for the presidency of Cape Verde by seventeen votes. He tied on 50 per cent of the vote with Carlos Roverto de Carvalho Veiga of the Movement for Democracy.

Newspapers love reporting close results. They screw up their deadlines and make them publish embarrassing headlines that get it badly wrong, like some of the classic confused headlines in the American press of November 2000. At least they make for good stories and that sells papers. One of the most embarrassing newspaper headlines of all time followed the narrow victory of Golda Meir in Israel: GOLDA WINS BY A NOSE. I bet they were pleased with that one.

One of my favourite close-vote stories occurred in Richmond-upon-Thames in a local council election in 1978. A Conservative won a seat in Barnes by a majority of just two votes, but the result was challenged by a voter who claimed to have been disenfranchised. A German couple turned up to vote despite not being British citizens and, therefore, not being registered. Quite what they thought they were up to I am not sure, but the clerk allowed them to vote as they happened to have a similar name to a couple living near them, and all three of them got confused in a mess of addresses and German accents. The genuine couple turned up later and were told they had already voted. The procedure in any case like this is to cast a tendered vote. This is kept separate by the clerk and not put in the ballot box. They can then be considered at a later point. It just so happened that a girl who was underage had also voted. As a person who would have her eighteenth birthday during the coming year, she was on the register with her birthdate alongside her name. Such people cannot vote if the election takes place before their birthday. She was wrongly advised by a Conservative agent, who may have been merely incompetent or may have guessed the result would be close. Some semicomatose clerk gave her a ballot paper and she cast her vote.

The relevant ballot papers were all dug up by court order and it was discovered that all three bogus votes were for the Tory; the tendered votes for the Liberal were allowed and the result was reversed.

PLEASE! SOMEONE'S GOT TO TURN UP!

The lowest turnout for a parliamentary constituency in Britain at a general election was in Kennington 1918 at 29.7 per cent. The national figure that year was only 57 per cent. There were clearly many reasons for it at that point in history, particularly with outdated registers. Despite growing waves of apathy, both those 1918 figures still just about stand as records to date. Several by-elections have seen lower numbers than Kensington. Indeed, Leeds Central set a postwar record in 1999 with a spectacularly poor 19.5 per cent. The biggest turnout, by the way, was Fermanagh and South Tyrone in 1951 at 93.42 per cent. Of course they have the advantage in Fermanagh that death does not stop you voting. The British people made a bold attempt to enter the record books in 2001 with a turnout that went barely over 58 per cent. Unluckily pipped at the post by 1918, when many of those on the register were either still abroad or lying dead on the fields of France after fighting for our right to enjoy democracy. Liverpool Riverside set the way with its 34.1 per cent. If anybody there under the age of 25 voted, can they please report to the City Hall for their cash prize?

The 1999 British elections for the European Parliament set new standards for low turnouts. We all thought we had seen low figures before, but the British people surpassed themselves as only about ten and a half million could be bothered – 24.1 per cent. Another of our special prizes is reserved for the reliably uninterested Liverpool Riverside, where they managed a truly pathetic 10.3 per cent turnout, just seeing off very close challenges from fellow Liverpudlians in Walton and West Derby. Only in Northern Ireland and rural parts of Wales was turnout anywhere near respectable. It has become one of the most oft-quoted and tedious clichés that more people voted for the winning housemate in the last episode of Channel 4's *Big Brother* than voted in the European election. It is probably not true, as we have no idea how many times some people picked up their phone to vote for Craig the builder. The point is that nobody cared enough about the European election to want to vote more than once.

New Labour's answer to reversing the decline in interest in elections has been to give us more of them! Not content with new elections in Scotland, Wales and Northern Ireland, we await new assemblies for the English regions. Several towns have also had the chance to decide if they wish to elect a mayor. Most have had dismal turnouts, and have either overwhelmingly decided they don't want one or have had a very even vote. Only Middlesbrough and Doncaster have emphatically embraced the idea, mainly because they were desperate to find any way they could to take power away from their sleazy Labour councils.

The greatest wheeze of them all was the idea to introduce an elected element to the reformed House of Lords. Yes, you lucky people can elect just 20% of the members, probably from a party list of has-beens and nobodies. They can then get overwhelmingly outvoted in a chamber still dominated by appointees, which possesses few powers except to hold up legislation and annoy the Government a bit.

If anyone can think of a single good reason why any of us should bother to turn up for that one, I would like to hear of it. If such an election ever takes place, prepare for some new broken records.

For those who are counting, the lowest turnout I have yet come across for a national election was 30 per cent in the Ivory Coast. That is staggeringly low, but at least it sounds more honest than some countries. It's another of those oddities – Ivory Coast. They achieved this figure as a country that allowed multiparty democracy, but somehow only one party contested the election. In fact in 1985, 546 candidates of the ruling PDCI contested the 175 National Assembly seats, showing they had the ingenuity to stand against each other, as nobody else was going to. Usually a one-party state gets turnouts of over 95 per cent, while the genuinely competitive elections get lower figures, in one of those perverse twists of logic that politics throws up. Ivory Coast seems to make more sense. Nobody wanted to stand. Nobody wanted to vote. As a multiparty system has developed there, the turnout has grown, but in 2001 they achieved a turnout of just 33.1 per cent partly helped by a boycott led by one of the main parties. Presumably, 67 per cent were not supporting the RDR's boycott. If they were, they should have just stood and won a landslide. Perhaps Ivory Coast just *is* the most politically apathetic country on the planet. That might make it one of the more attractive nations. By the way, the RDR still won five seats, despite not standing, and I'm not too sure how they managed that.

AN ODD ONE

A beautifully strange result was achieved in Denmark at their general election of 21 September 1971. Hilmar Baunsgard led his centre-right governing coalition back to the polls. There was a very close result as they gained 88 seats, while the Social Democrats and Socialists under Jens Otto Krag won 89 seats. The Folketing had 179 seats in total, so the result was still uncertain. The Faeroe Islands elected an Independent and everything was down to Greenland. It would be decided by a few thousand hardy characters living on the edge of an ice cap that, as a Danish protectorate, made up most of Western Europe's landmass (the largest noncontinental island in the world), though most would not recognise it as Europe at all. As was often the case, communications with the fisherfolk and skin traders of the Arctic were down again, and the Danish did not know who would represent their frozen compatriots. Would it be a

Baunsgard supporter or a Krag partisan? Who would govern Denmark? They would have to wait until the plane landed and the victor emerged with a victorious wave. The plane touched down and Denmark held its collective breath as an Inuit Eskimo Independent Marxist emerged in an enormous anorak, surprisingly elected on a wave of Euro-scepticism. Everyone scratched their head, deduced that he would probably not join the Conservative/Liberal coalition, and that Krag would become Prime Minister.

AND THE WINNER IS . . . THE LOSER

When you were taught that democracy was all about allowing the most popular candidate or party to govern, you were taught wrong. That happens in some systems, in some circumstances. In most systems, the winning party or coalition need not get a majority of votes, or even a plurality. In first-past-the-post elections, such as in the UK and USA, there is no mathematical reason why winning the most votes should get your party into government. If there is a decisive outcome it would usually follow, but if the result is close there is no reason why it should.

Everyone laughed at the opinion pollsters in 1992 who predicted either a small Labour majority or a hung Parliament at the general election. In fact they were nearly right. Although John Major's Conservatives won a healthy 8 per cent lead over Labour in the popular vote, they gained a small overall majority of 21 thanks to some tiny constituency majorities. If fewer than 1,500 voters had switched in the eleven closest fights, they would not have affected the 8 per cent lead at all, but would have given the country a hung Parliament. If a party cannot get its votes in the right places, it can still fail to win, unless its lead is of such landslide proportions that it does not matter.

Twice since World War Two, the party with the largest vote in Britain lost the general election. Most remarkably in 1951,

Clement Attlee's Labour Party polled 13,948,605 votes. This was 231,067 more than the Conservatives under Winston Churchill. Labour polled what was the highest popular vote ever at the time, and their percentage support of 48.8 per cent has never been bettered since. Yet they won 295 seats while the Tories won 321 seats and gained a majority of 17.

In the first general election of 1974, the tables turned as Edward Heath led his Conservatives into the general election on their worst campaign slogan of modern times: 'Who Governs Britain?' Any slogan that invites a facetious response is rubbish. Anyhow, 38.8 per cent of the voters decided that Heath could go on governing, while 38.0 per cent opted for Labour. This amounted to a national majority of 229,663. This time the electoral arithmetic turned out in Labour's favour. They failed to get an overall majority but won four more seats than the Tories. Experts consider that the electoral equation has moved steadily in Labour's favour over the years. The Tory vote tends to spread more evenly, which is useful if they win easily, but not if it is closer. They need to win an election by at least 8 per cent (like Major), to get a majority in Parliament. Labour have lots of very safe seats and lots of completely hopeless seats, and can concentrate on targeting the key marginals. It is easily possible for Labour to get a good working majority in Parliament with a tied popular vote.

Not only Britain produces such deeply unfair results. The American President is not elected on the basis of a popular vote either. Just as defenders of the British system argue that we don't directly elect a government, but rather we vote for local constituency MPs, the Americans point out that they have a federal system, in which it is important that a presidential candidate wins support across the states. He should not win simply by running up huge majorities in the few dominant States of the Union such as California and New York. There is certainly logic there, but it is worse than that. The system is rigged in favour of the little states. For example, California has

52 Congressmen to Wyoming's one. This represents an approximate population ratio of 52:1. However, electoral college votes for each state also include a representation of Senate seats. Every state has two Senators, whatever its size. Therefore California has 54 votes and Wyoming has 3. Any mathematician will tell you that 52:1 and 54:3 are two very different ratios. Most of the states have six Congressmen or fewer. Most of these are predominantly Republican inclined and the arithmetic stacks up impressively for them. As we all know, Al Gore won the popular vote in 2000 by a considerable margin with 50,996,116 votes (48.42 per cent) against 50,456,169 for George 'Dubya' Bush (47.90 per cent), and 3,874,040 (3.68 per cent) for others, 2,831,066 of that for Ralph Nader. That made a majority of 539,947, which is a lot of Americans by any measure. We deal with the whole Florida debacle in its own chapter, but, putting that to one side, Gore still won a clear victory and would have won an electoral college vote as well, if it had been calculated on a proper proportionate basis. Once again, America examines its constitution and ponders it for a bit, but we will see if it does anything about it.

Of course Bush was not the first. John Quincy Adams won the presidency in 1824 with 108,740 votes (only 30.5 per cent), well behind Andrew Jackson's 153,544 votes (43.1 per cent). He went on to become one of the country's most celebrated Presidents despite this terrible start. Rutherford Hayes 'won' the election in 1876 with 4,036,572 (48.0 per cent) against Samuel Tilden's 4,284,020 (51.0 per cent). Hayes was a reasonably successful president and you can read more about his election in the chapter on fraud and corruption ('Corruption, Fraud and Winning Dirty'). The last President to win by losing before Dubya was Benjamin Harrison in 1888 with 5,447,129 votes (47.9 per cent) against Grover Cleveland with 5,537, 857 votes (48.6 per cent). Harrison was not exactly an all-time star, but he did not too badly, either. Cleveland was the defending President, and he beat Harrison four years later. So he could claim to have 'won' three presidential elections in a row. Several other victorious candidates have had minority victories, and some have had very close-run fights, including Truman, Kennedy and Nixon. At least they all did manage to get more votes than anyone else.

PRIZE WINNERS OF THE NEW MILLENNIUM

Here are the special prizewinners for the most distinguished, pitiful performances in UK local council by-elections at the dawn of a new millennium for electoral disaster. I really am not going to plough through every vote from the main annual Council elections, as that would take forever to study tens of thousands of results, but by-elections generally produce the lowest turnouts anyway, and therefore the lowest votes. The years 2000 and 2001 produced some classy cases. Firstly, there was a very hot contest for the Lowest Turnout award. Throughout 2000, several inner city one-party domains and sleepy Town or Parish Councils hovered around the 10% mark, and some dipped below. Thurrock got off to a good start with an 8% turnout in January, but Camborne Town Council were not going to let them have it so easily. They forgot to send out any polling cards in West ward and saw 6.7% of their voters turn up on 27 April. As a consequence, Mebyon Kernow (Cornish Nationalists) beat the Labour candidate by 4 votes, which was very funny. This was a bit of a cheat, however, so it was only fair that they got beaten in the end. Uckfield Town Council East ward managed a turnout of only 6% on November 2. As the town spent much of 2000 being flooded, this was a reasonable sort of turnout for a fully submerged election. In a two-horse race, or a two-boat race if you prefer, Labour beat the Lib Dems by 27 votes (very decisive in these circumstances).

Nowhere could beat that in 2001. There were numerous contenders around the 10% mark, but Okehampton Town Council managed easily the lowest of the year with a 7% turnout on February 15, producing a Lib Dem win.

There is no question what was the worst Labour performance. They managed to get all of 13 votes in Pateley Bridge ward for Harrogate Borough Council in February 2000. This amounted to 1.5% of the vote and did not greatly trouble the Lib-Dems' 58.6%. Largo war on Fife Council challenged this with 34 votes (2.7%) in September 2001. The Lib Dems won that too. Labour got fewer votes, 23 of them (4.1%) in the same month in Compton ward Stratford-on-Avon DC – a Conservative win.

The Tories got 17 votes in Longview ward, Knowsley in June 2000, although the 45 votes they got in Park ward, Sheffield in October was marginally worse in percentage terms (2.5%). This is solidly Labour Sheffield Council Estate territory. However those records were smashed in 2001. Inverclyde Council cannot be bothered to name their wards, but one of these has made its mark by providing one of the worst results for an official Conservative candidate in the history of elections conducted under universal suffrage. Ward 4 elected a Lib Dem Councillor on September 6 with 569 votes. The Tory came in fourth with ten votes (0.8%)

As for the local by-election specialists, the Lib-Dems, they succeeded in getting 13 votes (1.3%) in the clumsily named Woodhead/Meikle Earnock ward of South Lanarkshire Council on 13 April 2000. Labour's 464 votes was beyond them. Priory ward Monmouthshire County Council 23 votes (2.4%) was the worst they could manage in 2001. The Tories won that encounter in March.

The minor parties and independents managed to produce many spectacularly poor performances over the two years in our study. But no Raving Loony, Natural Law, UK Independence or any other candidate could touch the achievement of an Independent candidate in Crown Ward for the Scottish Highland Council on 8 June 2000. Labour won the election with just 28.1% against no opposition from Conservatives, Lib-Dem or

SNP, but from 6 different independents! The split in the Independent vote let Labour through, but not much of it split for the sixth one, who got three votes (0.3%). Someone described as an Asian got 13 votes in the very well populated ward of Queensbury on Bradford City Council on 7 June 2001. That was an almost invisible 0.2%. Labour won with 3217 votes. Only 13 people saw any point in putting a UKIP voice into Birmingham City Council on October 11 (0.7%) in Kingsbury ward. Independents also got single figure votes in Goole and Brandon in 2001. The Lib Dem win in Brandon was also the most one-sided performance in a three corner fight in recent years – it helps when one of the three corners has folded.

All of these failed candidates were heroic. Maybe they were blindly optimistic, maybe they knew what was coming, but they showed true commitment to democracy when it would have been easier not to bother. I am sure they would all have made better Councillors than hundreds of others currently dozing in the Nation's Council chambers.

There were some pointless contests, such as Wem Rural Ward, North Shropshire, where a lone independent candidate united the entire anti-Conservative vote on 22 June 2000 to get all of 60 votes and see the Conservatives win this two horse race (1 thorough-bred, 1 lame donkey race) with 82.9%. To be fair, there have been much more one-sided races in the past. The last couple of years have been surprisingly short of them. The Tories can score higher shares in wards in Kensington & Chelsea in multi-party contests. Several wards across Northern England can give 90%+ support to Labour on a good day. Although this seldom happens in their former heartland of South Wales anymore. There was a late victory in this contest from Belmont Parish Council with Lib Dem 426 (85.4) Lab 73 (14.6) on 13 December 2001.

There were no ties in the by-elections we have been scrutinising, but Harrowby ward on South Kesteven District Council voted on 24 August when the more sensible voters were away sunning themselves on beaches. If one of these people had rubbed themselves down and found their way back to a polling station in their floppy hat, flip-flops and with stick of rock in hand, they might have overturned the Conservative's one vote majority over Labour. Probably the most remarkable result of any recent local by-election. Here it is:

Conservative	222 (24.7%)
Labour	221 (24.6%)
Independent Labour	213 (23.7%)
Liberal Democrat	181 (20.1%)
Independent	62 (6.9%)

How about that for a three- or even a four-way contest! To think, those people on holiday missed all that fun. On second thoughts, though, it's only a few seconds of fun, and even Skegness can offer more than that.

This was matched by St Thomas ward City of Wells PC on November 29 2001. Note that Wells is a city that only gets a Parish Council. That's what you get when you call a big Church and a few teashops a City. The Lib Dem got 372 (45.4%) Con 371 (45.2%). A majority of just one. The much more numerous Wymondham ward Norfolk County Council managed to produce Lib Dem 1736 (49.2%) Con 1734 (49.1%). A majority of just two on 2 August 2001. A Lib Dem gain from the Tories, who were somewhat miffed that Labour failed to find a candidate this time round. It's a fair bet they would have taken at least three votes off the Lib Dems if they had.

Becton ward on Newham London Borough Council may have had the most interesting local council by-election of 2001 as Labour saw off the challenge of the Christian People's Alliance by 58 votes in one of their safest local goverment strongholds in London with the BNP coming third, the Tories miles behind and the Liberal Democrats not standing.

Let the People Vote – So They Can Screw It Up!

The Strange Story of Spoiled Votes

'I am old now, and these same crosses spoil me. Who are you?
Mine eyes are not o'th' best, I'll tell you straight.'
– *William Shakespeare*, King Lear, *Act V, Sc. III*

Yes, this is a whole area that deserves a chapter to itself, and that is why I am giving it one.

Put simply, a spoiled vote is a ballot that is cast, but for some reason cannot be included in the count. That is, they are counted – but as a separate item and not added to any candidate's totals. There is a long and distinguished history here that stretches all the way back to the birth of the secret ballot. It is hard to see how people could have spoiled their votes in the days of voting by a show of hands in open hustings – perhaps they raised their arm in a strange and confusing way, or got muddled and raised the wrong body part altogether.

To get the boring bit out of the way, let's go through the acknowledged ways in which a ballot can be deemed to be spoiled, and therefore not counted. This is according to British electoral law, but most countries follow similar rules:

1. A blank ballot
2. Voting for more candidates than allowed (usually one)
3. Lack of clarity as to which candidate has been selected by the voter

4. Numbering of candidates rather than putting a mark (admissible as long as they have numbered only as many candidates as there are seats to be filled)
5. Any potential identification of the voter, such as a signature, address or detailed essay on the sexual perversions they believe the candidates have perpetrated
6. Lack of official mark
7. Lack of evidence that the voter is giving their chosen candidate a positive vote (e.g., an 'X' or a tick) rather than a negative comment (e.g. name scratched off ballot paper, death threat issued or brief Anglo-Saxon description of the sexual perversions they believe the candidate has perpetrated)

That just about covers it. We will return to each of these in detail. Some of these can be controversial of course. In these cases, the returning officer will allow candidates and agents to inspect the doubtful papers and usually they can agree on what to do with them. If they cannot, the returning officer makes a ruling. If anyone cannot accept the ruling, they can challenge it in court within a set time frame. In practice, they will do this only if it may affect the outcome of the election. It's a bit of a pointless waste of time and money otherwise.

Probably the most interesting variant we have on this when looking at other countries is the practice in some places, including parts of the USA, of allowing 'write-ins'. This allows for a kind of hybrid – an unspoiled spoiled vote if you like. In many places, you can write in the name of a candidate who is not on the ballot and vote for them. This is not really a spoiled vote because the vote will be included in the count, although a few dozen people who have voted for themselves are not really going to make any impact on the result and they may as well have been spoiled. However, there have been numerous examples of organised 'write-ins' and one or two campaigns for local offices have actually been successful. Also, we must acknowledge that if all the votes that Mickey Mouse has received over the years in this way were to be put together we would have to give him some sort of honorary international office. Some countries who practise compulsory voting allow voters to opt for 'none of the above', but this is really a cop-out. If voters do not want to vote for any of the above, they should be capable of finding a more satisfying way of doing it than that.

You can find the number of spoiled ballots for any election in the small print if you look hard enough, but it is rarely noticed by many people. So those voters who sit back triumphant in the thought that they really showed those people what they thought have not actually achieved anything unless there were thousands of them. Usually there are very few spoiled papers – less than one in a hundred or even less than one in a thousand, and most of these were a result of an accident rather than a deliberate decision. That hasn't stopped a handful of excellent cases happening over the years, some of which we will detail in a moment. Somehow the people of both East Berkshire and Bosworth in 1992 all managed to get it right, without a single spoiled vote. The UK record still stands with Belfast West in 1964 at 2,283 spoiled votes. Under current rules that would have saved the deposit for the 'Messed-Up Party'. Many of the largest figures come from seats where major parties were missing, such as where the main parties traditionally do not oppose the Speaker of the House, and some of the voters do not realise until they get to the polling station that they are virtually disenfranchised.

Of course, the whole USA Y2K cock-up gets star treatment elsewhere in the book. We will continue by returning to that list of methods of spoiling a ballot and looking at them a little more closely.

BLANK BALLOTS

These are often mysterious. Who are these strange people who breeze into polling stations, smile cheerfully at the tellers, give their names to the clerk, take a small piece of paper and put it straight into a box before going off to hand some blank cheques into the bank and carry an empty basket through the supermarket checkout? Sometimes there are concerns when there are a large number of these and questions follow as to whether there has been an administrative mistake. Fraud is unlikely, unless there is an extraordinarily sophisticated plot going on. In fact, these people are generally the most intelligent and thoughtful of conscientious active abstainers. They realise that a blank ballot is the most effective way of telling all the candidates they are hopeless, with no fear that their vote may be misread or reinterpreted in any way. If you wish to abstain in person at any election this is the professional way to do it.

It is a particularly satisfying tool to employ as a protest against any election you felt to be a waste of time and money such as an unnecessary by-election or an unwarranted referendum that you consider to be unfair, misleading or misconstrued. Surely some prize needed to be awarded to those who returned an envelope containing a blank ballot to the transport millionaire Brian Souter's completely ludicrous, personally financed postal referendum in Scotland on whether people wanted their schools to be stopped from 'promoting homosexuality'. Still no two people have agreed a definition of what that phrase means, which makes an intelligent, well informed referendum pretty well impossible. Those who attached their envelope to a heavy object to increase his postal costs further were even more creative in their opposition to silly exercises in promoting a rich man's prejudices. In actual fact, an official referendum can provide the occasion when a blank ballot is crucial to the outcome. Often a proposition has to reach a certain percentage of support to be enacted. Spoiled papers of any kind are added to the total vote, and thus reduce the chances of the proposition succeeding. This has been significant on some occasions, for example in delaying Ireland from bringing its divorce laws into the twentieth century before it finished. They got there in the end before the century was out.

IT'S SO HARD TO CHOOSE

In a society with so many choices, with ever-increasing ranges of products and a remote control to flick through hundreds of satellite TV stations, choosing just one person from a selection of rarely more than half a dozen, and often fewer, is too much for some people to handle. There are known to be some people who are so irrevocably nice they feel it would just be mean not to pick one of the candidates, so they vote for them all. Others who are torn between two think that they can register two votes, giving them an unfair advantage over the more decisive majority. Perhaps, they think their vote will be halved. Most of these are accidental spoiled papers, rather than purposeful ones. They are people who would be disappointed to know their vote was not registered.

The real fun starts when there are more seats than one to be filled. In a London borough election, for example, when three seats are filled in a ward in a single poll, the idea of perming three from twelve or more throws some electors into advanced psychotic reaction. Voters are given three votes to use. Most will use them to vote for all three candidates from their preferred party. Usually between 75 and 90 per cent will do that, though it is sometimes lower and observers have noted that the proportion has fallen on average. At the count, the votes for whole-party slates are stacked up and then begins the long painful process of counting the split votes. After observing many similar polls, let me introduce some of the typical aberrant specimens:

1. **The rational type**. Minor parties often field only one or two candidates. Indeed major parties may do so in seats that are hopeless for them and they ran out of arms to twist. Supporters of these parties use their surplus votes elsewhere. Alternatively, there is another rational explanation for splitting the vote, such as a popular candidate or well-known local councillor who has taken votes from other parties, or a well-known local prat who has lost them to other parties.

2. **The bigoted type**. One of the party's candidates seems to have significantly fewer votes than the others. On closer inspection it often turns out that they have a foreign-sounding name or revealed a non–fleshy-pink-coloured face on their election leaflet. Depressingly, this still happens in many places around the country and the candidates who receive the bonus votes feel sick about it – but a vote is a vote. Variants can include nonlocals (especially in some of the stranger rural corners of the land), gays or those suspected of being, or anyone who has just appeared to be different. Refreshingly, there is little evidence of age bias, much reduced evidence of class bias and the only evidence of possible gender bias may be that female candidates often do rather better than they would otherwise be expected to do.

   After studying the results of six different London boroughs in detail across three elections, I found a clear correlation that showed an advantage in fielding women. I also found that in most of the cases where a ward voted for split representation, the losing candidate of the more popular party was black. By all means encourage your local party managers with the first revelation, but don't use the second to plan your strategy. There are some lessons in politics that need learning by the voters even more than the parties.

3. **The bewildered type**: Counting to three can be challenging in the pressure cooker of a polling booth and for some it is just too much. Most common are those who voted for only one person, or occasionally two. It is pretty much certain that

most of these people did not know they had extra votes. They would have been told several times and it is printed on the ballot paper, but there will always be some who cannot be reached. A few may have chosen not to use all their votes, but not many among those who are supporting a party with a full slate. These are not technically spoiled votes of course, but they are partially wasted and so, in a sense, partially spoiled.

This phenomenon, together with some assistance from rational voters who split their votes for other reasons, gives rise to one of the great unnoticed bizarre features of British elections. If people are voting for only one candidate, they usually vote for the first candidate on the list from their party. If they are splitting their vote and dropping one candidate from their preferred party, it is usually the last one on the list. In other words, if you look at London councils or others where multimember wards are elected in single whole-council elections, there are plenty of Adamses, Allinsons and Armstrongs and precious few Zebedees. The electoral system is biased towards those with names that start early in the alphabet. In fact it is more complicated even than that and some serious studies have looked into it.

My example was not necessarily completely true. Being at the bottom of the ballot and having an unusual name can be advantageous. Let me illustrate the kind of thing that has often been observed with a fictitious example: Slightly Right Town is a Conservative-inclined ward, which can go Labour in a good year for them. Liberal Democrats are not active in the ward and there is no serious opposition from minor parties or independents. Davies is a Labour councillor who has held on in good and bad years and is popular. All the other candidates are first-timers – none of them are particularly well known or controversial. The ward votes narrowly for the Conservatives and the ballot paper appears as follows:

Adams	Conservative
Barlow	Labour
Davies	Labour
Edwards	Liberal Democrat
Johnson	Independent Local Strange Person
Smith	Say No to Planning Permission for the New Abattoir
Tayler	Conservative
Taylor	Independent Conservative
Tyler	Green
Watson	Labour
Yattleton-Twonk	Conservative

Other things being equal, Adams is a shoe-in. Top of the ballot and from the party getting the most votes. Davies is very likely to get back with a decent Labour core vote, a personal vote and a reasonable ballot position that is high up and next to the solitary Lib Dem candidate, which should lead to spare votes crossing over. Poor old Tayler can forget it. Two-thirds of the way down the paper (the graveyard slot), lost among minor candidates – two of whom have similar names, and with no obvious benefits from the position. The interest comes in the third place. It is clearly between Barlow and Yattleton-Twonk. Barlow has the advantage of being second on the ballot, between the two most popular candidates and near the lone Lib Dem. Yattleton-Twonk belongs to the more popular party, is at the bottom of the ballot (a spot some people look at first) and it is an interesting and unusual name (although not obviously foreign). This one could lead to recounts. If the Tory advantage is only very slim, Barlow might have a slight edge and squeeze the extra seat for the less popular party. So where was our discussion of council tax, local services, national issues, campaign strategies or candidates' competencies? They didn't figure. Voter psychology, ballot design and irrelevant trivia figured. That can be democracy sometimes.

IT'S OUR VOTE! NO, IT'S OURS!!

This one can be a dream! Some voters do not mark their votes clearly. These are often very elderly voters or others with difficulties of some sort. Some are just clumsy, careless or unsure what they are doing. People in difficulties can ask for assistance, but they rarely do – some out of pride, but most because they do not know they are in difficulties. In UK first-past-the-post elections, the traditional method of denoting support for a candidate is to put an 'X' by their name. In practice many variants are usually accepted, such as a tick, a number 1, or an underlining of the candidate's name. Unfortunately, ticks can fly off across a page, underlinings can turn into obliterations and nice big positive 'X's can cover half the boxes on the paper, while small faint 'X's can look like a pathetic scribbling from a weak and indecisive insect. These are the ballots that are cast into the 'doubtful' tray for perusal by candidates and agents. They love these. I have seen two respectable, intelligent men in Wiltshire arguing over a vote that was clearly spoiled as far as I could see. The voter had put a big 'X' through the whole ballot, but the centre of the cross went through one candidate's name and he wanted the vote. Later, the other one triumphantly found that a similar voter had done the same thing, but this time the centre of the cross went through *his* name. The candidates were each allowed the votes by the returning officer, and two voters who left the polling station happy that they had registered their protest had actually cast votes for these two. As I said, if you want to abstain in person, give them a blank ballot back. I tried my luck on one occasion as agent when a voter had commented on the supposed self-abusing nature of the candidates' personal recreational activities. This was hard to imagine of the candidates involved – particularly the very well known noble dame defending the seat. But the offending W-word did not reach to the top of the ballot where my candidate's name was. I argued, very plausibly I felt, that the voter was accusing the other candidates, but not my own. In effect this was a positive vote for him. I still feel that was the voter's intention. Unfortunately, the vote was invalid for at least three reasons and I lost my argument. We did not lose the seat by one vote, but it would have made a cracking good court case if we had. On second thoughts, we probably would have lost that as well, and at least there was no money at stake from spending thirty seconds arguing at the election count.

IT'S AS EASY AS 1, 2, 3

Not much to say on this one, except that it is surprising that some people unilaterally decide to introduce alternative voting or single transferable voting into a first-past-the-post election by numbering the candidates in order of preference. Some believe these may be Irish voters who are used to voting that way on the island, as many people are registered for both countries. Maybe others just think it is more fun. After all, going to all that trouble for one measly cross on the paper is a bit anticlimactic. Either way, on to the spoiled pile they go. Just not on I'm afraid.

AS I WAS SAYING ON MY LAST BALLOT PAPER . . .

Now we come to the serious nutters. Some voters still labour under the impression that the candidates read the messages they scrawl over their ballot papers and take them to heart. They are deeply wounded by the insults, moved by the tragic stories and inspired by the profound wisdom. Then the entire collection of papers is delivered to the winning candidate's home in several hundred bin liners, so they can read them in detail and take note of all the requests for special favours and the complaints about the noise from the playground over the road. After all, some people would get very cross if the victor did not realise their support was conditional on their meeting the request attached. Unfortunately, these people are sadly misguided and the winner does not get to keep the ballots after all. They are left in an enormous warehouse in Middlesex in carefully numbered sacks in case there is a query about the result months after the event. Of course, most of these comments are ignored by everyone, except maybe a very tired, bored teller at the count – apart from those that raise a laugh that gets spread around the hall.

Some of the best comments I have seen, or had reported to me, have been: 'I am 75' (no idea why they felt the need to tell us that); 'Don't vote! It only encourages them' (so why did you, then?); 'Where is Bruce?' (?); '**** off, you ****ers, you ****ing ****ing ****ers' (the Oscar Wilde Memorial prize, 1985); and 'I don't know why I am here' (my personal favourite).

The 1982 local elections across Britain took place as the fleet set sail towards war in the Falklands. I don't think any other war has promoted such an ugly mood in the country. Most of the population supported the struggle to get back the islands from Argentina, but the opposing minority were vocal and passionate and some of the supporters were nothing short of fanatical – egged on by the *Sun* and others in the most insane hour of our tabloid press. Every conflict Britain has ever been involved with has coincided with local elections or parliamentary by-elections. Some have even clashed with general elections. It has not really been a divisive factor on most of these occasions. This time it was not so much divisive as corrosive, and definitely decisive. There is little doubt that the Conservatives won back a lot of ground at that time and did much better in those elections than anyone had predicted they would even a couple of weeks earlier. As always, success could be mixed with the kind of problems voters could throw up.

I have never seen so many votes spoiled by electors' comments on the ballots at any other time. Most of these were by people who were in favour of the Falklands War, and presumably pro-government in most cases. Some made jingoistic references to 'Our Boys', but most opted for accusations of treachery against opposition candidates. Possibly Port Stanley was invaded by middle-aged university lecturers, who were running for the council as Labour candidates, or the Argentinian advance party on South Georgia was led by a group of retired librarians and other Social Democrats. The British fleet was clearly being sabotaged by bearded care workers from the Green Party. What these candidates actually thought about the Falklands War was of no significance. They were standing against Conservatives and that was treachery. Of course, the opposition parties were horrified to see the Conservatives picking up votes on an issue that had nothing to do with running Local councils, but they were delighted to see some of these votes go astray as they were accused of being 'Argie-lovers' by cranks who invalidated their votes. The depression for any non-Tories at the count in Wandsworth that year was partially alleviated by seeing that they might have actually lost a seat because of these people.

The Tories got some revenge a few years later, as hundreds of voters across the country used their ballot papers to tell us all where we could stick our Poll Tax bills. If those people had just used their votes to support anti-Poll Tax candidates, they might have gained another couple of councils. If those who did not vote, thinking they could avoid Poll Tax by hiding, had turned out, the outcome would have been catastrophic for the Tories and may have even set back their hopes for the 1992 general election. Another of those 'what-ifs'.

One oddity in this section is that of the people who sign their ballot papers. I suppose this is understandable in a way. It seems to be a formal business and we are used to signing our names on formal documents, so why not a ballot paper? The 1872 Ballot Act, a cornerstone of our system of representative democracy –

that's why. On to the spoiled pile, I'm afraid. Sorry.

A variation on this is the people who give their addresses – presumably, they are still awaiting a reply. Another lot for the discarded pile.

I cannot let this section go without giving a brief account of one of the best stories of recent years: A whole selection of legal precedent has built up over what is acceptable as a valid vote after dozens of court cases over the years. Still, slight variations are thrown up that seem to sit on the borderline. Sometimes an ingenious voter comes up with a brand-new approach and case law just does not cover it. Leicestershire County Council stood on a knife edge when a by-election was held in 1991 in Castle Donington. The council had been hung since 1981 as no party had managed to win a majority of seats, but the Tories had been dominant for most of this time. Now came a chance for a decisive shift of power to Labour. They could move to being almost neck-and-neck with the Tories and might be able to build a new coalition that could take control. After an amazingly tightly contested fight, Mr Wintle, the Labour candidate, and Mr Blunt from the Conservative Party both received the same number of votes and the returning officer declared the Labour candidate elected. Labour thought they had made a vital breakthrough. They had to think again. The Conservatives challenged in the Court by disputing a single rejected ballot paper that would change the result. A voter had abandoned the dull tradition of putting an 'X' by the chosen candidate and had opted instead for writing 'Yes Please' alongside the Conservative candidate together with a 'smiley face'. The ballot was deemed to be spoiled by the returning officer. Now, there is no problem with 'Yes Please' as far as I can see. Writing 'Yes' alongside the chosen candidate is established in case law as an acceptable vote. Adding 'please' simply indicates good manners as far as I can see. 'You are offering me this Candidate? How delightful! I would be very grateful, thank you very much.' It could be argued that at a certain point the text becomes a written message that invalidates the vote, as discussed earlier, and it was so argued. But two words that do not compromise the voter's anonymity and help to clarify their intention have to be acceptable, really.

The bigger problem was over the smiley face. Was this a kind of 'tag', a personal logo that someone used to identify themselves? A lot of people have the irritating habit of using some sort of scribble along with their signature, or even instead of it, to help identify themselves and show what a fun-loving, witty, fundamentally annoying person they are. If this was someone's personal identifying mark, the vote had to be invalidated. At the time the smiley face was very popular. It had been resurrected by rave culture and had become a symbol connected in some places with acid or ecstasy. Others used it more innocently and it frequently appeared scribbled on school books. Its very popularity helped the Conservatives to win the case. Even if it was someone's personal mark, there was no way of identifying them from that alone. A handwriting expert could analyse the words as well, but they would have to compare the writing with a sample from every voter in Castle Donington to hazard a guess. So in practical terms this was still a legal, private ballot. Mr Blunt took his seat in 1992, although Mr Wintle gained his revenge in a subsequent round of county council elections. The ruling now stands in all its majesty in British law as an example of precedent and you are at liberty to vote this way as well if you choose.

AND YOU SHALL KNOW THEM BY THEIR MARK

Before the voter receives their ballot paper from the clerk at the desk, a pattern of holes is punched into it using an unusual utensil that has no other purpose in life. I am not sure where they get these special franking machines from – they are not like the ones you would find in a post office, for example, but if you tried to use one as a regular hole puncher, a nut cracker, a weapon, or anything else, you would be very disappointed. The theory is that the returning officer has set a unique pattern for these holes, so that no one else knows exactly how they will appear on the ballot in advance. This removes the possibility of someone hi-jacking a number of ballot papers or forging them and stuffing ballot boxes. One of the things counters and tellers have to look out for at the count is to check that ballots have the mark. They generally try to spot those with no mark at all, but I have never seen anyone carefully scrutinising papers to check if it is an exact mathematical copy of a specimen to which they are constantly referring. As long as their mark is somewhere vaguely approximate to the official one, a fraudster could probably get away with it.

Of course, most of those papers that miss the mark are down to administrative error. The clerk simply forgot to stamp it and the fault is nothing to do with the voter, save that they did not notice and complain (frankly, how many people would?). Often there are none of these in a whole constituency and there are usually fewer than half a dozen. They are sad in that they invalidate someone's democratic right to vote, but as long as they do not impact on the result who really cares? Most vote totals are not entirely accurate anyway, as we know when recounts take place and always throw up a slightly different result. So they do not matter at all then? Step forward 'Winchester '97'

The 1997 general election set a number of records. One of these was the smallest Constituency majority in the UK for well over half a century. The result was the last to declare, at 6.15 p.m. the next day:

Mark Oaten	Liberal Democrat	26,100
Gerald Malone	Conservative	26,098
Patrick Davies	Labour	6,528
Richard Huggett	'Liberal Democrat'	640

An unexpected Liberal Democrat victory, taking a previously safe Tory seat in a year for terrible Conservative results. After recounts that sent the result in both directions, they settled on a majority of two. Richard Huggett ran as a bogus Lib Dem candidate. He features in the chapter on unusual candidates ('Stranger Gallery') – funny how familiar characters pop up. It was perhaps a little surprising that the Tories accepted the vote, given that an earlier count had gone to them by a bigger margin. The reason may have been that they were tired and fed up after their catastrophic election, or it may have been that they were already plotting their next move.

The battle moved to the courts. Fifty-five votes had been declared spoiled because they were not marked by a franking machine. This was unusually high for a parliamentary constituency, although not unique. There was no accusation of fraud, although some tried to spread rumours. It did appear that at least one official had been extremely remiss in their duties. The Tories had reckoned that these votes would give them the seat if counted and they wanted the High Court to let them prove it. The court ruled in their favour and the votes were dug up to indicate that they would have switched the result to a two vote majority for Malone. The Lib Dems argued that whichever party would have gained from the extra ballots was immaterial. They were spoiled papers and had to be discarded, as they would normally be. The Conservatives argued that, as the number was unusually high and the outcome of the election had been affected, the result should not be decided by an official's negligence. They also claimed a moral case that the voters had not been heard. They wanted the election declared invalid and a rerun ordered.

This was one of those cases where everyone loses. The Lib Dems lost their new seat, but the Tories had lost their chance of victory as well. They could not be awarded the seat on the basis of a revised count as the result had been declared already without their challenge. The judge ordered a fresh election. A constituency general election result was invalidated and ordered to be repeated for the first time in nearly a hundred years.

Ultimately the Tories were the real losers in dramatic fashion. Post-election depression in Conservative support, public antipathy to what they perceived as the tactics of sore losers and the usual exaggerated swings of support and evidence of tactical voting commonly associated with many by-elections combined to increase Mark Oaten's majority to 21,556.

This in turn led to fresh problems for psephologists and electoral pundits. The two-vote majority in May must have been a truer reflection of the mood of the constituency at the time, making it the most marginal seat in the country. However, the vote was invalidated and the vote in November was not strictly a by-election, but a very, very late result for the general election, which fortunately did not interfere with anyone's pools coupons. So was it the most marginal seat in the country or easily the safest Liberal Democrat seat? Who knows? Morally the former and technically the latter I suppose.

DO WE COUNT THE DEATH THREATS?

As we said earlier, a vote has to be clearly a positive expression of support to be counted. If it appears that it may be a negative remark, or is just completely unclear, it cannot be counted for any candidate. There is an immediate problem that leaps to our attention here. We all remember from school that an 'X' on your maths exercise book does not indicate a show of support from the teacher. So why do we use it? If a voter ignores the boxes and chooses to put a tick through their favoured candidate's name, or underlines their name, we can count that as a vote. But what if they put an 'X' through their name? Is that a vote or some kind of Mafia death sentence or voodoo curse? I have seen these counted as legal votes many times, but I am very unsure whether that was the intention of all these people. Names scribbled out or scratched off the paper are taken as signs of voters with red faces and steam pouring from their ears who exploded with rage shortly after leaving the booth and were found as a pile of smouldering ashes in the car park. They are not counted as positive votes. The vote in Coventry that I remember where someone had voted for every candidate bar one on the ballot and reserved a special four-lettered epithet for the remaining individual was also deemed to be spoiled. I have seen votes allowed where someone has voted for the correct number of candidates before giving a similar comment on one of the others. Again, these might have been challenged in court if they had mattered, but if 'Yes Please' is deemed clearly positive and does not give a clue to the identity of the voter, a much shorter comment can be clearly negative and equally anonymous.

Every vote counts in the end. Even the spoiled ones in their own way. Ask them in Leicestershire and Winchester and several other places besides. Ask them in Florida for that matter. It might be in your town next.

All-Time Greatest Mistakes

'Good nature and good sense must ever join; To err is human, to forgive, divine.'
— *Alexander Pope*, Essay on Criticism

To state that politicians are human may be the least remarkable revelation of this book, but many of them have put such effort into appearing to be more elevated than the rest of us that it is worth emphasising. We all make mistakes. Sometimes we are lucky and no one notices. Other times we have to apologise and clean up the mess. Following on from our initial idea that elections are an expression or even a celebration of all that it is to be human, we expect to see some mistakes. Dear Lord, do we find some mistakes!

YOU'RE ALL RI', YOU'RE ALL RI'

There is a lot of mythology that gets wrapped up with the 1992 general election. We deal with some of it elsewhere in the book. It is not surprising that people want to pore over the details of a campaign that threw up a result few had expected. Some people like to look at the various 'cock-up' theories: 'Major could never win the election unless the opposition really cocked up badly.' It is a fair theory and John Smith's unnecessarily detailed and honest shadow budget has been set up as one big error in the Labour campaign, as has the 'Jennifer's Ear' Party Political Broadcast, as have the confused messages about PR and dealings with the Lib Dems, as has Kinnock's verbose waffling, as has the

167

creepy bunch of spin doctors who made themselves visible like never before in a British election. Come to think of it, Labour's campaign was a big cock-up! Why did the idea ever get around that they did well?

The event that people most like to choose, however, is the Sheffield rally. Labour chose to hold an enormous rally for the party faithful in Sheffield Arena on Wednesday 1 April. Nice choice of date, you might remark. This was to be the biggest, most extravagant political mass rally in the UK since Oswald Mosley's gig at Olympia – a lovely comparison to contemplate. The original idea was that the polls were likely to be very close at this stage and the rally would play to the TV news audience as a reminder that Labour were on the rise; they had thousands of enthusiastic, energetic supporters and looked exciting and modern. When the evening came, Labour's two biggest poll leads had just been announced: 7 per cent for MORI in *The Times* and 6 per cent for Harris on ITN. The tide appeared to be turning and it was not surprising that some politicians were starting to get a little carried away with it all. Thousands of Labour activists gathered together in a state of high excitement, while Tories spent another night on the doorsteps and the phones. The showbiz stars were wheeled out. Several of the leading figures did their bit, including an overemotional Roy Hattersley. Then came Kinnock. The man who had worked so hard for years on reforming his party and presenting his new image as a statesman lost it big time. He breezed on to the stage to deafening music and applause. All he lacked was an electric guitar and the words 'Good evening, Sheffield! Are you ready to rock?' He managed to find something even more cringe-inducing as he shouted his repeated chorus of 'You're all ri', you're all ri',' as he waved his followers into near hysteria. It came across as a mixture of a revivalist black Pentecostal preacher from the Deep South and a drunken captain of the rugby club leading the after-match piss-up. Somehow the second example seemed more in keeping with the Kinnock image. He then went on to make a speech in which he announced that Britain 'will have a Labour government in nine days' time'. The country watched and thought, 'That's a bit of a cheek.'

Quite how damaging the Sheffield rally really was is a matter of some doubt. At first the press were neutral or even quite impressed by it. Apart from Matthew Parris, they saw it as a sign of the near certainty of a coming Labour victory, or at least a Tory defeat. This was one of those cases where TV images went over the heads of the hacks and straight into the minds of those watching in their living rooms. It was the voters who found the images distasteful. Some of them told their Labour candidates so both before and after polling day. I doubt whether one person switched their vote because of a silly rally, but images are important and that picture in their heads could have had almost a subliminal influence on many people as they finally made their minds up.

DISCUSSING TACTICS

Any country that has first-past-the-post elections will have tactical voting. It is just a fact of life. Whether it is parties endlessly repeating that a vote for Party X is a wasted vote, or people realising that their preferred candidate has all the chances of a cow in the Grand National. What is amazing is that there is not more tactical voting. The only reasons why lots of people do not vote tactically, or indeed bother to vote at all in safe seats, are that they are so tribal they will never vote any other way; they think the leading candidates are so poor they cannot bring themselves to support them; they have no idea what support the parties have locally; or they are so ill-informed that they do not understand how the parliamentary system works. It is only because there are millions of people like that that we do not get results that are even more distorted than they are already, with no-hope candidates scarcely getting any votes at all.

It took until 1997 for the *Mirror* to get the idea of tactical voting. They still did not quite understand it. On the eve of the general election they produced a guide for their readers to explain how it worked. Most people had long before worked out the idea, but the *Mirror* decided some of their voters needed help, and in particular they might not have the information required to work out how best to oust the non-*Mirror*-reading Tory in their constituency. The idea was very simple. If you were a Liberal Democrat supporter you were advised to vote for Labour in places such as Brecon and Radnor, which the Lib Dems won, and Norfolk North, which they might have won if you had not wasted your votes on tactically switching to Labour, who came well back in third place. You would also have been pretty peed off as a Liberal in Oldham East and Saddleworth advised to stop the Tory, who came in a poor third, just to help Labour unseat your own MP! Things did balance out partially. Labour supporters would have been annoyed at the advice to vote Lib Dem in Colchester and destroy their good chance of winning it. At least there was still a strong Tory vote to worry about there. The real *Mirror* clincher was in Hastings and Rye. Here they advised Liberal Democrats to vote Labour and Labour supporters to vote Lib Dem. Hastings has not seen such confusion since Harold's last stand. Somehow, after all the promiscuous vote swapping had sorted itself out, Labour won the seat by 2,560 votes.

After the event, the *Mirror* managed to claim the kind of triumph that their bitter rivals at the *Sun* had claimed five years earlier. Their tactical masterplan had worked and they were obviously much cleverer than the other tabloids, who had merely encouraged people to vote for their chosen party with no consideration of tactics. They underlined the success by pointing to Torbay with its 12-vote majority for the Lib Dems over the Tories. They did not point to Winchester, Kingston, Eastleigh, Northavon, Sutton, Carshalton or other seats where the Lib Dems had to crawl in with small majorities without the *Mirror*'s help. They missed Wellingborough, Romford, Lancaster, Harrow West, Wimbledon and many others where Labour narrowly made it without the *Mirror* readers getting their tactical briefing. More significantly, they missed dozens of seats such as Dorset South, Teignbridge, Hexham and Totnes, where a few tactical votes could have knocked out the Tories. Anyway, at least they had Torbay. As they pointed out, 'Lib Dem Adrian Sanders beat Rupert Allason by 12 votes. If just six Labour voters had not switched, Mr Allason would still be an MP.' Run that by me one more time! By my maths, if six Labour switchers had gone back to third-place Labour, the Lib Dem majority surely would have been six. If six Labour supporters decided to vote tactically for the Lib Dems, but then changed their minds at the last moment and decided to vote Tory instead, it might work out. I have no idea why anyone would do that, though. Tactical voting is a simple idea, but still beyond the grasp of well-paid political journalists from national newspapers.

Besides, everyone knows that Rupert Allason lost in Torbay because he annoyed the staff in a constituency restaurant on the eve of the election and they all agreed to vote against him. Tactically.

The more opaque kind of tactical voting that the Tories hinted at in 2001 came in the final week, when all of them bar William Hague effectively admitted they were going to lose. They put out the unusual posters encouraging voters to BURST TONY BLAIR'S BUBBLE. Apparently, the aim was to get voters to take pity on them and reel back in distaste at the thought of the grin on Blair's face with a second landslide. Whether this was a tactical own goal, or a brilliant use of the 'Queensland' ploy that had caused an upset in a state election in Australia in a similar situation, was open for debate. If it worked at all it was only to encourage further the rampant abstentionism, so we can call it a mistake now.

ORANG-UTANS AND PENGUINS

Politicians realised in the early days of mass media that the rules of the game had changed. The increase in the franchise made it impractical to get to know or attempt to bribe all the electors. The campaign meetings were already dying. The newspapers were taking over the campaign, followed in due course by radio and television, and now by all the various aspects of new technology. The result was that almost each successive election got dumbed down further and further. Most people complain that the politicians do not put their ideas across. This is not entirely true. Some of them may not be very good at doing it, but they certainly try. The truth is that most people do not want to read a manifesto, gather detailed evidence or engage in serious, informed debate. That is fair enough. Most people have other things to do. The media know this and the politicians have gradually cottoned on to the idea as well. So now we have the elections of photo opportunities and sound bites. Never give the people a detailed critique of the flaws in the government's health policy and the precise reasoning behind your own. Just get a picture in the papers of your candidate standing outside a closed hospital wing, endlessly parrot some meaningless phrase like 'Health, health, health' and try to get one of the nurses from *Casualty* or *ER* on the TV to back your campaign – she'll make more impact than a real nurse. The politicians all know it's crap, the media all know it's crap, the public all know it's crap, but it is like one of those game-theory problems where nobody is able to break out of the pattern. Whoever jumps first and does something different is the loser.

It did not take politicians long to realise that a picture speaks a thousand words, and as photos became more common and more prominent in newspapers, and TV invaded the world's living rooms, they had to attempt to get this to work for them. Cue the dawning of the era of the photo opportunity. This is an attempt to save the photojournalists the trouble of working out their own ideas for a good picture, and mounting some sort of stunt loosely based around a campaign theme, with the central purpose of setting up a photo that the papers would want and a few seconds of footage that the TV news will run.

Thankfully, for our purposes in investigating electoral weirdness, there are two promising areas to explore here: the stunt that goes wrong and the stunt that was a really bad idea in the first place.

By 1983, the Conservative Party machine had learned from the USA how to play this game properly. Even countries such as Germany and Australia were ahead of the UK before then. The Tory campaign strategists worked out Mrs Thatcher's itinerary in exacting detail. They knew what stories they wanted and what images they wanted every day, and most days they got them.

Even for them, things could still go wrong, as Margaret Thatcher admitted in her autobiography *The Downing Street Years*:

> I left after the press conference for my first campaign tour, which was in the West Country. At 10.45 a.m. we drove from Central Office to Victoria Station, and from there went by train to Gatwick to catch the flight to St Mawgan in Cornwall. A Group of around 40 or 50 journalists joined us, sitting together at the back of the plane. It was a pleasant rural day. I visited the fish market at Padstow Harbour and went on to Trelyll Farm, near Wadebridge. There I was caught out by the press. I was standing on a heap of cut grass and the *Daily Mirror* photographer asked me to pick some up. I saw nothing wrong with that, and so I obliged. He took the Photograph – and the picture duly appeared the following day with the caption 'Let them eat grass'. It does not do to be too co-operative.[1]

---

[1] Margaret Thatcher, *The Downing Street Years*, pp. 294–5, HarperCollins, 1993.

The SDP/Liberal Alliance could not match the might of the Tory machine, but they got the hang of it pretty well. Of course, with two leaders conducting two national campaigns, the media could safely ignore whichever one had a good campaigning day with some nice photo opportunities, and focus on the one who had a lousy day, got followed everywhere by hecklers and looked completely fed up.

The real lessons were learned by Labour. If the Tories fought a 1980s campaign and the Alliance fought a 1980s campaign on a shoestring, there was still no chance of dragging Labour out of the 1950s. Michael Foot and Enoch Powell are widely regarded as the greatest parliamentarians of the postwar era. However, they both took to modern mass-media election campaigning much as a fish takes to motor cycling. Every night on TV news the country would watch Thatcher, Jenkins and Steel out on their media-friendly, glitzy campaign tours. Then we would watch poor old Mr Foot in his donkey jacket addressing a small group of activists in a school hall. The microphone would pack up. Then the table would fall off the stage. After a few weeks of this it was not surprising the people decided Labour was probably not up to governing a country at the time.

The shockingly silly photo opportunities continued unabated in 2001. Of all the crass attempts at eating chips, drinking beer or buying reggae CDs at market stalls that the politicians went through in order to pretend they were normal people, the best two were down to mistakes again. First, there was the mistake only narrowly stopped from turning into a disaster when William Hague spoke outside an aircraft museum in Essex. A smart aide noticed that he was speaking in front of a World War Two Luftwaffe plane. Only the strategic movement of a few supporters and their placards made sure that he did not appear in the next day's papers against a backdrop of swastikas. The best came on the opening of the Tories' desperate campaign to get back on the map in Scotland. Malcolm Rifkind proudly unveiled the first Scottish campaign poster in front of assembled hacks and their cameras with its clever, if subtle, message, TESCO BROADWATER RETAIL PARK. NOW OPEN 24 HOURS. It was one of the best posters any party produced during the campaign, but a little man hastily tried to paste up the proper one while Rifkind joked his way out of it.

There was one tremendous case of photo-opportunity madness in 1992 when the president of the Board of Trade and Industry, Ian Lang, went to support the Edinburgh Conservative MP James Douglas Hamilton in his re-election campaign. Now what could we pick for a nice Edinburgh landmark for the photo opportunity? You could probably think of a dozen, admittedly most of them not in the right constituency – but that does not matter too much. They opted to take the Scottish press with them to Edinburgh zoo. The idea was to have a photo taken with the zoo's famous orang-utan, even though the ape had always kept quiet about its views on political matters. Unfortunately, they discovered the orang-utan had died eight years previously and they had their photo taken with a few penguins instead. A bad idea, badly researched, badly executed and a five-star cock-up. I don't care how many politicians have posed for pictures outside schools, hospitals, businesses and so forth that their party policies were in the process of closing down. Edinburgh zoo was the worst photo-opportunity mistake and it wins the prize.

GETTING TIRED AND EMOTIONAL

British party leaders have got used to smear tactics thrown at them partly by their opponents, sometimes by their own party, but mostly by the press. As they face this assault, while tiring from the rigours of being on the road nonstop, it can get to them, as Frank Johnson reported about Michael Foot in his study of the 1983 election year:

He must still have been talking about smears before we caught up with him in Croydon. For, difficult though it may be for the reader to believe, Mr Foot, standing on the back of a lorry with a candidate named Mr Ian Smedley at his side demanded: 'I want to hear three cheers for Ian Smear's victory on June 9. Hip hip . . .' Difficult to believe, but understandable. For we could all sympathise with Mr Foot's preoccupation with smears.

So Mr Ian Smedley, or Mr Ian Smear, got his three cheers for victory on June 9, as he would have got had Mr Foot been under the impression that he was Mr Ian Scare or Mr Ian Slander . . . Mr Foot is not unusual among politicians in being in the grip of one overpowering concern, in his case 'smears', which intrudes itself even when he is talking about something, or somebody, completely unconnected with it.

For example, soon after the first evidence emerged that President Nixon had indeed committed some sort of crime in Watergate, the President, while speaking in support of a Governor Evans, several times referred to 'Governor Evidence'. Perhaps an obsessive personality is what draws such figures as Mr Nixon and Mr Foot to politics in the first place.'[1]

When we look to tired politicians reaching the end of their ability to endure, there is always the old favourite of falling over. Stylish campaigning falls by Margaret Thatcher, Nancy Reagan, Lionel Jospin and Robert Dole have been repeated on TV on numerous occasions, but the complete disappearance of Senator Henry Jackson through the stage floor at a campaign rally in Washington State must have been a special moment. He climbed back and blamed the Republican planks on the platform.

[1] Frank Johnson, *Election Year*, Robson, 1983, pp. 165–6.

IT IS NOT MY POLICY IN THIS ELECTION TO HIT THE VOTERS

That sentence was one of several genuine witticisms that the Tory leader William Hague came up with in the 2001 election. Hague and the Lib Dems' Charles Kennedy never had any difficulty beating Tony Blair in the comedy stakes. It referred, of course, to the most memorable moment of the campaign. In many years to come, they will make nostalgic TV programmes on the lines of "I Love 2001" and little known TV personalities and minor journalists will forget the images of New York and Afghanistan the rest of us will all remember from that year and just remember the fun parts, as they always do on nostalgia shows. They will fondly recall Butt Ugly Martians, Celebrity Big Brother, Text messaging, Hear'Say, Germany 1 England 5 and the day that John Prescott thumped an egg throwing Welsh bloke with a 1980s haircut. The thing that took all his opponents by surprise was that the incident not only made no dent on Labour's lead, but turned Prescott into a new folk hero. Polls showed that working-class men and young voters were particularly impressed by the speed of the left jab, and they were two groups that Labour needed to get out on polling day. If the punch added half a percentage point to the turnout in the end, it was probably the most effective tactic of the entire campaign.

The general consensus was that if an egg hits you at great speed from about a foot away, the instant reaction from the victim might be that it was a fist or a stone, and it is not surprising that they might lash out in response. True enough, but if Prescott were a schoolteacher, a policeman or a nurse in a similar situation and he had failed to control himself he would soon be looking for a different job. A good thing he was only Deputy Prime Minister, as we should not expect such high standards from senior politicians. There was some speculation as to whether anything like this had happened before. Of course if you go back centuries to the kind of election that Hogarth illustrated and Dickens wrote about, it was the normal form of political debate. Indeed egg throwing was a regular feature of British elections until the postwar period, when rationing meant that people valued their farm produce rather more highly. Politicians and their supporters would often respond in kind until they started learning about public relations and the TV cameras started following them. A candidate for Congress in 1860 took the option of taking out a knife, then cutting up and eating an apple thrown by a protestor.

Scenes like the showdown in Rhyl have become rarer in modern elections, although Denis Healey still boasts about the time he threw a protestor off the stage at an election rally. Maybe we will see the start of an interesting new trend. At least the event spawned a couple of great Internet games in which you got to throw eggs at candidates and attempted to dodge the blows. They gave me more pleasure during the general election than reading any of the manifestos.

If you worry about the example politicians set the young these days, look back to the campaign song of the Primrose League in 1930s Folkestone. The Primrose League were an adjunct of the Tory Party committed to old-fashioned values. They had flourished in urban, working-class communities more than much of the party and they had very active youth sections at the time, like a kind of Young Conservatives Juvenile Division. Maybe they ought to think about bringing them back. After all, it was young children who went about the streets singing:

> *Vote, vote, vote for Sassoon;*
> *Chase old Ellis out the town.*
> *If it wasn't for the law*
> *I'd punch him on the jaw –*
> *Vote, vote, vote for Sassoon.*

What a pity the young are so politically apathetic these days.

WORST CAMPAIGN COMMUNICATOR EVER?

It is a bold assertion to make, but there is much to support it. Entire books have been written about the rubbish Dan Quayle managed to spout while campaigning as George Bush's running mate in 1988 and again in 1992. Of course he actually won the first time, proving that being that bad does not really matter, particularly as nobody is quite sure why they bother to elect a vice-president anyway. Unless the president dies, most Americans are not clear what they actually do, apart from chair debates in Senate. We have not got the space to give you another entire book, so here are a couple of choice Quayle campaign favourites:

- 'The Nazi holocaust was an obscene period in our country's history, well, not our country's history, this century's history, we all lived in this century, I didn't live in this century.'
- 'Republicans understand the importance of bondage between parent and child.'

Yes, this was the man who campaigned in a school, telling the children to spell potato with an 'e' on the end.

Of course, George Bush Jr has tried hard to steal the title from his dad's number two. His inability to name leaders of major world nations showed real promise, as did quotes such as, 'If you say you're going to do something and don't do it, that's trustworthiness. I don't think we need to be subliminal about the differences between our views'; and 'I want to reduce our own nuclear capacities to the lever commiserate with keeping the peace.' He also made one of the greatest campaign goofs with his comment on an election rally platform to Dick Cheney that a well-known journalist was a 'major-league asshole', unaware that the microphone was on and transmitting this message both to the audience at the rally and to the world's TV screens.

I have wondered about this curious phenomenon. For years now, the Republicans have specialised in fielding candidates that appear to be total idiots, but Bush has a fairly distinguished academic record, including a Harvard MBA. Are they actually all pretending to be stupid to win votes? If so, what does that tell us about Americans? The nation that turned Forrest Gump into an icon of modern America is the richest society on Earth, and one of the best educated, but it has a deep suspicion of intellectuals. Perhaps there is something in the idea that Americans like to feel they are smarter than the president. Perhaps Republicans are clever enough to have worked that out and they play stupid, but the Democrats still field boring policy wonks like Al Gore, who like to pretend they are cleverer than they actually are.

TELLING IT LIKE IT IS

Few candidates are truly candid in telling the whole truth. Some minor, maverick candidates like to boast that they always tell it like it is. Note there the words 'minor' and 'maverick', however. No one ever votes for people who tell the truth and they are regarded as freakish.

The Natural Law Party made one of the most honest admissions of any party political broadcast when their leader Geoffrey Clements said that five hundred scientific experiments had looked at their programme and over forty of them had shown that their methods were effective. He did not even need to push the point to the viewer that, presumably, over 450 of them had not.

As always, *The Simpsons* had its finger on the American pulse when it had the 1996 presidential candidates, Clinton and Dole, taken over by two morphing aliens who started astonishing people with their frank approach to electioneering:

KENT BROCKMAN: Senator Dole, why should people vote for you instead of President Clinton?

DOLE/KANG: It makes no difference which one of us you vote for. Either way, your planet is doomed! Doomed!

KENT BROCKMAN: Well, a refreshingly frank response there from Senator Bob Dole.

. . .

CLINTON/KODOS: I am Clin-Ton. As overlord, all will kneel trembling before me and obey my brutal commands. End communication.

MARGE: Hmm, that's Slick Willie for you, always with the smooth Talk.

Some might say that the most colossal electoral mistake of recent times was the London Conservative Party's choice of Jeffrey Archer as candidate for Mayor. Why Tory leaders and membership alike continued to be charmed by the man for many years after the rest of the country had sussed him was a very great mystery indeed. And those who *had* seen through the man probably felt smugly vindicated in their views the following year, when Archer was sent down for perjury and perverting the course of justice. At least they were able to change their minds in time. Labour had more than enough problems in choosing their own candidate, as Tony Blair persevered with his unique theory of devolution, where regions of the country had the right to have his personal selection of leader imposed upon them. Their candidate Frank Dobson claimed on the BBC, 'Not a single human being has asked me about the selection process – only journalists.'

THE GIFT OF THE PRINTED WORD

I was once nearly responsible for publishing the most inaccurate election address ever delivered. The candidate had spent far too long writing it and I was starting to worry greatly about printing deadlines. After we had just about managed to get it to the printers before the final date possible, we had to make another visit for the usual formality of checking the final copy, as laid up by the printer. We expected to make a couple of minor adjustments about colour tones or headline sizes, but had not anticipated that the designer had decided to rewrite much of the copy before laying it out on the page. Our Election address now claimed:

1. There were only two science teachers in the country
2. Our bar chart showed that nobody voted Labour in the previous election
3. Our party would create jobs and inflation
4. We would spend £1 more on the health service

Altogether we spotted about twenty mistakes including misspellings of words such as 'environment' and of one of the towns in the constituency. There were a couple of cases of complete gobbledegook and a reference to the sitting male Member of Parliament as 'she'.

Unfortunately, this was a year or two before computers took over the printing and designing process. Now it would need a few prods at a keyboard to put something like this right. Then it took a couple more days to mock up a corrected version and our printing schedule was falling apart.

Eventually, they were dragged off to the presses, hurried off for addressing, dumped off at the post office with many of them unsorted, taken away and resorted and then delivered to a grateful public a few days before polling. I was reliably informed that a village in the north of the seat received empty envelopes from us. At least they never received the first version of the leaflet.

We managed to stop it and did a little better than the Liverpool Labour Party, whose election leaflet called for 'a 35 hour *wee*, with no loss in pay', or the Conservative candidate who claimed, 'I come from a rural background, having lied in the area for 35 years'. The London leaflet for the Liberal Democrats'

European election campaign of 1999, which featured Paddy Ashdown visiting a school that Richmond's Lib Dem council had just closed, was quite a good one as well.

The best effort of the 2001 campaign was surely the leaflet from Essex that complained about the government's 'poultry handouts to pensioners'. Now if Labour had thought of giving a frozen chicken to every senior citizen, they really would have been on a winner.

HERE'S ONE WE FILLED IN EARLIER

It is not just the politicians who can get it wrong. The administrators are well capable of doing so. Not only can they forget to book halls, lose ballot boxes, neglect to train staff properly, send postal ballots to the wrong places or put children on the register – among many other well-attested mistakes – but their bosses in the Home Office can get it terribly wrong as well.

There was a great worry that British voters would not cope with their first taste of proportional representation at the European election of 1999. In the end, most of them did not bother. The choice of system did not help, as the only option we had was to choose from a set of impersonal party lists. This led to some very large ballot papers, but not exactly confusing ones. The fact that only 25,812 votes were spoiled (0.26 per cent), as against 90,288 votes (0.28 per cent) in the 1997 general election proved that there was no widespread confusion. Usual Home Office nannyism had struck, however. It was probably the same people who commission public information films to tell us not to set fire to our sofas or let small children play with power tools who decided we needed a special leaflet to point out the dangers of the European election ballot paper. Their leaflet attracted more interest and argument than all the political leaflets put together – admittedly not difficult for this dull election. Let's try to summarise the things that went wrong.

First, the leaflet was blue and looked like a Tory leaflet; then they magnified the three main party lists and grouped them together just so the mock-up paper looked nothing like the real thing; they made up some fictitious parties for the leaflet but left off the Greens and the UK Independence Party, who both won seats (they complained and threatened to sue); they advertised a hotline for minority language leaflets and staffed it completely with people who spoke only English. Apart from the leaflet, they rounded things off nicely with the guidance on the London ballot paper that helpfully pointed out how to mark the British National Party list. A flawed voting system, very large ballot papers, but nothing complicated until the Home Office tried to make it seem worse. At least the Post Office managed to fail to deliver the leaflet to much of the country where it was never received, so that saved some confusion.

THE BIGGEST CLANGER OF THEM ALL

To find the worst individual mistake any candidate has ever perpetrated is a very tricky business. We can worry about injudicious manifesto promises elsewhere, but it is in the campaign rally or media event that the poor candidate can come truly unstuck. The list of candidates who have forgotten where they are and addressed the audience wrongly could fill a book. In some countries this has even meant making a speech in the wrong language. Perhaps the most gut-tightening, embarrassing moment came in 1969 as Democrat candidate for mayor of New York, Mario Procaccino, proclaimed boldly to an audience of black voters, 'My heart is as black as yours.' You can just imagine one of those moments when a few hundred people go completely silent.

The Eyes of the People, the Voice of the Swine

Media Coverage of Elections

'Publish and be damned'
 — *Arthur Wellesley, Duke of Wellington*

'Murder, robbery, rape, adultery and incest will be openly taught and practised, the air will be rent with the cries of distress, the soil soaked with blood, and the nation black with crimes. Where is the heart that can contemplate such a scene without shivering with horror?'

The verdict of the press on the imminent election of:

a) Ken Livingstone as Mayor of London?
b) Shirley Williams at the Crosby by-election?
c) Rodrigo Borgia as Pope?
d) None of the above?

The answer is 'd' of course. That was *The New England Courant* in 1800 about Thomas Jefferson, admittedly not the most morally upright person ever to hold high office, but now revered as a Founding Father of the American Nation. Maybe some of the prophecies came true, but they probably weren't Jefferson's fault. It is interesting to consider what exactly the editor was playing at with a comment like that. It does not seem to have been intentionally humorous. Did he actually believe it? Did he expect his readers to believe it? Did he know it was nonsense, but hated Jefferson so much and expected most of his

185

readership to do so, too, that he was fair game for whatever the editor wanted to say?

Newspapers, journals and all their latter-day cousins such as magazines and Internet websites have long delighted in providing biased, unreasonable and bigoted coverage of elections. Finding truth is always the biggest problem for any voter. If you do not feel able to trust the candidates, you can be sure you cannot trust the printed media. Sometimes broadcast media are better, but not always. In the UK the bias is at its most obvious when each paper delights in announcing whom it is supporting, and whom it has chosen to ridicule. The *Sun* has always liked to follow the honourable principle of supporting the winner. In 1992 it famously told us IT WAS THE SUN WOT WON IT after showing a picture of Neil Kinnock with a light-bulb in his head on election day with the words, 'If Kinnock wins today will the last person to leave the country please turn off the lights.' The *Daily Mail* likes to support the winner, too, and, when it decides it cannot, it pretends the election is not happening. In other countries the situation can be even more extreme. Of course there are plenty of nations left where only the governing party gets favourable coverage. In others it is whoever has the money and the influence. The most striking recent example of a media mogul who showed the value in his media empire was Silvio Berlusconi – a man who used his background as a football chairman to call his new party 'Forza Italia' after a football chant. After two general election defeats the Conservatives might consider ''Ere we go, 'ere we go, 'ere we go' or 'You'll Never Walk Again'.

THE ITALIAN JOB

The rest of the Western world beat their breasts and worried deeply about the future of democracy as the man who dominates the Italian media headed for the premiership. In Italy they did not all worry so much about Berlusconi. Imagine a world in which Trevor McDonald or Michael Buerk comes nightly on to the telly and enthuses about his wonderful leader on the news while making snide remarks about the opposition. That is what anchormen like Emilio Fede do on Retequattro, just one of the TV networks Mr Berlusconi owns alongside Canale 5 and Italia 1, not forgetting the major newspaper *Il Giornale* and the big publishing interests. Berlusconi was Prime Minister before and his administration collapsed amid financial scandal, but his media have spread the word that this was all down to corrupt rumour-mongering by the Socialists and his other enemies.

Many countries would simply not allow anyone with these media and business interests to take high office, notwithstanding the long string of financial scandals. Even those that have no constitutional bar against such a conflict of interest could rely on their voters to balance out the powers. But this sort of success is almost worshipped in Italy, and the whiff of wrongdoing just makes him that much more sexy. Certainly, plenty of Italians are very scared of him. Society was split almost down the middle and a reasonably impressive 81 per cent turned out in the 2001 general election to take sides. They were keeping some polling stations open until two in the morning to allow the queues to reach their end. In Britain some polling station officers must have been tempted to shut up shop at two in the afternoon. Berlusconi has promised that there will be no conflict of interests. We shall have to wait and see.

The media carve-up led to radical measures from the Radical Party. With Forza Italia and its allies plugged by Berlusconi's Mediaset channels and the Socialists and their friends relying on the RAI channels, The Radicals found themselves squeezed out along with several other minor parties. If the TV will not put your party on the news, you have to *create* news, so their leading figure, Emma Bonino, went on hunger strike. As she started to get sick, even the President called for more publicity for the Radical Party to stop her losing any more weight. At least they got noticed.

ROLLING AND POLLING

In the UK there are strict guidelines about TV coverage of elections. Reporting must be seen to be impartial and all parties must be given fair publicity. There is no end to the arguments as to whether this is ever achieved, but many countries do not pretend to try. For a long time British TV kept as clear of politics as it could. It was not felt that it was possible to cover elections equally and fairly and TV was a vulgar little nonentity anyway. By-elections were not even mentioned in the news until the Rochdale by-election of 1958. Granada decided to cover it. They found that they did not get prosecuted under Representation of the Peoples legislation and the BBC and other broadcasters joined in after that. The 1959 general election was the first to be properly covered on British TV.

Now that campaigns are largely fought on the TV screens, the whole style of electioneering has changed much as they had feared all those years ago. Now we have rolling news, there is endless scope for detailed analysis of policy and explanation of the politicians' arguments. There is endless scope, but it never happens. In the US individual news items rarely last more than ninety seconds, even if the news goes on for ever. They do not tend to last much longer in Britain or elsewhere. Politicians have learned the art of the sound bite to cope with this need to get themselves across rapidly. Did you know the average politician's sound bite lasted 42 seconds in 1968 and it now lasts about seven seconds? Try to sum up some great address such as Christ's Sermon on the Mount, Mark Antony's Funeral Oration from *Julius Caesar* or Lincoln's Gettysburg Address in a seven-second sound bite. If you can get over the true meaning without making it sound fatuous or ridiculous you should go into politics. Winston Churchill is one of the few people who ever lived who had the knack of regularly saying something profound in a single simple sentence. These days they get advertising copy writers to do it for them. Thankfully our wartime leader did not exhort us to greater efforts with breakfast cereal ad-lines.

HELP ME MAKE IT THROUGH THE NIGHT

Election Night TV coverage has become a national institution in most parts of the world. The American presidential election of 2000 showed us how disturbingly powerful this coverage can become. At least in the UK the truth is in the hands of 659 returning officers who tell us what the real results are. The Americans get a confusing mess of partial ballot returns, exit polls and computer readings that are provided by a shadowy and highly controversial private news service (VNS). The public rely on CNN, CBS, NBC, Fox and all the rest to make sense of it for them. The real results do not come out for weeks, so what Dan Rather says is the word of God. This time God got it wrong, then got it wrong again, and the nation trembled as they witnessed their hi-tech media screw-up as they never believed possible.

The UK started its overnight coverage of general elections in 1950. It was an amazing achievement by the producer, Grace Wyndham Goldie, to get this made, as there had been no coverage at all of the election campaign prior to this. Also, the BBC always turned itself off at around 10.30 p.m. anyway and going live overnight for any reason sounded far too dangerous. The show was presented by Chester Wilmot and there was one outside broadcast from Trafalgar Square. There were no live declarations, no predictions, no penetrating interviews with politicians, no swingometers. There was already a young David Butler, though. In 1955 a few more cameras went outside, Richard Dimbleby compered and Robert McKenzie appeared with his little homemade swingometer. Real election night telly had arrived. ITN joined in the fun after that and pushed the use of outside broadcasts from the town halls. Then Robin Day led the new generation of interviewers. So the election night extravaganzas grew from there.

They still follow a familiar pattern. The first hour is heavily prepared, with well-organised items, a good airing for all the graphics and a tour of all the main OBs and key politicians who are available. From about 12.30 a.m. onwards it is a deluge of results, chaotic analysis and endless gaffes. My favourite period is round about 11 p.m., when there is some real information to go on, but precious little, and everyone tries to make of it what they can. 1979 was a great year for this when the Glasgow Central result came in about half an hour before any others. There was hardly any swing at all in one of the safest Labour seats anywhere, and they spent ages trying to think of something interesting to say about it, without finding a single thing, before some more results came to rescue them and start to show the tide turning for Thatcher.

Still the most memorable election night was that brought to us by *Monty Python* in their famous General Election sketch, originally broadcast in 1970. Absurd as it was, the parallels with real election night coverage before and since were uncanny.

John Cleese anchored the proceedings in the frantic style of a presenter who wanted to be seen to be in charge, while he was clearly getting hopelessly lost in a maelstrom of information overload that was getting him just a bit too excited. Neither Eric Idle, Terry Gilliam nor Graham Chapman would say anything of any use, while Terry Jones's swingometer was falling apart and a little man called Colin kept trying to get a word in about how this was his first time on TV. Michael Palin gave us one of the best election night lines ever when he told us that the result was pretty much as he expected except that the Silly Party won, and this was mainly due to the number of votes cast.

Apart from the fact that we were observing a national fight between the Silly Party and the Sensible Party, with a few Very Silly or only Slightly Silly candidates thrown in, this could have looked just like the media election coverage of the real thing. It was almost so close to the truth that it was imitative rather than satirical.

Real British TV coverage has been just as impressive as that, from Robin Day's legendary arguments with George Brown, through Bob McKenzie and his ground-breaking swingometer to Jeremy Paxman's cruel demolition of any politician who had just been beaten, Peter Snow's maniacal dances around his virtual-reality universe and David Dimbleby's Mars bars. ITV and Sky News produce their own shows of course, but they never quite achieve the same level of fun that the Beeb manage.

If you love watching an endless supply of gaffes on live TV, there is no substitute for Election Night programmes. Jonathan Dimbleby admitted he was a complete 'nana for screwing up the story from the Torbay declaration, but not for announcing to the world that this was the general election of the year 200,001. ITN still continue to follow the American model of calling results before they have been officially declared. This has led to their getting seats wrong on numerous occasions, such as when they ran the story for a while in 1997 that Simon Hughes had lost his Bermondsey seat. Sky News had a few blips in 2001. There was no way the A team of Adam Boulton and Michael Thrasher were going to get thrown by being told that the Tories had gained Stoke South on a night that was going against them badly. They had the sense to rubbish that immediately. The regular after-noon presenters the next day blathered on for a minute about Ian Paisley losing North Antrim after his party had just gained two seats, before David Butler stepped in and pointed out that this was probably nonsense.

Hundreds of OBs from around the country mean that the broadcasters have to drag in everyone to help, from sports reporters to the newest recruits getting their first network break. This gives us some excellent moments like the woman reporting from Cornwall in 1997 who spoke in completely disjointed gibberish, let down by her technology and her vocabulary, and the excited young reporter on the BBC from Torbay in 2001.

She had discovered the exclusive news that this race was so close that 'the Lib Dems are taking down numbers from the voters at the polling station, checking against lists of party members in their offices [I guess she meant party voters] and calling on them to see if they have voted and if they need a lift'. She had uncovered an amazing story about something that had gone on in every election for over a hundred years, but it was her first starring role on the box and this was her big moment – so don't be cruel to her. She may be anchoring it all in a couple of decades.

Meanwhile, the radio continues to give us its cosy chat through the night that you can follow comfortably from beneath the duvet. Many local stations turn out their own parochial report from the local counts and studio chat from obscure local figures with a presenter who would normally spend their small hours playing Carpenters tracks and chatting on air to local insomniacs, who are trying to win the phone-in competition and expose their personality disorders. The election experience usually throws them. Over on Radios 4 and 5 Live the professionals get to work and they usually manage to get the politicians a little more relaxed. Neil Kinnock was sounding just a little too relaxed in the 2001 broadcast – like several units over relaxed. The running joke this year was for James Naughtie to ask Mark Mardell for a comment and then interrupt him after four words with, 'And now we must go over live to Leicester'. It took a while for Naughtie to realise how many times he had done this and have a little laugh about it. I am not sure that Mardell was entirely convinced about the comedy of the situation.

NEW MEEJA

So has the advent of new technology changed the face of democracy? In its defence, it has opened up important new sources of information, particularly for developing countries and anywhere where political information is regarded as state property. The Internet cannot be controlled by politicians and that is why they are deeply worried by it. It has also allowed new debates and forums to open up, including staging debates with politicians. Anyone who tried to ask a question of Clinton, Blair or Putin in any of their webcast discussions had to wait in line behind a few thousand others and a host who chose the questions they wanted, so it does not get you as intimate with the powerful as you might wish.

As for campaigning, the Americans claimed that it was a vital part of the 2000 presidential election campaign. The British parties all jumped on board, but I am sceptical at this stage. All our parties set up fancy websites. The Conservatives had the most groovy graphics. The DUP had the best jokes. They all sent out emails to anyone on their list, but there is the point – you got their emails only if you wanted them. You were either a supporter already or you were curious, like me. If they had got your address from somewhere without your consent, you would probably not be happy and you could always block them. Going on nearly all the mailing lists I can report that hardly any of the emails were interesting. They were all copies of what was in the papers anyway. Labour and Tories sent piccies as well, many that would not load. The Lib Dems nearly sent me mad by sending as many as six emails a day at one stage in the campaign. The only party that had a mailing-list facility that I opted not to join was Sinn Fein. They were the only ones that asked for payment first. Call me an old-fashioned reactionary, but I can remember those jars they used to have on the bar in some Tooting pubs for the republican cause and I still worry a little about where the money goes.

Labour led the way in text-messaging young supporters. However, 'X LBR 2day if ur up 4 it' would still appear on your mobile only if you had registered with them. If gibberish like that appeared on someone else's Cellnet they would assume it was going wrong and give it a smack. If they think this is the way to the hearts of the young they ought to GAL (little joke only text fans will understand).

Maybe in a few years nearly everyone will be on the Net and they will have solved the security problems to allow us to vote there. Until then there is a long way to go, but they are trying.

JUST A FEW MORE MINOR AWARDS

Enlightening Comment Award: We all still miss the reporting of John Cole, who would give us such gems in his beautiful Ulster accent as, 'We're a year nearer the general election than we were this time last year.'

Interesting Misprint Award (lots of contenders for this one): The *Western Daily Press* had an interesting spin on one election when they reported: 'Mr Freeson, 59, an ex-Housing Minister, won the seat with a 4,834 vote majority in a sex-cornered fight at the last election.'

Pompous Patronising Comment on Other Countries' Elections Award: 'It's hard to make serious study of an adolescent nation, which selects according to emotions.' (*Le Libre Belgique* on the Slovakian elections 1994.)

WHEN CAN WE STOP THIS?

You have to have some sympathy with the media. They have to give a lot of prominence to elections, but they know that they do nothing for their audience figures. Most newspapers report falls in their circulation during election campaigns, and TV news ratings fall. They might go up a bit for the actual results. The *Daily Mail* managed a first for a supposedly serious mainstream newspaper in Britain during the 2001 campaign. Bar a very few exceptions, they kept the election off their front page through-out. They always pride themselves on being in touch with middle Britain, and this time they tried to catch the mood of pretending the election was not happening.

People love to complain that elections are boring. They also like to complain that they do not know enough about what the politicians stand for, so the politicians tell them and people complain they are boring again. It's a very unfortunate circular argument.

We even got scientific evidence in 2001, when *Channel Five News* reported on a study that showed that a group of viewers responded with higher pulse rates and blood pressure while watching paint dry than while watching election broadcasts. As half of the TV output these days consists of programmes about decorating bedrooms or other similarly dull activities, this was hardly surprising.

Apathy is the big fear these days, particularly with regard to the young. The media and the politicians all wondered about why we were expecting that well under half the first-time voters would actually bother. The most stunning example came with a vox pop interview early in the campaign when a young man looked into the camera with a drowsy expression and mumbled, 'Well, I'm a student, so I'm not interested in politics.' I must admit I sat there in stunned silence for a while, before the anger set in. Could we have imagined anyone saying that a few years ago? I decided there was no point in worrying about tuition fees and grant abolition any more. I had this guy in my mind's eye now and I just thought, 'Good. Serves you right!' Maybe in a few years' time there will be a government that will introduce public flogging and ritual humiliation for every tenth student and they will all be there with their dead-eyed expressions saying, 'Well, I'm a student, so I'm not interested in politics.'

Prophets, Seers, Sages and . . . Opinion Polls

'If one tells the truth, one is sure, sooner or later,
to be found out'
– *Oscar Wilde*, Phrases and Philosophies for the Use of the
Young

The first modest attempts at opinion polls began in the nineteenth century, with papers publishing straw polls. They were not very scientific, but did manage to predict results fairly accurately in some cases. You might say that this is not that impressive when there were so few voters to survey anyway.

As the millions were enfranchised, and as social scientists began to work out the theory behind good polling, the polls took root. Of course, they were led by the commercial world as it sought to find more accurate ways of discerning what the consumers were thinking. They discovered market research and the political pundits spotted its use in their field. It was particularly useful when they discovered that you do not have to poll tens of thousands of people. If your sampling is careful, much smaller numbers can be just as accurate.

The moment when the world looked up and took serious notice of opinion polls was with the American presidential election of 1948. The polls had pointed clearly to victory for the New York Republican and 1944 presidential runner-up to Roosevelt, Thomas Dewey (known as 'the Man on the Wedding Cake'). So sure were the experts that many Americans woke up to newspapers the next morning that declared DEWEY WINS. If they turned on their radio they got a different story. As we know now, Dewey was actually beaten by the Missouri Democrat and outgoing Vice-President

Harry Truman. The result was not even close with Truman getting over 57 per cent of the vote and 303 electoral college votes to Dewey's 36 per cent and 189 votes. Even with the loss of four Southern states to James Strom Thurmond's intervention for the Southern racist 'Dixiecrats', Truman won the election easily without sweeping the traditionally Democrat South.

As is often the case, it is when something fails that real progress is made. In this case, pollsters learned that voters can switch late and that it was a bad idea to continue to include old data instead of kicking it out when new data was gathered. They also learned a lot more about sampling and realised that they were interviewing a disproportionately upper-class selection and they were doing some very strange things with undecided voters.

Gallup made their debut in British elections in 1945 and got it very nearly right, although everyone thought they were talking rubbish at the time, as even ardent socialists did not think Churchill was going to lose. Other pollsters joined the fun in 1950 and UK opinion polls were generally pretty accurate until 1970. Even then the ones that surveyed late (such as ORC, Harris and NOP) were not all that far out. There was clearly a late swing and poor Gallup and Marplan were left high and dry with their predictions of 7 per cent and 8 per cent leads for Labour respectively as Ted Heath made it home with a lead of 3 per cent. Then they went on to get it right again in the years after. MORI could even get smug about getting all three elections from 1979 to 1987 right to within one point for each party with their final results. So the opinion polls established themselves as a serious, credible, scientific tool of political analysis – utterly worthy of respect. Oh, there was 1992, wasn't there?

OOPS! CAN WE TRY BEST OF THREE?

Sometimes opinion polls can get it badly wrong. However much money is thrown at them, however carefully they are constructed and executed on scientific principles, however well trained and diligent the interviewers may be, sometimes they are well and truly botched. This is not just the odd rogue poll that goes up the wall, with a result way out of line from anything else; or the ridiculously unreliable phone-in polls conducted by newspapers, radio or TV stations. Anyone who believes stuff like that deserves to be left with egg on their face.

In 1992 pollsters were left to lick their wounds and explain why they cocked it up well and truly. Through most of the campaign, a Labour victory was predicted. Bar a couple of polls dismissed as rogues, there was never a Tory lead of more than 1 per cent shown throughout the campaign. About 80 per cent of the dozens of polls conducted by the major, reputable polling organisations during the campaign showed a Labour lead of anything between 0.5 per cent and 7 per cent. All of the 'Big Five' even managed to screw up their exit polls on election day itself, so they could not simply blame a last-minute swing as they did, probably correctly, when they screwed up in 1970. MORI predicted a 1 per cent lead for Labour; NOP stuck their neck out on a 3 per cent lead for Labour – giving the BBC their inaccurate hung Parliament prediction; ICM had the parties neck and neck and let Sky News predict that Labour would be the largest party on that basis; only Gallup had the Tories leading by just 0.5 per cent – which would still leave the Commons hung. ITN's favoured pollsters at Harris were quiet about their figures, but they too predicted a hung Parliament – albeit a bit closer to the result than the others.

John Major beat Neil Kinnock by 8 per cent. This was way outside the realms of any margin of error. However, he scraped in with a Commons majority of only 21, thanks to a few very close votes in marginal seats. This did illustrate one factor: Labour did do much better in marginals than elsewhere and the concentration of polling in marginal seats was an issue for some of the polls. Dozens of other theories were put forward as to why this all went so badly wrong. The theory that the whole business of opinion polling was utterly unreliable was not allowed to be seriously discussed, as too many careers and reputations were tied up in it. After all, if market researchers cannot get their highest profile cases right, why should anyone trust their analysis of marketing campaigns for baked beans or health insurance? Then we would live in a world with fewer market researchers and you can ponder for a while whether that is a bad thing.

This is not the place to get into a detailed look at all the theories put forward to explain the errors, but one of them was generally agreed to be true and it is fascinating: Tories are shy! There are always a large number of people who refuse to take part in an opinion poll. There are then a few others who take part in the rest of the survey, but refuse to answer the one key question as to how they intend to vote. Pollsters had always assumed that we could safely guess that these people's party allegiances would break down in the same proportions as the rest of the respondents – that is that there was no particular party preference among the shy. Some had queried this before, particularly noting that the elderly are much more likely to refuse to answer questions and they are more prone to Conservative support as a group.

Closely allied to the shy Tory is another phenomenon that was posited: the lying Tory. It was now assumed that some Conservative voters were actually lying about their voting intentions. Why? One idea was that some people were ashamed to admit that they were going to vote Conservative for purely personal, financial reasons when it might have appeared to be more 'socially responsible' to vote Labour. There was more of a feeling at the time that voting Labour was the fashionable, cool thing to do and that voting Tory was somehow embarrassing. Pete Davies had an interesting take on this in his book *This England*, where he drew the enlightening comparison between voting Tory and wanking. We know there must be millions of people out there doing it, but very few will own up.

There might be some dispute as to whether the shameful problem was essentially with voting Tory or specifically with voting for the government, but perhaps a Tory government provides us with a kind of double whammy. This phenomenon does not occur in other countries in quite the same kind of way as far as I can see. In America, for example, right-wingers are probably more vocal and proud of their position than liberals, if anything. Perhaps quiet conservatism really is a key facet of the British personality. It can be a real pain to opinion pollsters, though, who have devised different ways of skewing the result to exaggerate the Tory vote since 1992.

ONLY THE AVERAGE COUNT

In some ways opinion polls do seem to be a bit of a mystery. A lot of people get very miffed that they have never been polled. 'How do they know what I think? They have never asked me!' The answer is that we do not care what you think. You are only one person and we have asked scores of people who represent every stratum of society that could be held to be representative of you – your sex, your age group, your socioeconomic group, your region and so on. If you just happen to be the only person in Britain from your sociological pigeonhole who is intending to vote for the Institutional Revolutionary Party of Mexico then you are just unrepresentative. The IRP has always been one of my favourite party names, by the way – how can you be an institutional revolutionary?

I have been lucky enough to have been polled on my voting intentions twice – and I lied only once. I also spent a short time on the other side of the fence as a telephone researcher. Most of the work was commercial. My special responsibility was helping to construct the computer game sales chart: 'So that was two "Revenge of the Alien Mutant Goats from Outer Space", was it?' But I did get to do a little political polling as well. I can vouch for the care that is put into ensuring that the sample is completely balanced. We would struggle on into the night to get the quotas filled. I can tell you the group you can never find at home – young women. When you are a young man phoning strangers in Glasgow or Exeter to ask them if there are any young women there, you soon learn how hard market research can get. Some people never even answered. They just slammed the phone down.

We are not going to get into a detailed lecture on statistical theory here, because statistical theory is not very funny. However, polls operate on a margin of error. They are set so that there is a probability of 95 per cent, or even as much as 99 per cent, that the results are accurate to within three percentage points. If you want 99 per cent certainty you just have to ask a lot more people. You may wonder what happens with those 5 per cent (or at least 1 per cent) of polls that are wrong. These are what we know as rogue polls. There has to be some possibility that all the people you interviewed just happened to be Green voters, even though the sampling was properly handled. Maybe the Labour voters just happened in every case to be the next one in line that you did not speak to. Many of these polls never see the light of day, because someone in the company is sufficiently awake to see that the result is daft. Some do make it, like the one that showed Labour winning in 1979. Occasionally they are right – it's all the others that are wrong. In Florida even the rogue polls are regarded as actually being more accurate than the official results.

THE LATEST NEWS ON POLLS

Perhaps the most telling point from the opinion polls leading up to the 2001 general election in Britain was that raised by the Gallup poll in the *Daily Telegraph* that showed that 66 per cent of the public agreed that William Hague came over as 'a bit of a wally'. The percentage did not really matter. Most politicians would have scored quite badly. The point was that the question was asked at all – and for a survey in a Conservative-supporting paper at that! That sort of impression that is passed around the media becomes common currency and can destroy a politician. Liars, crooks and cheats have a better chance of fighting their way to a comeback than a wally. Perhaps this is one of the best examples of opinion polls taking their place as one of the tools of the media that have been used to make the life of the modern politician pretty near impossible. They never used to give them this sort of shabby treatment: 'Excuse me, sir, would you say that Winston Churchill is a nutter?' 'Pardon me, madam, do you agree with the statement that Clement Attlee is a loony?' These were questions that were never asked and would not have been considered, even when any particular politician was generally unpopular.

On the whole, the pollsters continued to recover their credibility in 2001. Poor old Bob Worcester's MORI was the exception, as they changed their methods halfway through the campaign as their polls were consistently out of line with every one else's, showing ridiculous Labour leads that would probably have knocked Hague out of Richmond if they were true. They had to make the decision as to whether to annoy their clients at that stage, or after the results when it was too late.

All the organisations predicted a comfortable Labour win. There were only two exceptions I noticed. First there was the reliably wayward ITV Teletext phone poll, which had been hijacked by the Tory Party for years without the Teletext folk noticing. It predicted the same overwhelming support for the Tories that it had for every one of their policies for some time. Secondly, a phone poll conducted by the *Sun* in the final week showed a surprising landslide result for the Tories. It may have been more hijacking, or it may simply have been that the model with the blue rosette, promoting the poll on the front page of the paper, had the most prominent assets of the three shown. Maybe she should have been the party leader.

You Can't Make It Up

The Story of Voting Through Fiction

Having looked at the media's attempts to get to grips with elections, we can move sideways and look at the fictional arts. There has been quite a bit of stuff done on elections over the years, particularly in literature and cinema, a bit less on television, less still on the stage and I would be delighted if anyone can suggest a great piece of architecture, sculpture or postmodern installation art that deals with an electoral theme. Remember we are not counting newspaper content, grand portraits of successful politicians or anything else that is literal and factual. We are looking for imaginative, artistic and essentially fictional exploration of voting rather than reporting and analysis. Most of what we are about to discuss has a *basis* in fact of course: some of it is very thinly disguised satire on real people and situations. That is fine. After all, any arts that have no basis in reality would be meaningless.

Some areas of the arts have brushed the surface of the topic. Theatre has given us hundreds of political dramas and comedies. We can find plenty of examples from classical Greece to contemporary cutting-edge theatre. We could look at the work of Stoppard, Shaw or Brenton or look abroad to Dario Fo or most of the writers of the Absurd school. The most recent hit has been the West End comedy *Feelgood* by Alistair Beaton. However, dramatists still consider that elections are either too difficult to stage convincingly or are not sufficiently useful as vehicles to explore their interest in either micro or macro political behaviour.

203

BOOKS

Yes, politics is prevalent through much of English literature, and in some other parts of the world. Elections have featured in modern novels by such as Michael Dobbs and Chris Mullin. Jeffrey Archer gave us *First Among Equals*. This was what they call a 'page-turner'. Eventually you turn the last page and discover that the Labour MP has become Prime Minister (sorry to spoil it). In the American edition you turned the last page and it was the nice Tory. Very little else was changed in the book to get us to that point. You could have turned the page and found it was the SDP MP or the nasty Tory and been similarly unbothered. It did not really make any difference. Therefore low marks for plot and character development, but full marks for accurate portrayal of British politics.

Here we will concentrate on the best of political fiction. I have picked what may be the best selections from the three finest examples in the field. No less a hero than England's greatest novelist gave us an account of elections in his time in *Pickwick Papers*. The Pickwickians have arrived in Eatanswill in time to observe the election. The whole town is deeply divided between the Blues and the Buffs, who will take contrary positions on anything.

'You have come down here to see an election – eh?'
　Mr Pickwick replied in the affirmative.
　'Spirited contest, my dear sir,' said the little man.
　'I am delighted to hear it,' said Mr Pickwick, rubbing his hands. 'I like to see sturdy patriotism, on whatever side it is called forth; – and so it's a spirited contest?'
　'Oh yes,' said the little man, 'very much so indeed. We have opened all the public-houses in the place, and left our adversary nothing, but the beer-shops – masterly stroke of policy that, my dear sir, eh?' – the little man smiled complacently, and took a large pinch of snuff.

'And what are the probabilities as to the result of the contest?' inquired Mr Pickwick.

'Why doubtful, my dear sir; rather doubtful as yet,' replied the little man. 'Fizkin's people have got three-and-thirty voters in the lock-up coach-house at the White Hart.'

'In the coach-house!' said Mr Pickwick, considerably astonished by this second stroke of policy.

'They keep 'em locked up there till they want 'em,' resumed the little man. 'The effect of that is, you see, to prevent our getting at them; and even if we could, it would be of no use, for they keep them very drunk on purpose. Smart fellow Fizkin's agent – very smart fellow indeed.'

The tale goes on as we learn of the attempts at bribery through the provision of large numbers of parasols, the fights, the doping of opposition voters and the sabotage of a coach, which is ditched into a canal – a hat belonging to one of the voters is found, but we are not sure whether his head was in it or not. The following day the candidates appear before the crowd for their nomination, the first literary example of politicians kissing babies appears, some very long boring speeches are made and there are more fights.

Then Horatio Fizkin, Esquire, of Fizkin Lodge, near Eatanswill, presented himself for the purpose of addressing the electors; which he no sooner did, than the band employed by the honourable Samuel Slumkey, commenced performing with a power to which their strength in the morning was a trifle; in return for which, the Buff crowd belaboured the heads and shoulders of the Blue crowd; on which the Blue crowd endeavoured to dispossess themselves of their very unpleasant neighbours the Buff crowd; and a scene of struggling, and pushing, and fighting, succeeded, to which we can no more do justice than the Mayor could, although he issued imperative orders to twelve constables to seize the ringleaders, who might amount in number to two hundred and fifty, or thereabouts. At all these encounters, Horatio Fizkin, Esquire, of Fizkin Lodge, and his friends, waxed fierce and furious; until at last Horatio Fizkin, Esquire, of Fizkin Lodge, begged to ask his opponent the honourable Samuel Slumkey, of Slumkey Hall, whether the band played by his consent; to which the honourable Samuel Slumkey declining to answer, Horatio Fizkin, Esquire, of Fizkin Lodge, shook his fist in the countenance of the honourable Samuel Slumkey, of Slumkey Hall; upon which the honourable Samuel Slumkey, his blood being up, defied Horatio Fizkin, Esquire, to mortal combat. At this violation of all known rules and precedents of order, the Mayor commanded another fantasia on the bell, and declared that he would bring before himself, both Horatio Fizkin, Esquire, of Fizkin Lodge, and the honourable Samuel Slumkey, of Slumkey Hall, and bind them over to keep the peace.

Eventually order is restored, the candidates make their pompous speeches and the vote on a show of hands is too close to call. Polling takes place over the next few days amidst much corruption and drunkenness and a few independent voters are found at the last minute by Slumkey's agent – assuring his election.[1]

It is worth noting that Dickens worked as a political reporter during the most violent election in British history – the 1835 election. He reported mostly in East Anglia and it seems likely that many of his stories of Eatanswill were based on fact and probably only slightly exaggerated. Was Eatanswill really Bury St Edmunds, Chelmsford or any of the other places he visited at the time?

Then there is Trollope, perhaps the finest political novelist.

Our antihero Melmotte is running for Parliament for the Westminster constituency. His financial crimes are catching up on him and rumours have spread across the constituency. Many of his party have deserted him and he faces the ballot wondering when the police will knock on his door – a situation experienced by several nonfiction election candidates.

He went up into Covent Garden, where there was a polling booth. The place seemed to him, as one of the chief centres of a contested election, to be wonderfully quiet. He was determined to face everybody and everything, and he went up close to the booth. Here he was recognised by various men, mechanics chiefly, who came forward and shook hands with him. He remained there for an hour conversing with people, and at last made a speech to a little knot around him. He did not allude to the rumour of yesterday, nor to the paragraph in the *Pulpit* to which his name had been attached; but he spoke freely enough of the general accusations that had been brought against him previously. He wished the electors to understand that nothing which had been said against him made him ashamed to meet them here or elsewhere. He was proud of his position, and proud that the electors of Westminster should recognise it . . . It was asserted afterwards that this was the only good speech he had ever been known to make; and it was certainly successful, as he was applauded throughout Covent Garden . . . At two or three o'clock in the day, nobody knew how the matter was going. It was supposed that the working classes were in favour of Melmotte, partly from their love of a man who spends a great deal of money, partly from their belief that he was being ill-used, – partly, no doubt, from that occult sympathy which is felt

---

[1] Charles Dickens, *Pickwick Papers*, Wordsworth Editions Ltd, 1993 (1837), Chapter 13, pp. 162–3, 175–6.

for crime, when the crime committed is injurious to the upper classes.

After receiving a demand for £80,000 from a firm of solicitors, he discovers that he has beaten his opponent, Mr Alf, by less than a thousand votes – against the predictions of the day's papers.

It was very much to be member for Westminster. So much had at any rate been achieved by him who had begun the world without a shilling and without a friend – almost without education! Much as he loved money, and much as he loved the spending of money, and much as he had made and much as he had spent, no triumph of his life had been so great to him as this. Brought into this world in a gutter, without father or mother, with no good thing ever done for him, he was now a member of the British Parliament, and member for one of the first cities in the empire. Ignorant as he was he understood the magnitude of the achievement, and dismayed as he was to his present position, still at this moment he enjoyed keenly a certain amount of elation. Of course he had committed forgery – of course he had committed robbery. That, indeed, was nothing, for he had been cheating and forging and stealing all his life. Of course he was in danger of almost immediate detection and punishment. He hardly hoped that the evil day would be very much longer protracted, and yet he enjoyed his triumph. Whatever they might do, quick as they might be, they could hardly prevent his taking his seat in the House of Commons. Then if they sent him to penal servitude for life, they would have to say that they had so treated the member for Westminster![1]

---

[1] Anthony Trollope, *The Way We Live Now*, Penguin Classics, 1875, pp. 483–94.

Our final selection here is from *Dubliners* by James Joyce. The short story 'Ivy Day in the Committee Room' from that collection may be the best writing about elections in the English language, so let's have a short extract:

– Well I did a good day's work today, said Mr Henchy, after a pause.

– That so, John?

– Yes. I got one or two sure things in Dawson Street, Crofton and myself. Between ourselves, you know, Crofton (he's a decent chap of course), but he's not worth a damn as a canvasser. He hasn't a word to throw to a dog. He stands and looks at the people while I do the talking.

Here two men entered the room. One of them was a very fat man, whose blue serge clothes seemed to be in danger of falling from his sloping figure. He had a big face which resembled a young ox's face in expression, staring blue eyes and a grizzled moustache. The other man, who was much younger and frailer, had a thin, clean-shaven face. He wore a very high double collar and a wide-brimmed bowler hat.

– Hello Crofton! said Mr Henchy to the fat man. Talk of the devil . . .

– Where did the boose come from? asked the young man.

– Did the cow calve?

– O, of course, Lyons spots the drink first thing! said Mr O'Connor, laughing.

– Is that the way you chaps canvass, said Mr Lyons, and Crofton and I out in the cold and rain looking for votes?

– Why, blast your soul, said Mr Henchy, I'd get more votes than in five minutes than you two'd get in a week.

– Open two bottles of stout, Jack, said Mr O'Connor.

– How can I, said the old man, when there's no corkscrew?

– Wait now, wait now! said Mr Henchy, getting up quickly. Did you ever see this little trick?

He took two bottles from the table and, carrying them to the fire, put them on the hob. Then he sat down again by the fire and took another drink from the bottle. Mr Lyons sat on the edge of the table, pushed his hat towards the nape of his neck and began to swing his legs.

- Which is my bottle? he asked.

- This lad, said Mr Henchy.

Mr Crofton sat down on a box, and looked fixedly at the other bottle on the hob. He was silent for two reasons. The first reason, sufficient in itself, was that he had nothing to say; the second reason was that he considered his companions beneath him. He had been a canvasser for Wilkins, the Conservative, but when the Conservatives had withdrawn their man and, choosing the lesser of two evils, given their support to the Nationalist candidate, he had been engaged to work for Mr Tierney.

In a few minutes an apologetic *Pok!* was heard as the cork flew out of Mr Lyons's bottle. Mr Lyons jumped off the table, went to the fire, took his bottle, and carried it back to the table.

- I was just telling them, Crofton, said Mr Henchy, that we got a good few votes today.

- Who did you get? asked Mr Lyons

- Well, I got Parkes for one, and I got Atkinson for two, and I got Ward of Dawson Street. Fine old chap he is, too – regular old toff, old Conservative! *But isn't your candidate a Nationalist?* said he. *He's a respectable man,* said I. *He's in favour of whatever will benefit this country. He's a big ratepayer,* I said. *He has extensive house property in the city and three places of business and isn't it to his own advantage to keep down the rates? He's a prominent and respected citizen,* said I, *and a Poor Law Guardian, and he doesn't belong to any party, good, bad or indifferent.* That's the way to talk to 'em.

- And what about the address to the King? said Mr Lyons, after drinking and smacking his lips.

- Listen to me, said Mr Henchy. What we want in this country, as I said to old Ward, is capital. The King's coming here will mean an influx of money into this country. The citizens of Dublin will benefit by it. Look at all the factories down by the quays there, idle! Look at all the money there is in the country if we only worked the old industries, the mills, the ship-building yards and factories. It's capital we want.

- But look here, John, said Mr O'Connor. Why should we welcome the King of England? Didn't Parnell himself . . .

- Parnell, said Mr Henchy, is dead.[1]

MOVIES

If you look through a list of the greatest films ever made, it is surprising how many of them are overtly political at least in part. This is especially strange when you consider that politics is widely considered to be one of the surest routes to box-office death for a movie. *Citizen Kane*, *The Godfather*, *Schindler's List*, *Duck Soup*, *Dr Strangelove* and *'Z'* could head a list of hundreds that would have to include most of the best historical epics, many of the films of Renoir, Bunuel, Eisenstein and numerous other world cinema giants and even many block busters that are shot through with political plot lines such as several Bond films, *Jaws*, *Independence Day*, *Gladiator* and even *Star Wars*. However, we have to set limits. We will concern ourselves only with films that have featured elections as a central part of the movie. This excludes all those that deal with only general political themes or real or imagined political figures, or that feature an election only as a minor detail. For example, I do not include *All*

[1] James Joyce, 'Ivy Day in the Committee Room', from *The Dubliners*, Jonathan Cape 1967, pp 145-148.

the President's Men, which was a great movie with a memorable ending as Dustin Hoffman and Robert Redford tap away on their typewriters to bring about the downfall of Nixon, whose election victory is being reported on the television as they speak. I would include Redford's other 1970s political movie, *The Candidate*, which was very commendable, but unfortunately not as good.

Among the movies that have dealt with elections are several excellent films such as *The Manchurian Candidate*, *State of the Union*, *The Great Man Votes*, *The Great McGinty* and *The Candidate*. Even Woody Allen meets one of his former girl-friends in *Annie Hall* at an Adlai Stevenson campaign rally. The movie *Election* was ostensibly a teen flick about a high school student election, but the parallels are clear and fairly well drawn.

If you are going to watch only one great old movie on an electoral theme, I would advise you to make it *All the King's Men*. It won the Oscar for best picture in 1949 but tends to be unjustly forgotten today when people remember the classics. Directed by Robert Rossen, it was taken from a book by Robert Penn Warren that was blatantly based on the life of the controversial Southern governor Huey Long. As the hero, Willie Stark, Broderick Crawford plays the honest local campaigner who fights his way up from obscurity and against terrible opposition, only to become as much a monster in the end as those he had sought to defeat. I won't give away the ending in case you have not seen it. For any who know Mercedes McCambridge only as the voice of the demon in *The Exorcist*, it is worth seeing that she can be just as scary in the flesh as the young political aide from hell.

Bulworth and *Primary Colors* are two terrific modern films that deal with elections well. They are both hilarious as well as intelligent and moving. Warren Beatty's performance, as a Senator who goes through some kind of a breakdown during his re-election campaign, was one of the best of his career. He knows he is finished, has hired a hit man to kill him and has sunk so low that he starts to actually tell the truth in public, to the horror of his campaign team. Some have found the scenes when Beatty raps and attempts to 'get down with the homies' too embarrassing to handle. They do not seem to realise that is the point. *Primary Colors* was based on the anonymous novel that was eventually revealed to be the work of Joe Klein. If anyone had not got the message already that Jack Stanton, the Southern governor with a heart of gold, but an uncontrollable libido, was meant to be Bill Clinton, John Travolta rams the point home by playing the character with a perfect Clinton hairstyle and accent. We follow him through the Presidential Primaries as his team and his wife (Emma Thompson) try to keep him on course. Every campaign team should have a character like the one played by Kathy Bates – a manic, psychotic lesbian who has a unique way of getting an opponent to admit he had faked a compromising phone recording of Stanton. Watch it and learn. In the end we all stand in the shoes of Henry, the idealistic young black aide, as he looks into the eyes of Stanton and decides whether he can continue to serve on his team. I think most of us would have come to the same decision.

Sadly, British movies have tended to leave politics alone, with some brief references in historical films and rather a lot about the problems of Ireland. *Scandal* was probably the best British political movie. As for electoral stories, *Left, Right and Centre* and *The Rise and Rise of Michael Rimmer* were about as near as British cinema got to films along the lines of those we have just mentioned. They were both terrible.

TELEVISION

There have been loads of TV shows about politics, including *House of Cards*, *Yes, Minister*, *The New Statesman*, *GBH* and the televised version of Chris Mullen's *A Very British Coup*. You could go on for ever about the programmes that have dealt with the issue to some extent. Americans had less enthusiasm for a while, but eventually got the bug and then gave us loads of them, from *Spin City* to *The West Wing*. However, again elections have not featured so heavily in these programmes.

Britain's soaps *EastEnders* and *Coronation Street*, as well as radio's *The Archers*, have often dabbled with politics. *Coronation Street*, in particular, has heavily featured the exploits of councillor Alf Roberts over the years, and then the succession to the throne of his widow, Audrey. The 2001 election saw Audrey come under threat from a smarmy newcomer. Early in the campaign, we saw a debate between the two of them, chaired by Audrey's campaign manager Norman 'Curly' Watts. The audience started out sympathetic to Audrey until she turned up late and then sank under the pressure of the other chap's oily charms. Then she cleared off, claiming to be sick, and Curly stopped chairing the event to take her place! He won a slanging match with 'Mr Slimeball' and the audience changed sides again.

Then the next day he got himself nominated as a candidate. Presumably she had a few days left to withdraw her nomination, but Audrey remained a candidate while campaigning for Curly. On election day, Mr Slimeball canvassed for votes at the polling station door, for which the police should have carted him away. Then the candidates had an argument inside the polling station, for which they should all have been carted away. Curly won the vote in the end, although none of the candidates seemed to know the result before it was announced – more dramatic, but unreal.

Now, soap writers are usually spot on when it comes to dealing with social realism. Give them a political storyline and they write absolute garbage like that. This book may be full of strange election stories, but that lot was just impossible.

ART

If there has been any claim to have created great political art that has dealt with electoral themes it has to come from that hybrid form of art and populist ephemera – the political cartoon. Two names stand out as men who went well beyond the realms of mere transient journalism and were great artists and painters as well. They are William Hogarth and James Gillray.

William Hogarth (1697–1764) was one of Britain's finest artists. He was also a great satirist and some of his best-remembered work deals with his devastating attacks on the social evils of his day. Work such as *A Rake's Progress, Marriage à la Mode* and *The Shrimp Girl* are well admired to this day and work such as *Gin Lane* shows us the kind of desperate squalor that common people endured in eighteenth-century Britain. He painted for the King and moved in high society but kept his feet on the ground as well. For our purposes it is the series of engravings about the Oxfordshire elections of 1754 that interest us. The first, which is entitled *An Election Entertainment*, shows the two Whig candidates throwing a party for the voters. We can see the scene of bribery and treating and one self-sacrificial candidate even goes so far as to let a hideous old woman kiss him. In the second plate, which shows us how canvassing proceeded in those days, we see a voter being bribed while the tavern doubling as the Whig HQ is attacked by a mob of Tory supporters down the road.

In the third print, the candidates argue at the hustings while the insane and the dying cast their votes. The two Tories who have won the election are carried off in a triumphal procession in the fourth print led by a lunatic fiddler and obstructed by various animals and people fighting. There may be no photographs or newsreel footage of the 1754 election, but who needs them when Hogarth's engravings are so much richer?

James Gillray (1757–1815) was probably the greatest of all satirical cartoonists. The fact that he got away with publishing such grotesque caricatures of all the major politicians and royal figures of his day without being executed showed that Britain was a far more tolerant nation at the time than anywhere else in the world. The likes of Charles Fox, Tom Paine and William Pitt were regularly targets of his venom. Come election time he would generally show his favouritism towards the Tories. Although he was liberal in his views on many issues, he became a friend of Pitt and reasoned that Tories were wealthier, and therefore better able to buy pictures from him.

The French artist Honoré Daumier followed in the steps of these two with his satirical study of politics and society through the turbulent period of mid-nineteenth-century France. He used his art to help support democratic principles through all the revolutionary changes of the time and was probably the first notable satirical sculptor.

Since these trailblazers left their mark, satirical artists have left theirs all over the world. A few of them have even matched the brilliance of these giants, though very few can claim to have been so original. Of course, it is largely through the newspapers that they have plied their trade, just as Gillray found employment with *The Times*. Perhaps people like Steve Bell in the *Guardian* carry the torch today for this unique art form. It takes talent to sum up a man like John Major simply with a pair of grey Y-fronts and forever associate the two together in the minds of so many.

MUSIC

I am not aware of any classical music that was composed specifically about elections. As with the other areas we have looked at we can think of operas with political themes by Wagner and Verdi, and there is even Gilbert and Sullivan, but democracy was not prevalent in Valhalla or in most other operatic settings.

Popular music is another matter. Politicians have probably used campaign songs since elections began. We know they were used in the nineteenth century. From the earliest nursery-rhyme tunes with lyrics that would fail to reach such high standards, to the efforts of latter-day pop composers, campaign songs have been uniformly awful. Maybe Adlai Stevenson's presidential campaign of 1952 hit an all-time low with a little number featuring couplets like 'Didn't know much about him before he came; Now my heart is the ballot that bears his name.' Everyone can join in the chorus of 'Adlai, I love you madly.' Of course he lost. Some politicians have tried to get around that by pinching existing songs with uplifting lyrics, a catchy tune and a driving beat. Bill Clinton established the idea of playing a song to death with Fleetwood Mac's 'Don't Stop' in 1992. It is impossible now to remember that D:Ream's 'Things Can Only Get Better' was actually a reasonably good dance record until New Labour made everyone completely sick of it. Labour went a little more reflective in 2001 with 'Lifted' by the Lighthouse Family. Their earlier choice of 'Reach' by S Club 7 was dropped after the three boys in the band had their drugs-bust episode. Meanwhile, the Lib Dems joined in the party with 'New Beginnings' by Stephen Gately from Boyzone. As discussed in the earlier chapter, 'Just Say Cheese and Pray that it Works', Conservatives have a problem with credible celebrities, as most of them prefer not to be associated with right-wing causes. Some artists have threatened to sue when any ideas were put abroad that their songs were being considered for campaigns by politicians they did not approve of. The British Conservative Party end up being reduced to commissioning Andrew Lloyd Webber or Mike Batt to write forgettable dirges for them. Even with the musical genius behind the Wombles on board the Tories still failed to win in Wimbledon!

Away from the real campaigns, elections have even featured as themes for pop songs. We could probably even put together a reasonable compilation album from the following:

'I Wanna Be Elected' – Alice Cooper
'Election Blues' – Canned Heat
'Election Day' – Arcadia

'Election's Just a Farce' – DBF
'General Election' – Lord Beginner
'Throwing the Election' – Game Theory
'Ain't Gonna Vote No More' – Mick Warrington
'Always Tell the Voter What the Voter Wants to Hear' –
    Chumbawumba
'Don't Vote' – Flash and the Pan
'One Man One Vote' – Frank Zappa
'Right to Vote' – Laura Nyro
'Vote' – Little Steven
'Vote for Me' – Clint Eastwood & General Saint
'Vote for Mr Rhythm' – Ella Fitzgerald
'Vote With a Bullet' – Corrosion of Conformity
'Ballots not Bullets' – 24-7 Spyz
'I'm a Conservative' – Iggy Pop
'Young Conservatives' – Kinks
'Love Me, I'm a Liberal' – Phil Ochs
'Socialist' – Public Image Ltd
'Electioneering' – Radiohead
'Futurist Manifesto' – Be-Bop De Luxe
'Manifesto' – Roxy Music
'Smear Campaign' – Rory Gallagher
'Candidate' – David Bowie

There are at least half a dozen really good songs there. The rest may be pretty obscure or just very poor, but it is not an exhaustive list, particularly if you want to start including songs that are more loosely related to elections and those that have been used as themes or have any other connection. So how about it, then: 'Now That's What I Call Suffrage'?

Lest They Be Forgotten

There are some little nuggets about elections that do not fit neatly under any of our headings, so we will put a few of them together in a brief look through those miscellaneous oddities.

DITCHING THE BOSS

Arthur Balfour was the first of two twentieth-century British prime ministers to succeed in achieving the outstanding failure of losing their own seats at a general election. Balfour (or Pretty Fanny, as his rather scary nickname had it) lost his seat of Manchester East in 1906 as his Conservatives and Unionists were thrashed in the landslide election of 1906 by Campbell-Bannerman's Liberals. Remarkably, he came back almost straightaway in a by-election for the City of London and remained as party leader. Modern parties would be far more cruel.

The other failure was achieved by Ramsay MacDonald. He had lost a seat once before. That was in 1918, after he was accused of treason for commenting that World War One need never had happened if the government had not made so many mistakes. How dare he suggest all those men could have missed their chance for a patriotic death if politicians had exhibited a degree of competence? Where's the glory in that? MacDonald moved on from Leicester to represent Aberavon from 1922 and immediately became Labour leader. That indicates that we are looking at an impressive man and a deeply unimpressive parliamentary party. In just two years he led them into government. But he moved on again to Durham Seaham in 1929, and soon had the Labour Party standing against their former leader, who now stood as one of the National Labour members of the coalition government. In 1935, Manny Shinwell thrashed him by more than two to one. He remained part of the government and won a by-election to represent the Scottish Universities the following year, but the first Labour Prime Minister had turned against the bulk of his party and they had turned against him.

PICKING THE DATE

Many heads of government around the world envy the right of a British prime minister to pick their own re-election date. It is one of many nonsensical features of our constitution. Only some of those states that have adopted their constitution from the British model have similar arrangements. Robert Mugabe has always been very grateful for this. This Ministerial power can lead to some very odd examples of decision making. For example, Margaret Thatcher opted for 9 June 1983, rather than the 16th or 23rd, reasoning that the public would be getting extensive coverage of Ascot Week on the TV if they delayed, and all the toffs in hats at the races would put the voters off. As if all those working-class Tories would forget about their council house purchases and share-owning ambitions and flee back to the class war at their first sight of a ridiculous four foot wide hat covered in fruit. Actually, she probably had a point: although it would not be the working class that would be the problem, but the middle-class voters, bitter that they did not get corporate hospitality tickets, as Roger and Hermione did across the road.

John Major liked the idea that as he visited the Queen to seek the dissolution of Parliament, her corgis were in attendance, making these animals and their owner the first to know outside the Cabinet. He got on very well with the corgis.

BROTHERLY STRIFE

Strangest election of recent years? A possible contender is the 2000 election for coroner in Jasper County, Missouri. The incumbent, Ron Musbaugh, held this vital position for the Republicans, but faced a new challenge from Don Musbaugh for the Democrats. Yes, Ron and Don are identical twins. The same womb; the same home; the same career and ambitions for the same office. Somehow they even had the same campaign manager! How did that work? Perhaps the poor soul did not even realise he was working for two people: 'Hell, I thought it was the same guy. It's not like they were ever in the same room together.' In the end Ron held on to his position in one of the Republicans' notable achievements of 2000. How do you campaign for county coroner? 'If elected I promise that I will always remember to wash my hands.' Maybe.

THE RETURNS OF THE LIVING DEAD

Spare a thought for Alfred Dobbs, the Labour MP who won his first election for Smethwick on 26 July 1945 in the Labour landslide. As he travelled to Westminster the following day to claim his new seat, filled with enthusiasm and anticipation for all the possibilities for his future, he died in a car accident. Of all the political records Mr Dobbs might have wanted to set, the shortest ever parliamentary career was the one he would have liked to have gone without. Bobby Sands's 25-day career as an MP serving as an IRA prisoner on hunger strike takes a very distant second place. Three members of Labour's new intake of 1945 were dead before the year was ended, which was a remarkably unlucky turn of events.

In Britain, returning officers have traditionally been allowed some discretion over what to do about dead candidates. In all honesty, if a candidate for a minor party dies a week away from polling there is little point in cancelling it and making new arrangements. It might seem to be a bit disrespectful, but life has to go on. However, if someone who looks like a potential winner dies they will try to call it off if there is still time to delay. The last time this happened was at the 1951 general election in Barnsley, when the defending MP, the Labour candidate F Collindridge, died nine days before polling. In 1923 they managed to postpone the event with only two days' notice in Derbyshire West when the outgoing Liberal MP C F White died.

This is not the way things work in the States. As there are no by-elections in America, the poll has to go ahead whatever has happened to the candidates. If a dead candidate winds up getting elected, it is normally the job of the state governor to appoint a replacement until the next round of elections. Of course dead politicians have been elected all over the world, but America seems to be particularly keen on doing this. It may have something to do with the American love of nonintrusive government – dead politicians don't interfere.

In 2000 there was a much-celebrated race for the position of Senator for Missouri. This was one of the very rare cases in which a candidate was killed as a result of their campaigning, rather than an unrelated illness or accident. Rare, that is, in relatively peaceful democracies where candidates are not routinely murdered. The Democrat challenger Mel Carnahan died in a plane crash while touring the state. The governor who had succeeded Carnahan announced before the poll that he would award the seat to Mel's widow Jean should he win the election. This assurance was enough to tip the race to the deceased candidate, so the right-wing Republican Senator John Ashcroft was ousted from the Senate just as his hero was stumbling into the White House. Ashcroft was later seen heading for Dubya's cabinet, while the Senate was deadlocked with an equal split between the parties thanks to a couple of near ties and the posthumous election of Mel Carnahan.

Carnahan was the latest in a long list of posthumous victories. One of the most impressive came when the voters of San Mateo County, California, elected Brendan Maguire as their sheriff in 1986 despite the fact that he had been dead for two months, having given plenty of opportunity for people to notice his new circumstances and nominate an alternative person. Another possible world record, unless anyone can point out a better example.

WHAT HAPPENS NEXT?

Not content with horse racing or card playing, gamblers moved in on elections a long time ago. More respectable pundits back up their own powers of prophecy with academic argument, detailed analysis of records and insight gained from years of research. Racing fans just call that studying the form. We have looked at opinion polls and media elsewhere and have touched on the folly of predicting election results. It is a wonder why sensible bookmakers allow people to bet on an area where so many have inside knowledge, but that does not always help. I was tempted to use my inside knowledge in 1992. Having just seen the postal votes being checked a day before polling day, I saw that Labour were well ahead of the Tories in a key marginal seat that the bookies still thought the Tories would hold. I knew Tories were generally better at getting postal votes, so this seemed to be a winning bet. It was probably only because I was in a hurry and I did not pass a bookie on the way home, that I resisted the temptation. As it turned out I received the clearest confirmation the following day that Major won the election with a late swing, because the Tories held the seat. Somehow bookies get a more accurate picture than those of us who merely look at how people have already voted.

Much in the way that others look at tealeaves, some like to predict election results on the basis of expecting certain parties to do well in particular circumstances. The most logically argued of these theories is that Labour do well in good weather when it is easier to get their less enthusiastic voters out. A lot of dumb theories circulate about which conditions lead to which sorts of results, so I have produced a definitive ready reckoner for you to produce your own theory of synchronicity. I provide all you need to know about the general elections from 1945 onwards and suggest a few clues to help you construct a plausible theory that might get you a couple of minutes of attention on a talk-radio station:

The Strangebullet Election Ready Reckoner
(designed for the use of all who wish to construct an electoral theory of synchronicity)

1945   Date: July 5 (result announced 26 Jul – 23 seats voted later but no votes were counted until all the results were received from servicemen overseas). Zodiac sign: Cancer
Result: Lab. maj. 146 (Lab. 393, Con. 213, Lib. 12, Others 22). Lab. – Attlee, Con. – Churchill, Lib. – Sinclair (who lost his seat)
Weather: Clear and fair
Top non-election-related news stories: Allied troops begin occupation of assigned regions of Berlin (Potsdam Conference and the Iron Curtain by time of results)
Number-one record: No chart (perhaps 'We'll Gather Lilacs in the Spring Again')
Top box-office movie: No weekly figures, top film of year – *The Seventh Veil*
Team on top of English League: League suspended (Everton champions from 1939, Blackpool were leading 39–40 when it was suspended after just three rounds of matches)

1950   Date: 23 February. Zodiac sign: Pisces
Result: Lab. maj. 5 (Lab. 315, Con. 298, Lib. 9, Others
3). Lab. – Attlee, Con. – Churchill, Lib. – Davies
Weather: Mild, sunny, heavy rain in the evening in
some areas
Top non-election-related news stories: British and
American spies Sanders and Vogeler jailed in Budapest;
US naval attaché, a friend of Vogeler, killed on Orient
Express
Number-one record: 'Dear Hearts and Gentle People'
(sheet-music chart)
Top box-office movie: No weekly figures, top film of
year – *The Blue Lamp*
Team on top of English League: Liverpool

1951   Date: 25 October. Zodiac sign: Scorpio
Result: Con. maj. 17 (Con. 321, Lab. 295, Lib. 6,
Others 3). Con. – Churchill, Lab. Attlee, Lib. – Davies
Weather: Foggy and frosty in morning in some parts,
clearing and fair for rest of day
Top non-election-related news stories: Tension in Suez
as British troops and ships head for area and relations
with Egypt break down
Number-one record: 'Too Young' (sheet-music chart)
Top box-office movie: No weekly figures. Top film of
year: *The Great Caruso*
Team on top of English League: Bolton Wanderers

1955   Date: 26 May. Zodiac sign: Gemini
Result: Con. maj. 58 (Con. 344, Lab. 277, Lib. 6,
Others 3). Con. – Eden, Lab. – Attlee, Lib. – Davies
Weather: Fine and sunny day, scattered showers in
evening
Top non-election-related news stories: Alberto Ascari
dies in crash while testing car at Monza; Freddie
Palmer rides Phil Drake, owned by Mme Leon
Volterra, to win the Derby

Number-one record: 'Stranger in Paradise' – Tony
Bennett
Top box-office movie: *The Dam Busters*
Team on top of English League: Chelsea

1959 Date: 8 October. Zodiac sign: Libra
Result: Con. maj. 100 (Con. 365, Lab. 258, Lib. 6,
Others 1). Con. – Macmillan, Lab. – Gaitskell, Lib. –
Grimond
Weather: Dry typically autumnal day
Top non-election-related news stories: Death of Mario
Lanza; Leakey's skull of earliest known man is
exhibited in London; a rhinoceros is elected in São
Paulo, Brazil
Number-one Single: 'Here Comes Summer' – Jerry
Keller ('Only Sixteen' – Craig Douglas in some charts)
Number-one album: *South Pacific* – original
soundtrack
Top box-office movie: No weekly figures. Top film of
year – *Carry on Nurse*
Top of TV ratings: *Double Your Money* (quiz show with
Hughie Green – sometimes people won £32!)
Team on top of English League: Wolverhampton
Wanderers

1964 Date: 15 October. Zodiac sign: Libra
Result: Lab. maj. 4 (Lab. 317, Con. 304, Lib. 9, Others
0). Lab. – Wilson, Con. – Douglas-Home, Lib. –
Grimond
Weather: Lots of rain for most of the country through
much of the day
Top non-election-related news stories: Khrushchev
ousted in Kremlin coup – replaced by Brezhnev and
Kosygin; Mary Rand wins long jump in Tokyo
Olympics; Queen Elizabeth ends tour of Canada
Number-one single: 'Oh Pretty Woman' – Roy Orbison
Number-one album: *A Hard Day's Night* – Beatles

Top box-office movie: top films of year – *Goldfinger*, *A Hard Day's Night*

Top of TV ratings: *Coronation Street* (Len Fairclough, Elsie Tanner, Ena Sharples, Albert Tatlock, Minnie Caldwell, Annie and Jack Walker)

Team on top of English League: Chelsea

1966   Date: 31 March. Zodiac sign: Aries

Result: Lab. maj. 96 (Lab. 363, Con. 253, Lib. 12, Others 2) .Lab. – Wilson, Con. – Heath, Lib. – Grimond

Weather: Mild day with a few light showers, heavy rain in northern Scotland

Top non-election-related news stories: Verwoerd's National Party wins South Africa's election; British Airports Authority formed; French announce plans for military withdrawal from NATO

Number-one single: 'The Sun Ain't Gonna Shine Anymore' – Walker Brothers

Number-one album: *The Sound of Music* – original soundtrack

Top box-office movie: *The Sound of Music* (for the millionth week)

Top of TV ratings: *Mrs Thursday* (series of dramas starring Kathleen Harrison)

Team on top of English League: Liverpool

1970   Date: 18 June. Zodiac sign: Gemini

Result: Con. maj. 30 (Con. 330, Lab. 287, Lib. 6, Others 7). Con. – Heath, Lab. – Wilson, Lib – Thorpe

Weather: Nice fine day everywhere

Top non-election-related news stories: Charles Manson trial; Communists close road from Phnom Penh to Saigon with mortar attack; Rover launches the Range Rover; England still mourning World Cup quarter final defeat by West Germany four days earlier

Number-one single: 'In the Summertime' – Mungo Jerry

Number-one album: *Bridge Over Troubled Water* – Simon and Garfunkel

Top box-office movie: *M*A*S*H*

Top of TV ratings: *Shadows of Fear*: 'Did You Lock Up?' (episode in series of single dramas starring Michael Craig and Gwen Watford)

Team on top of English League: Everton

1974 (i) Date: 28 February. Zodiac sign: Pisces

Result: No overall majority (Lab. 301, Con. 297, Lib. 14, Others 23). Lab. – Wilson, Con. – Heath, Lib. – Thorpe

Weather: Showers all over the country, very heavy in the southwest

Top non-election-related news stories: Seven Watergate conspirators indicted; UK is still on three-day week and prepares to return to 10.30 p.m. TV curfew lifted for the election campaign; USA and Egypt restore diplomatic ties

Number-one single: 'Devil Gate Drive' – Suzi Quatro

Number-one album: *Old, New, Borrowed and Blue* – Slade

Top box-office movie: *The Sting*

Top of TV ratings: *This is Your Life* (presented by Eamonn Andrews, victims – John Dankworth on 27th, Richard Gordon in a special on 28th)

Team on top of English League: Leeds United

1974(ii) Date: 10 October. Zodiac sign: Libra

Result: Lab. maj. 3 (Lab. 319, Con. 277, Lib. 13, Others 26). Lab. – Wilson, Con. – Heath, Lib. – Thorpe

Weather: Cloudy day with some showers, occasional outbursts of heavy rain in parts

Top non-election-related news stories: IRA kill five in Guildford five days before election and they plant two

bombs in London as the results are still being counted; seven hostages freed in Dominican Republic; Croydon is enjoying Britain's first McDonald's
Number-one single: 'Annie's Song' – John Denver
Number-one album: *Rollin'* – Bay City Rollers
Top box-office movie: *Emmanuelle*
Top of TV ratings: *Man About the House* (sitcom starring Richard O'Sullivan, Paula Wilcox, Sally Thomsett, Brian Murphy and Yootha Joyce)
Team on top of English League: Ipswich Town

1979   Date: 3 May. Zodiac sign: Taurus
Result: Con. maj. 43 (Con. 339, Lab. 269, Lib. 11, Others 16). Con. – Thatcher, Lab. – Callaghan, Lib. – Steel
Weather: Fair day, only Scotland and West Country had any significant rain
Top non-election-related news stories: Fighting continues in Rhodesia as rebels refuse to accept new parliamentary elections; bombing campaign continues in Paris by Corsican Nationalists; Red Brigade bomb Christian Democrats HQ in Rome
Number-one single: 'Bright Eyes' – Art Garfunkel
Number-one album: *The Very Best Of* – Leo Sayer
Top box-office movie: *California Suite*
Top of TV ratings: *Coronation Street* (Alf Roberts, Stan and Hilda Ogden, Emily Bishop, Mavis Riley, Eddie Yeats)
Team on top of English League: Liverpool

1983   Date: 9 June. Zodiac sign: Gemini
Result: Con. maj. 144 (Con. 397, Lab. 209, Lib./SDP 23, Others 21). Con. – Thatcher, Lab. – Foot, Lib. – Steel, SDP – Jenkins
Weather: Cloudy with some light showers, warm in most parts
Top non-election-related news stories: Clive Sinclair is

knighted; Bernadette McAliskey is refused entry to USA; elections in Norway and Portugal

Number-one single: 'Every Breath You Take' – the Police (from the album *Synchronicity* – spooky or what?)

Number-one album: *Thriller* – Michael Jackson

Top box-office movie: *Return of the Jedi*

Top of TV ratings: *Coronation Street* (Deirdre and Ken Barlow, Mike Baldwin, Brian Tilsley)

Team on top of English League: Liverpool

1987   Date: 11 June. Zodiac sign: Gemini

Result: Con. maj. 102 (Con. 376, Lab. 229, Lib./SDP, 22 Others 23). Con. – Thatcher, Lab. – Kinnock, Lib. – Steel, SDP – Owen

Weather: Cool day with showers, some thundery and heavy, dry and warm in west

Top non-election-related news stories: Princess Anne given title 'Princess Royal'; Britain expels two Iranian envoys; student riots in South Korea

Number-one single: 'I Wanna Dance with Somebody' – Whitney Houston

Number-one album: *Whitney* – Whitney Houston

Top box-office movie: *The Morning After*

Top of TV ratings: *EastEnders* (Den and Angie Watts, Pauline and Arthur Fowler, Pete and Kathy, Ian, Mark, Michelle, Sharon, Colin, Wicksy, Lofty, Dot and Nick)

Team on top of English League: Everton

1992   Date: 9 April. Zodiac sign: Aries

Result: Con. Maj. 21 (Con. 336, Lab. 271, Lib Dem 20, Others 24). Con. – Major, Lab. – Kinnock, Lib Dem – Ashdown

Weather: Fine sunny day, cloudy in Scotland, some showers in North

Top non-election-related news stories: Yasir Arafat survives plane crash in Libya; General Noriega of

Panama convicted of drug trafficking; Arthur Ashe tells the world that he has AIDS; two killed in London bomb blast evening after election while celebrating Tory victory

Number-one single: 'Stay' – Shakespeare's Sister

Number-one album: *Adrenalize* – Def Leppard

Top box-office movie: *Bugsy*

Top of TV ratings: *Coronation Street* (Bet Gilroy, Reg Holdsworth, Betty Turpin, Curly Watts, Percy Sugden)

Team on top of English League: Manchester United

1997 Date: 1 May. Zodiac sign: Taurus

Result: Lab. Maj. 179 (Lab. 419, Con. 165, Lib Dem 46, Others 29). Lab. – Blair, Con. – Major, Lib Dem – Ashdown

Weather: Sunny and dry everywhere, unseasonally hot in all parts but southern coast

Top non-election-related news stories: Ellen Morgan comes out as the first lesbian lead character in a prime-time US TV series; mass murderer 'Mad Dog' McCafferty deported back to Glasgow from Australia; Hubble Telescope scientists say the world is at least 13 billion years old; England beat Georgia 2-0 in World Cup qualifier, Scotland lose to Sweden; lots of reports about production problems on the movie *Titanic*, which everyone agrees looks likely to be a very expensive flop.

Number-one single: 'Blood on the Dance Floor' – Michael Jackson (replacing the much more New Labourish 'I Believe I Can Fly' by R Kelly)

Number-one album: *Tellin' Stories* – the Charlatans

Top box-office movie: *The Empire Strikes Back* (new edition)

Top of TV ratings: *Coronation Street* (Vera Duckworth, Gail Platt, Roy Cropper, Rita Sullivan)

Team on top of English League: Manchester United

2001   Date: 7 June. Zodiac sign: Gemini
Result: Lab. Maj. 167 (Lab. 413, Con. 166, Lib Dem 52, Others 28). Lab. – Blair, Con. – Hague, Lib Dem – Kennedy
Weather: Cool with occasional showers all over the country, some heavy in northwest England and Scotland.
Top non-election-related news stories: Arrest of Michael Barrymore on drug charges following investigation into death of a man at his house; riots in Leeds – following those in Oldham; unrest in Nepal after massacre of royal family by Crown Prince; continuing Jeffrey Archer trial; tabloids still excited about first eviction in second series of *Big Brother*; England beat Greece 2-0 in World Cup qualifier; a draw for Wales and a defeat for Northern Ireland.
Number-one single: 'Angel' – Shaggy
Number-one album: *Hot Shot* – Shaggy
Top box-office movie: *The Mummy Returns* (Thatcher returns from the dead but cannot revive the Tory Party; instead they sink as disastrously as the US Fleet in *Pearl Harbor*, released in election week.)
Top of TV ratings: *Coronation Street* (again!) (Battersby family, Audrey Roberts, Ashley Peacock, Alma Halliwell)
Team on top of English League: Manchester United (again!)

I will leave it to you to construct your single unifying theory of electoral synchronicity, but I will point out one or two observations for the more casual reader. First, we hereby explode the myth that Labour does better in nice weather. The first of May 1997 was a beautiful day, but good Labour performances have tended, if anything, to be on wet days. There is plenty of ammunition for Tories to point at omens in the pop charts when Labour is elected: 'The Sun Ain't Gonna Shine Any more', 'Devil Gate Drive', 'Blood on the Dance Floor' all show deep foreboding. Whereas we should all have known Major would be re-elected in 1992 with 'Stay' remaining at number one for ages. Remember Thatcher's piercing blue 'Bright Eyes' in 1979!

There was some fuss during the 2001 election about an academic who found that FA Cup holders could reliably predict the winner of a general election. The idea was that pre-dominantly red teams predicted a Labour win, while blue or white teams led to a Tory win. This led to speculation that the election was not postponed because of foot-and-mouth disease, but because Chelsea would still have been the holders on 3 May, while the upcoming final between Arsenal and Liverpool meant that Labour could not lose.

There is a decent correlation, certainly much better than league leaders, but it was not perfect, as all the papers claimed. First, you have to cheat by giving Labour the gold shirts of Wolves in 1950 and the claret of West Ham in 1964. Then you let the Tories have the black and white of Newcastle in 1951 and 1955. After that it still falls down with Portsmouth in 1945, Nottingham Forest in 1959 and Manchester United in 1983. It works perfectly for the other nine elections, though. Before you start getting confused, an election before Cup Final day means we count the previous year's winner.

I have had real trouble trying to find any links with the star signs, news stories or football league leaders; perhaps the last one would work better with the Scottish League or the cricket County Championship, but someone else can work those out. Some of the movies work out quite nicely, particularly Labour's 1997 comeback with *The Empire Strikes Back* and *The Mummy Returns* in 2001, which Margaret Thatcher had chosen to bring to the campaign mythology herself in her comeback speech. It was the more recent deadly apparition of New Labour that returned in the end rather than the original 'Mummy'.

I would invite anyone who wants to try it to produce something similar for another country of your choice. Most have fixed terms of course, so that is a variable factor you will not have, but there are bound to be some incredible coincidences to uncover out there. After all, it would be an incredible coincidence if there weren't any.

USA 2000

It's a Done Deal!

> 'This thing is so wild, wacky and woolly, nobody knows how it's going to come out.'
> – *Dan Rather (CBS News on election night)*

So we come to Florida! Already, the American Presidential election of 2000 has become part of legend and it has spawned millions of words of comment. There have been a number of books produced on the subject. We do not have room to deal with everything in depth here, but we will try to make a brief journey through the highpoints of strangeness, dubious behaviour and downright lunacy that characterised it. The whole election was very odd, but it was Florida that stole the show, and that is where we will concentrate our attention.

I don't know whether you go along with any of the conspiracy theories that have become connected with the 2000 vote. There have been arguments put forward by both sides. I personally find it hard to go along with any idea of an all-embracing conspiracy. This is simply because there were so many amazing, apparently unconnected things going on that I tend to feel that anyone who was able to coordinate all that lot would have to be the most brilliant campaign genius of all time – move over Alexander the Great. However, that some individual aspects of the nonsense were deliberately contrived by various people seems certain. Other aspects were just down to good old incompetence or unlucky accident.

Whether it was all a big plot or not, the election was an utter shambles and any tiny, impoverished emerging nation can hold their head up high the next time they get lectured on democracy by the USA and they can ask America when they are going to learn how to run elections properly themselves. If it wasn't a fix, then it was a national humiliation. If you still don't believe me, let's go through some of the evidence.

SHAKING LIKE JELL-O

Florida was always going to be a pivotal state. With its 25 electoral college votes, it is one of the Big Seven. As Gore was sure to win New York and California and Bush was bound to win on his home turf in Texas, Florida stood there as the biggest challenge to them both. For Bush it had its wealthy neighbourhoods, the continuation of the Deep South Bible Belt to the north of the state, the fanatical support of the Cuban exile community and brother Jeb as Governor; for Gore it had some of the poorer communities in the States, the sprawling cosmopolitan metropolis of Miami, large black and Jewish communities and many areas of Democratic control at local level. Many thought that if the election was tight, it would be settled here. The Sunshine State is both a microcosm of the USA and a yet a state unlike any other in America.

On election night the network news channels declared that Gore had won Florida. The arguments started immediately as they did not even wait for voters in the heavily Republican northern area of Panhandle, which is in the Central time zone, to finish voting before the exit poll result was announced. There was no doubt in anyone's mind that Gore had won. They declared a result on the basis of the exit poll alone only if a candidate was at least ten points ahead. Otherwise it would be declared too close to call until sufficient district returns came in. Gore had just carried Pennsylvania as well, so the experts started counting it up on their fingers and worked out that Bush would have to win just about every state left apart from

California and Hawaii. As you flicked through the channels, many were on the verge of giving it to Gore.

Then the real results started to trickle in and some computer operators nudged their producers to point out that Bush was actually doing rather well in Florida. He was scoring more than the polls said he should be. One by one, CNN, Fox, NBC and the rest told us that they were changing Florida to 'too close to call'. By now we knew that Bush had taken Tennessee and Arkansas and the Midwest was solid for him. Gore's camp started to sweat. The legendary CBS anchorman, Dan Rather, was going into overdrive by now: 'This much tension you can't cut with a saw, it requires a blowtorch'; 'Bush has had a lead since the start, but his lead is now shakier than cafeteria Jell-O.' However, his description of Gore and Bush as being locked together 'spandex tight' was the most unpleasant image of the whole campaign. Then came the bombshell. Florida was going to Bush and there was no way Gore could now win without it. We had a winner and the papers started to write their headlines. Gore called the Bush team on his mobile and got in his car to make his concession speech.

Then the Internet made its first historic intervention in electoral politics. A Gore aide was following the Florida Secretary of State's web page and he saw the Bush lead suddenly drop from 50,000 to 6,000 before his eyes as the page updated. He knew the media were wrong again and this was in no way over. He frantically called Gore in his car and told him to turn round. Gore called Bush and took his concession back. Bush was not happy. Gore told him not to get 'snippy'. Later, America woke up to utter confusion. Many of the papers declared Bush the winner, but Florida had not declared. Several other states, such as Iowa, New Mexico, Oregon and Wisconsin, were also incredibly close and it even looked as though the Senate was likely to be tied. What had been one of the dullest election campaigns ever had turned into the most fascinating aftermath of them all.

As more results trickled in, Bush's lead in Florida was set at 1,784 votes. This was a minute amount for a state of nearly 16 million souls. As there were still some results to come in and several days to wait for the overseas postal vote deadline, the final result would have to be delayed. Sure enough, the next few days saw the Bush lead dip to just 327. Now there was time to start to hear some of the horror stories about what had happened in Florida on election day.

FLOAT LIKE A BUTTERFLY

The first big complaint was over what came to be known as the Butterfly Ballot. Every county has the right to design its own version of the ballot paper and officials in Palm Beach thought they would help their large number of elderly voters by giving them a design that put the candidates into two columns, enabling them to use larger print. Party workers had not objected to this because they assumed Palm Beach County would follow the explicit state law that stated that the boxes for marking the choice of candidate should be to the right of the name. At the last moment someone decided to break that law. Instead they placed all the boxes in the middle of the ballot with the boxes corresponding to the candidates' names alternatively from each column. It was easy to vote for Bush, who was at the top, as the representative of the party that held the state governorship. However, Gore's name was second, but his box was third – after the box for Pat Buchanan, who was top of the list on the right hand side of the page.

Complaints started flooding in on the morning of the election as people feared they had voted for Buchanan by accident. As an ultra-right-wing candidate who had recently made some very controversial apologist statements for Hitler, Buchanan did not expect to win many votes in this heavily Jewish county. In the end he received 3,704 votes, over three times as many as he received in any other Florida county and even he admitted that all bar a few hundred of these were obviously mistaken. In addition to this, 5,200 votes were discarded for 'overvoting'. These people had voted for both Buchanan and Gore. Presumably these were mostly people who had made a mistake and attempted to correct it. It is reasonable to assume that Gore lost about 8,000 votes because of the Butterfly Ballot. They would have put him into the White House with ease. If anyone doubted this argument they could look at an experiment conducted in a shopping mall, in which people were given a ballot paper identical to this one and then asked how they thought they had voted afterwards. All the Bush voters had got it right. A staggering 7 per cent of the people who thought they had voted for Gore had got it wrong. The legal challenges dragged on about the case and we can be sure that the butterfly ballot will never see the light of day again, but it is too late now for the 2000 election.

DON'T LET 'EM DO IT

Among the more controversial methods of ensuring that some of the people of Florida would not get to vote at all was the radical policy to bar convicted felons from voting. This may be considered suspect enough on its own merits. When someone has served their sentence there seems to be little justification in banning them from their fundamental rights and duties as a citizen for the rest of their days. It was also well noted that this would disproportionately affect young urban black males – not a noted base of support for Republican candidates.

However, the case was made much worse by the fact that a commercial company, Database Technologies (DBT), was hired by the state to research the names of all the felons and facilitate the amendments to the register. The real reason why this company went bananas, cutting thousands of names off the list who either had no criminal record at all, or had minor traffic or drug offences that should not have counted, remains unclear. If you had a similar name to a convicted felon, you could be in trouble, as their sophisticated techniques did not stretch to realising some people share the same name. Some of the counties saw that DBT's work was rubbish and ignored them, but others used their research and neither Jeb Bush nor Katherine Harris did anything to stop them. DBT still got paid handsomely for their completely incompetent work, and the lawyers continue poking around to see what can be done. Many people turned up to vote to find that they were off the register on account of their criminal behaviour. Willie Whiting is a gentle, elderly pastor of an evangelical house church. He was very surprised to find that he was in this situation, as nobody had told him that he had a criminal record. Of course, this was because he hadn't.

Others were told that they had no vote because they had received an absentee ballot, even though they had not requested or received one. Some of the more determined were prepared to take up to ninety minutes arguing for their right to cast a ballot. Most, of course, did not – and they frequently reported that the officials were totally unhelpful. Several polling stations in Miami closed early and voters were turned away if they had no ID, even though there was no legal reason why they needed it. It was overwhelmingly African Americans who experienced these problems. Some of the older voters among them wondered whether this was 21st-century Florida or still 1960s Mississippi.

The Florida Highway Patrol found other ways of stopping people. Road blocks were set up along major highways in predominantly black areas where there had been no road blocks for years. The police took a sudden interest in wanting to check drivers' papers. It was confirmed later that there had been no plans for widespread road blocks that day, but some individual officers had decided to take their own initiative, entirely contrary to proper procedure. This could have only one effect. The delays that they caused would have put some people off, but they particularly put off any people who knew they had problems with their insurance or their licensing, or those who were habitually distrustful of police anyway. There is no way of knowing how many people turned round and gave up because of this tactic.

Stories of more old-fashioned intimidation abounded as well. Several black voters complained of intimidation, threats and even actual violence from some enthusiasts who were keen to put them off the idea of going to poll. There was particular concern about the activity of some Cuban gangs who were determined to add their little bit of help to the campaign.

THE STORY OF CHAD

The word that sticks in everyone's head after the election of 2000 is 'chad'. Prior to this, most of us did not know there was a word for the little piece of paper or card that is knocked out by a hole-puncher.

The voting machines used in many counties in Florida were old contraptions designed by the Votomatic company. A voter puts a punch card into a holder, held by two pins. A punch tool then makes a hole in the card in the appropriate place. The voter can then turn the page to move on to the next offices for election.

Unlike the chads that are left by a standard hole-puncher, these ones were square. If the chads are not punched through cleanly the votes are not recorded in the mechanised counting process. Some have assumed that the problems with chads that are not punched through arise because of weak voters who have not pushed properly. This might be possible, but more likely causes are misalignment of the machine or ageing parts. Votomatic also say the machine must be cleaned after every election and Florida officials admitted that in many cases they were not.

So we were left with the new vocabulary of Chadspeak. A

hanging chad is still attached (purists define three different stages of hanging including the swinging chad and the tri-chad). A pregnant chad is one that is indented, but still attached. Some would call these dimpled chads, while others use either term depending on the degree of indentation. Are you still with us here?

Nobody is entirely clear why Americans still use these ridiculous machines. As far as I can work it out, they result in an inaccurate and nontransparent counting procedure that is also very slow after all the checks and recounts have been made. If they do not feel they are yet ready to move to a fully computerised system, pencil and paper remains a strong alternative.

Let's take a look at how inaccurate these machine counts can be. One very small precinct in Deland, Volusia County, had given 9,888 votes to James Harris, the Socialist Worker candidate, while somehow subtracting 16,000 votes from Al Gore. Officials spotted that this was an unusual result to say the least, so they inserted a new disc into the system and got the more believable result of Gore 193, Bush 22 and Harris 8. Everyone laughed. It's just like those times that someone gets sent a gas bill for £1 billion and it gets put on the news for everybody's entertainment. The thing is that you then stop and wonder how many people got sent a bill that was wrong, but still within the bounds of credibility. If a counting system is not transparent, we simply do not know if it is getting it right until it does something obviously crazy. People make mistakes, but other people notice. Some people still do not seem to understand that machines go wrong as well, and they will not always be noticed.

Immediately as the post-election crisis started to emerge, Bush and Gore sent their high-powered teams to Tallahassee to fight their corners. Two former Secretaries of State, James Baker and Warren Christopher respectively, went to represent their candidates backed with armies of lawyers and political strategists. The rumour mill went haywire over what was going on and many people were convinced that one side or the other was going down south to steal ballots or to magic up new ones. In fact Christopher determined primarily to obtain hand counts on those counties where it was reckoned Gore had lost thousands of votes because of problems with chads – Volusia, Broward, Palm Beach and Miami Dade. Baker's team were there primarily to stop them.

This was the point at which we got into the obscure legal battles over what could be recounted and what could not. Warren Christopher's lawyers argued that there were thousands of undervotes (that is people who had not completed their ballot, in most cases missing the presidential election). They claimed that most of these were as a result of faulty machines rather than a desire to vote on obscure county offices, but not President. They wanted manual checking of the ballots. James Baker's team argued that there was no agreed criteria for deciding what to do about chads and that repeated handling would result in interference with the ballots.

The recounts started at amazingly slow speed, then they stopped while Republicans started a disturbance here or there. They started again slightly slower than before, then they were stopped as a judge ruled them illegal. Then they started again as Florida Supreme Court ruled they were legitimate. Meanwhile, judges and lawyers argued over whether pregnant chads could be counted or not and at what point pregnant became hanging. 'Can you call it hanging if you can see light through it when you hold it up?'

Extra votes trickled in for Gore as the process painfully plodded on, between hold-ups. With hindsight, Gore's people would have done better to insist on further machine checks instead, as there was no reason to delay these with legal challenges and the more times they went through the machines the more chads would be knocked out.

DECLARING A WINNER

Fingers had been pointing at Jeb Bush, George's little brother who was the Governor with overall responsibility for all this. As Jeb is widely regarded as smarter and more hard-working than his brother, and without the wayward-youth episode as well, you might wonder why he would have been so keen to get his brother elected anyway. He was within his rights to feel aggrieved that it was not him running for the office. This whole episode has not helped any ambitions of his own. However, he started to get let off the hook in many people's estimation because a new star was emerging to take the flak. The immaculately presented figure of Katherine Harris served as Florida's Secretary of State. This meant that the management of the electoral process was one of her responsibilities. Oddly, she was also chairwoman of George W Bush's Florida campaign. If the phrase 'conflict of interests' ever had any meaning it was sitting in an office in Tallahassee. People around the world scratched their heads, as no mature democracy would ever think of allowing such a state of affairs.

Katherine Harris took her moment in the sun with glee, as she appeared on everyone's TV set looking like an extra from *Dynasty*. America split down the middle as to whether they loved her or loathed her, much as they had with Hillary Clinton. She liked to take charge and tell everyone how matters would proceed, apart from when she was giving testimony to judges in the court hearings – then it was all someone else's job. In particular she was adamant that it was her job to declare the final result on her set deadline of Sunday 26 November. The overseas ballots had all been in for over a week, and the final deadline for accreditation of electoral college members was looming. After 19 days of much-interrupted counting, Palm Beach had very nearly finished a full manual recount. They asked for a delay of a few hours, but Harris would not give it. She took her moment of historic drama to tell the world that Bush had finally won by 537 votes. He would be the President. At the point at which they lost the race to complete, Palm Beach had found a net gain for Gore of 192. Observers said there was a net gain for Gore of 846 in the dimpled-chad ballots that were not counted. Miami Dade also did not finish on time, and there was at least a net gain of 157 votes for Gore that was not included.

TELL IT TO THE JUDGE

After contradictory rulings by court judges, it was the Florida State Supreme Court that had come to the rescue of Gore by upholding the recounts. This had surprised people, as the general view of experts was that the court would not want to interfere in such a way. Republicans charged that the court was all Democrat-appointed, but at other times it was not helpful to Gore at all, particularly over the Butterfly Ballot and over complaints about absentee ballots.

If there was going to be closure it was going to come from the US Supreme Court, the highest federal legal institution in the land. Eventually they ruled on Tuesday 12 December, 35 days after polling. They ruled to stop all recounts, thereby handing the election to Bush. It was argued again that there was no agreed standard for approving ballots in a manual count and that the recounting could go on for ever if it was not stopped now. Furthermore, we were almost at the point at which Florida would be disenfranchised from the electoral college altogether and the election would be settled in a very messy fashion on the floor of the House of Representatives.

So Bush won, not by 537 votes in Florida, or by five electoral votes, but by one vote on the Supreme Court. The 5–4 majority among the judges stopped the recounts that were pushing the result towards Gore. The judges broke down pretty much across their expected ideological fault line. The four judges in the minority position all wrote strong dissenting opinions. For example, this from Justice John Paul Stevens: 'Although we may never know with complete certainty the identity of the winner of this year's presidential election, the identity of the loser is perfectly clear. It is the nation's confidence in the judge as an impartial guardian of the rule of law. I respectfully dissent.'

THE BEST OF THE REST

We have nowhere near enough space to cover everything that went wrong. Much of it was thoroughly covered in the international media, some was not. We should also not forget the very close results such as Gore's 366-vote majority in New Mexico and the arguments about irregularities in various places around the USA. Among the dafter things to happen in Florida, we had the faulty voting machines in Duval County, where 27,000 votes were discarded. Most of these were invalidated because two names had been pressed. These occurred mainly in predominantly black areas of Jacksonville. They joined the ranks of the forgotten as they were not challenged by Christopher's team. It is also believed that some of the overvotes were caused by misleading guidance from well-meaning campaigners who encouraged people to vote on every page. As the presidential ballot was spread over two pages in Duval, many voted for a minor candidate on the second page as well as Gore on the first. Some wrote in Gore on the second as well as voting for him on the first – even that was invalidated on the machines. One of the big mistakes for Gore's people was to put insufficient effort into challenging overvotes as well as undervotes. Election law says there should have been checks to see signs of intent from those who wrote in their choice, but it did not happen. The *Washington Post* checked 2.7 million computer votes: Gore had 46,000 overvotes to Bush's 17,000. The *Orlando Sentinel* counted undervotes and overvotes in Orange County and found a 203 net gain for Gore. If you have been adding all these numbers from the start you will begin to get the picture that the exit polls were right – Florida thought it had voted for Gore and the pollsters had recorded the result more accurately than the election officials.

If Gore had just called for a full recount across the state, they could at least not be accused of purely choosing Democrat areas and might have got the ruling in their favour, even if the workload would have been colossal.

Seminole County joined in the fun with its own controversy. Democrats wanted all the overseas ballots there thrown out because their applications had been tampered with by officials. Gore kept away from this dispute because it contradicted the aim to count every vote, but others pursued it. It was common practice for parties to send out forms for absentee votes that their supporters could complete to get their ballots. In Seminole a design problem led to most of these being left incomplete. Democrats were furious when Republican campaign workers were allowed to set up shop in the county offices with their laptops at the ready in order to complete the details of their supporters that were missing. Republicans were annoyed that so much fuss was made of this, as there was no suspicion of any corruption and many of the votes were from military personnel. However, Democrats saw that fussy legal arguments were being used against them elsewhere, so they decided to have a go. If they could get all the Seminole absentee votes thrown out for their technical errors, the drop in the Bush vote would be another, albeit the least satisfactory, way to give the election to Gore. Again they failed.

Legal challenges continue on some of these and other issues pertaining to the Florida election. It is still possible that any one of them may yet come back to give Bush's administration another nightmare.

We have covered a lot of ground in this book, and given awards to some of the oddest examples of electoral practice we have seen around the world. There can be no question as to where the prize for 'The most disgracefully handled cock-up of a so-called election' goes. Katherine Harris can walk up to the stage to take the award and give thanks to Governor Jeb, the police, the judges, the lawyers, the election officials, the private investigators and all the others who contributed so much to this catastrophe. In defence of America, it has to be said that it is impressive they have taken the whole affair in such good humour. If you are being cynical you could say that it is important for the elite to close ranks and put the whole affair to bed, after learning the lessons. It would be bad for all of them to rock the boat too hard. You could also say that the average American voter may still have only a hazy idea of exactly what happened, given the simplistic and insufficient information that was disseminated on American TV. However, you have to ask how many countries of the world would have been pushed into civil war for less?

Elections are at the heart of our society. They show us at our best some times, and at our worst too often. Stronger yet stranger than the bullet, the ballot is here to stay. When something like Florida 2000 comes along it gives everyone a lesson in how precious their vote is, yet how life goes on whatever the outcome. After all, when there is another election coming up, there is always hope.

Bibliography

Some of the books that were used for facts, ideas, quotes or general background info, in addition to those already quoted in the text:

Ackroyd, Peter. *Dickens*. Sinclair-Stevenson, 1990, p. 161

Amrine, Ed Dougles. *Reader's Digest: Did You Know?*. Reader's Digest, 1990, p. 250.

Ashdown, Paddy. *The Ashdown Diaries*, Vol. 1. Allen Lane (Penguin), 2000, p. 152.

BBC Election Series.

Black, Jeremy. *Pitt the Elder: The Great Commoner*. Sutton Publishing, 1999, pp. 10, 11, 70.

Blake, Robert. *The Conservative Party: From Peel to Major*. Arrow, 1998.

British Parliamentary Election Results. Various volumes.

Brogan, Patrick, and Garratt, Chris. *Introducing American Politics*. Icon/Totem, 1999.

Brunson, Michael. *A Ringside Seat*. Coronet, 2000.

Bullock, Alan. *Hitler and Stalin: Parallel Lives*. Fontana, 1991, pp. 182, 256–7, 608–10.

Butler, David, and Stolman, Anne. *British Political Facts 1900–1979*. Macmillan, 5th edition, 1980.

Butler, David, and Kavanagh, Dennis. *The British general election of 1992*. Macmillan, 1992, pp. 135–42, + loads more.

Butler, David, and Westlake, Martin. *British Politics and European Elections 1999*. Macmillan, 2000, pp. 212–14, 227, 231–2.

Cathcar, Brian. *Were You Still Up for Portillo?*. Penguin, 1997.

Curtis, Richard, and Elton, Ben. *Blackadder: The Whole Damn Dynasty*. Michael Joseph, (Penguin) 1999, pp. 244–6.

Chronicle of the 20th Century. Longman, 1988.

Dale, Iain. *The Unofficial Book of Political Lists.* Robson, 1997.

Davies, Pete. *This England.* Abacus, 1997.

Derbyshire, J Denis, and Derbyshire, Ian. *Political Systems of the world.* Chambers, 1989.

Dorril, Stephen, and Ramsay, Robin. *Smear! Wilson and the Secret State.* Grafton, 1991.

Eccleshall, Robert, and Walker, Graham (eds). *Biographical Dictionary of British Prime Ministers.* Routledge, 1998.

Encyclopaedia Britannica.

Encyclopaedia Britannica Year Books.

Fenton, James. *All the Wrong Places: Adrift in the Politics of Asia.* Penguin, 1988.

Guardian Election Guide Series.

Guinness Book of Records, 1996

Hamilton, Neil. *Great Political Eccentrics.* Robson, 1999.

Healy, Denis. *The Time of My Life.* Penguin, 1989.

Thomas Hobbes. *Leviathan.* Everyman, 1651.

Johnson, Paul. *Political Anecdotes.* Oxford, 1986.

Jones, Nicholas. *Campaign 1997.* Indigo, 1997, pp. 118–19, 144–6.

Jones, Nicholas. *Campaign 1997.* Indigo, 1997, pp. 118–19, 144–6.

Kane, Joseph Nathan. *Presidential Fact Book.* Random House, 1998.

Kleinman. *The Saatchi and Saatchi Story.* Pan Books, 1987.

Knight, Greg (comp.). *Parliamentary Sauce.* Robson, 1993.

Lee, Stephen J. *Aspects of British Political History 1815–1914.* Routledge, 1994.

Leonard, Dick. *Elections in Britain Today.* Macmillan.

MacIntyre, Donald. *Mandelson and the Making of New Labour.* HarperCollins, 1999.

McPhee, Nancy. *The Complete Book of Insults.* Book Club Associates/André Deutsch, 1982.

Mitchell, Paul, and Wilford, Rick (eds). *Politics in Northern*

Ireland. Westview Press, 1999, pp 67–73

Complete Monty Python Scripts, The. Mandarin, 1990.

Moon, Nick. *Opinion Polls History, Theory and Practice.* Manchester, 1999.

O'Farrell, John. *Things Can Only Get Better.* Black Swan, 1998, pp. 87–8.

O'Rourke, P J. *Parliament of Whores.* Picador, 1991.

Parris, Matthew, and Mason, Phil. *Read My Lips.* Penguin, 1996.

Pile, Stephen. *The Book of Heroic Failures.* Futura, 1979, pp. 177–8.

Pile, Stephen. *The Return of Heroic Failures.* Penguin, 1988, pp. 83, 158.

Plato. *The Republic.*

Rallings, Colin, and Thrasher, Michael (eds). *British Electoral Facts.* PRS (Ashgate), 2000.

Rees, Laurence. *Selling Politics,* BBC Books, 1992.

Richard, Paul. *How to Win an Election.* Politicos, 2001.

Rousseau, Jean Jacques. *The Social Contract.* Everyman, 1762.

Russell, Bertrand. *A History of Western Philosophy.* Unwin, 1946.

Schama, Simon. *Citizens: A Chronicle of the French Revolution.* Viking, 1994, pp. 644–6, 515–17

Richmond, Ray, and Coffman, Antonia (eds). *The Simpsons: A Complete Guide.* HarperCollins, 1997.

New York Times correspondents. *36 Days: Complete Chronicle of the 2000 Presidential Election Crisis.* Times Books, 2001.

Thompson, Hunter S. *Better Than Sex.* Black Swan, 1994.

Thompson, Leonard. *A History of South Africa.* Yale University Press, 1995, esp. pp. 150, 190, 225, 237, 254.

Tibballs, Geoff (comp.) *The Ultimate Lists Book.* Carlton Books (Siena), 1998.

The Times House of Commons, 1950.

Vankin, Jonathan, and Whalen, Jonathan. *The Giant Book of Conspiracies.* Paragon, 1998.

Walker, John (ed.). *Halliwell's Filmgoer's Companion*, 10th Edition. HarperCollins, 1993.

Wallechinsky, Wallace, I, Wallace, A. *The Book of Lists.* Corgi, 1977.

Wallechinsky, Wallace, I, Wallace, A, Wallace, S. *The Book of Lists 2.* Corgi, 1980.

Waller, Robert, and Criddle, Byron. *The Almanac of British Politics* (various editions).

Whitaker, Brian (comp.). *Notes & Queries Vol. 3.* The *Guardian.* Fourth Estate, 1992, pp. 169–73.

Thanks to . . .
Every national UK paper except the *Daily Sport*. They all helped somewhere along the line, as did many magazines, journals and party propaganda (including manifestos).

Websites
Agora Elections Around the world, Vote Finder, Politicos, Demon Politics Site, BBC, Channel 4, Media Channel, *Times*, *Guardian*, CNN, *LA Times*, *Miami Herald*, Labour Party, Conservative Party, Liberal Democrats, George W Bush, Al Gore, Greens, BNP, Official Monster Raving Loony Party, several other parties and numerous international sites, some of them written in alphabets my computer could not download.

The most striking website I came across in my research was Terminator3Armageddon, especially its Vladimir Zhirinovsky fan club page. The most obsessive was Political Graveyard with its complete listing of the cause of death and final resting place of every politician there has ever been in the state of Michigan (six died while campaigning in an election).

Thanks also for assistance from several individuals and for information from:

Conservative Party, Labour Party, Liberal Democrat Party
Association of Liberal Democrat Councillors
Leicestershire County Council